Practice*Pla[...]*

Arthu[...]

Helping therapists help their clients . . .

TheraScribe®

The Treatment Planning and Clinical Record Management System for Mental Health Professionals.

Thera*Scribe*®—the latest version of our popular treatment planning, patient record-keeping software. Facilitates intake/assessment reporting, progress monitoring, and outcomes analysis. Supports group treatment and multiprovider treatment teams. Compatible with our full array of **Practice*Planners*®** libraries, including our *Treatment Planner* software versions.

- This bestselling, easy-to-use Windows®-based software allows you to generate fully customized psychotherapy treatment plans that meet the requirements of all major accrediting agencies and most third-party payers.

- In just minutes, this user-friendly program's on-screen help enables you to create customized treatment plans.

- Praised in the *National Psychologist* and *Medical Software Reviews,* this innovative software simplifies and streamlines record-keeping.

- Available for a single user, or in a network version, this comprehensive software package suits the needs of all practices—both large and small.

Treatment Planner Upgrade to Thera*Scribe*®

The behavioral definitions, goals, objectives, and interventions from this *Treatment Planner* can be imported into Thera*Scribe*®. For purchase and pricing information, please send in the coupon below or call 1-866-888-5158 or e-mail us at planners@wiley.com.

For more information about **Thera*Scribe*®** or the Upgrade to this *Treatment Planner,* fill in this coupon and mail it to: R. Crucitt, John Wiley & Sons, Inc., 7222 Commerce Center Dr., Ste. 240, Colorado Springs, CO 80919 or e-mail us at planners@wiley.com.

❑ Please send me information on **Thera*Scribe*®**

❑ Please send me information on the *Treatment Planner* Upgrade to **Thera*Scribe*®**
Name of *Treatment Planner* _____

❑ Please send me information on the network version of **Thera*Scribe*®**

Name _____

Affiliation _____

Address _____

City/State/Zip _____

Phone _____ E-mail _____

For a free demo, visit us on the web at: therascribe.wiley.com   Ⓦ**WILEY**

Practice*Planners*® Order Form

Treatment Planners cover all the necessary elements for developing formal treatment plans, including detailed problem definitions, long-term goals, short-term objectives, therapeutic interventions, and DSM-IV™ diagnoses.

❏ **The Complete Adult Psychotherapy Treatment Planner,** Third Edition
 0-471-27113-6 / $49.95

❏ **The Child Psychotherapy Treatment Planner,** Third Edition
 0-471-27050-4 / $49.95

❏ **The Adolescent Psychotherapy Treatment Planner,** Third Edition
 0-471-27049-0 / $49.95

❏ **The Addiction Treatment Planner,** Second Edition
 0-471-41814-5 / $49.95

❏ **The Couples Psychotherapy Treatment Planner**
 0-471-24711-1 / $49.95

❏ **The Group Therapy Treatment Planner**
 0-471-37449-0 / $49.95

❏ **The Family Therapy Treatment Planner**
 0-471-34768-X / $49.95

❏ **The Older Adult Psychotherapy Treatment Planner**
 0-471-29574-4 / $49.95

❏ **The Employee Assistance (EAP) Treatment Planner**
 0-471-24709-X / $49.95

❏ **The Gay and Lesbian Psychotherapy Treatment Planner**
 0-471-35080-X / $49.95

❏ **The Crisis Counseling and Traumatic Events Treatment Planner**
 0-471-39587-0 / $49.95

❏ **The Social Work and Human Services Treatment Planner**
 0-471-37741-4 / $49.95

❏ **The Speech and Language Treatment Planner**
 0-471-27504-2 / $49.95

❏ **The Continuum of Care Treatment Planner**
 0-471-19568-5 / $49.95

❏ **The Behavioral Medicine Treatment Planner**
 0-471-31923-6 / $49.95

❏ **The Mental Retardation and Developmental Disability Treatment Planner**
 0-471-38253-1 / $49.95

❏ **The Special Education Treatment Planner**
 0-471-38872-6 / $49.95

❏ **The Severe and Persistent Mental Illness Treatment Planner**
 0-471-35945-9 / $49.95

❏ **The Personality Disorders Treatment Planner**
 0-471-39403-3 / $49.95

❏ **The Rehabilitation Psychology Treatment Planner**
 0-471-35178-4 / $49.95

❏ **The Pastoral Counseling Treatment Planner**
 0-471-25416-9 / $49.95

❏ **The Juvenile Justice and Residential Care Treatment Planner**
 0-471-43320-9 / $49.95

❏ **The Psychopharmacology Treatment Planner**
 0-471-43322-5 / $49.95

❏ **The Probation and Parole Treatment Planner**
 0-471-20244-4 / $49.95

❏ **The School Counseling and School Social Work Treatment Planner**
 0-471-08496-4 / $49.95

❏ **The Sexual Abuse Victim and Sexual Offender Treatment Planner**
 0-471-21979-7 / $49.95

Progress Notes Planners contain complete prewritten progress notes for each presenting problem in the companion Treatment Planners.

❏ **The Adult Psychotherapy Progress Notes Planner**
 0-471-45978-X / $49.95

❏ **The Adolescent Psychotherapy Progress Notes Planner**
 0-471-45979-8 / $49.95

❏ **The Couples Psychotherapy Progress Notes Planner**
 0-471-27460-7 / $49.95

❏ **The Child Psychotherapy Progress Notes Planner**
 0-471-45980-1 / $49.95

❏ **The Addiction Progress Notes Planner**
 0-471-10330-6 / $49.95

❏ **The Severe and Persistent Mental Illness Progress Notes Planner**
 0-471-21986-X / $49.95

Name_____

Affiliation_____

Address_____

City/State/Zip_____

Phone/Fax_____

E-mail_____

*Prices subject to change without notice.

To order, call 1-800-225-5945

(Please refer to promo #1-4019 when ordering.)

Or send this page with payment* to:
John Wiley & Sons, Inc., Attn: J. Knott
111 River Street, Hoboken, NJ 07030

❏ Check enclosed ❏ Visa ❏ MasterCard ❏ American Express
Card #_____

Expiration Date_____

Signature_____

On the web: practiceplanners.wiley.com

*Please add your local sales tax to all orders.

Practice Management Tools for Busy Mental Health Professionals

The Psychopharmacology
Treatment Planner

Practice*Planners*® Series

Treatment Planners

The Complete Adult Psychotherapy Treatment Planner, 3e
The Child Psychotherapy Treatment Planner, 3e
The Adolescent Psychotherapy Treatment Planner, 3e
The Continuum of Care Treatment Planner
The Couples Psychotherapy Treatment Planner
The Employee Assistance Treatment Planner
The Pastoral Counseling Treatment Planner
The Older Adult Psychotherapy Treatment Planner
The Behavioral Medicine Treatment Planner
The Group Therapy Treatment Planner
The Gay and Lesbian Psychotherapy Treatment Planner
The Family Therapy Treatment Planner
The Severe and Persistent Mental Illness Treatment Planner
The Mental Retardation and Developmental Disability Treatment Planner
The Social Work and Human Services Treatment Planner
The Crisis Counseling and Traumatic Events Treatment Planner
The Personality Disorders Treatment Planner
The Rehabilitation Psychology Treatment Planner
The Addiction Treatment Planner, 2e
The Special Education Treatment Planner
The Juvenile Justice and Residential Care Treatment Planner
The School Counseling and School Social Work Treatment Planner
The Sexual Abuse Victim and Sexual Offender Treatment Planner
The Probation and Parole Treatment Planner
The Psychopharmacology Treatment Planner
The Speech and Language Pathology Treatment Planner

Progress Notes Planners

The Child Psychotherapy Progress Notes Planner, Second Edition
The Adolescent Psychotherapy Progress Notes Planner, Second Edition
The Adult Psychotherapy Progress Notes Planner, Second Edition
The Addiction Progress Notes Planner
The Severe and Persistent Mental Illness Progress Notes Planner
The Couples Psychotherapy Progress Notes Planner

Homework Planners

Brief Therapy Homework Planner
Brief Couples Therapy Homework Planner
Brief Child Therapy Homework Planner
Brief Adolescent Therapy Homework Planner
Brief Employee Assistance Homework Planner
Brief Family Therapy Homework Planner
Grief Counseling Homework Planner
Group Therapy Homework Planner
Divorce Counseling Homework Planner
School Counseling and School Social Work Homework Planner
Chemical Dependence Treatment Homework Planner
Child Therapy Activity and Homework Planner
Addiction Treatment Homework Planner, Second Edition
Adolescent Psychotherapy Homework Planner II
Adult Psychotherapy Homework Planner

Client Education Handout Planners

Adult Client Education Handout Planner
Child and Adolescent Client Education Handout Planner
Couples and Family Client Education Handout Planner

Documentation Sourcebooks

The Forensic Documentation Sourcebook
The Psychotherapy Documentation Primer
The Chemical Dependence Treatment Documentation Sourcebook
The Clinical Child Documentation Sourcebook
The Couple and Family Clinical Documentation Sourcebook
The Clinical Documentation Sourcebook, 2e
The Continuum of Care Clinical Documentation Sourcebook

PracticePlanners®

Arthur E. Jongsma, Jr., Series Editor

The Psychopharmacology Treatment Planner

David C. Purselle

Charles B. Nemeroff

Arthur E. Jongsma, Jr.

WILEY

JOHN WILEY & SONS, INC.

Published by John Wiley & Sons, Inc., Hoboken, New Jersey.
Published simultaneously in Canada.

For general information on our other products and services please contact our Customer Care Department within the United States at (800) 762-2974, outside the United States at (317) 572-3993 or fax (317) 572-4002.

Wiley also publishes its books in a variety of electronic formats. Some content that appears in print may not be available in electronic books. For more information about Wiley products, visit our Web site at www.wiley.com.

Library of Congress Cataloging-in-Publication Data:

Purselle, David C.
    The psychopharmacology treatment planner / David C. Purcelle, Charles B. Nemeroff, Arthur E. Jongsma, Jr.
        p. cm. — (Practice planners series)
    ISBN 0-471-43322-5 (pbk. : alk. paper)
    1. Mental Illness—Chemotherapy—Handbooks, manuals, etc. 2. Psychopharmacology—Handbooks, manuals, etc. 3. Medical protocols. I. Nemeroff, Charles B. II. Jongsma, Arthur E., 1943- III. Title. IV. Practice planners.

    RC483.P876 2003
    616.89′18—dc21

                                                                    2003053480

Printed in the United States of America.

10 9 8 7 6 5 4 3 2 1

To Dr. William VanEerden, a psychiatrist whose deep knowledge of psychotropic medications is only surpassed by the strength of his commitment to his patients.

—A.E.J.

To Buffie, a wonderful person, whose encouragement and patience has helped me through many endeavors.

—D.C.P.

To my wife Gayle, thank you for all of your help and support that makes projects like this possible.

—C.B.N

CONTENTS

PRACTICE*PLANNERS*® SERIES PREFACE

The practice of psychotherapy has a dimension that did not exist 30, 20, or even 15 years ago—accountability. Treatment programs, public agencies, clinics, and even group and solo practitioners must now justify the treatment of patients to outside review entities that control the payment of fees. This development has resulted in an explosion of paperwork. Clinicians must now document what has been done in treatment, what is planned for the future, and what the anticipated outcomes of the interventions are. The books and software in this Practice*Planners* series are designed to help practitioners fulfill these documentation requirements efficiently and professionally.

The Practice*Planners* series is growing rapidly. It now includes not only the original *Complete Adult Psychotherapy Treatment Planner*, third edition, *The Child Psychotherapy Treatment Planner*, third edition, and *The Adolescent Psychotherapy Treatment Planner*, third edition, but also Treatment Planners targeted to specialty areas of practice, including: addictions, juvenile justice/residential care, couples therapy, employee assistance, behavioral medicine, therapy with older adults, pastoral counseling, family therapy, group therapy, psychopharmacology, neuropsychology, therapy with gays and lesbians, special education, school counseling, probation and parole, therapy with sexual abuse victims and offenders, and more.

Several of the Treatment Planner books now have companion Progress Notes Planners (e.g., Adult, Adolescent, Child, Addictions, Severe and Persistent Mental Illness, Couples). More of these planners that provide a menu of progress statements that elaborate on the client's symptom presentation and the provider's therapeutic intervention are in production. Each Progress Notes Planner statement is directly integrated with "Behavioral Definitions" and "Therapeutic Interventions" items from the companion Treatment Planner.

The list of therapeutic Homework Planners is also growing from the original Brief Therapy Homework Planner for adults, to Adolescent, Child, Couples, Group, Family, Addictions, Divorce, Grief, Employee Assistance, and School Counseling/School Social Work Homework Planners. Each of these books can be used alone or in conjunction with their companion Treatment Planner. Homework assignments are designed around each presenting problem (e.g., Anxiety, Depression, Chemical Dependence, Anger Management, Panic, Eating Disorders) that is the focus of a chapter in its corresponding Treatment Planner.

Client Education Handout Planners, a new branch in the series, provides brochures and handouts to help educate and inform adult, child, adolescent, couples, and family clients on a myriad of mental health issues, as well as life skills techniques. The list of presenting problems for which information is provided mirrors the list of presenting problems in the Treatment Planner of the title similar to that of the Handout Planner. Thus, the problems for which educational material is provided in the *Child and Adolescent Client Education Handout Planner* reflect the presenting problems listed in *The Child* and *The Adolescent Psychotherapy Treatment Planner* books. Handouts are included on CD-ROMs for easy printing and are ideal for use in waiting rooms, at presentations, as newsletters, or as information for clients struggling with mental illness issues.

In addition, the series also includes Thera*Scribe*®, the latest version of the popular treatment planning, clinical record-keeping software. Thera-*Scribe*® allows the user to import the data from any of the Treatment Planner, Progress Notes Planner, or Homework Planner books into the software's expandable database. Then the point-and-click method can create a detailed, neatly organized, individualized, and customized treatment plan along with optional integrated progress notes and homework assignments.

Adjunctive books, such as *The Psychotherapy Documentation Primer*, and *Clinical, Forensic, Child, Couples and Family, Continuum of Care,* and *Chemical Dependence Documentation Sourcebook* contain forms and resources to aid the mental health practice management. The goal of the series is to provide practitioners with the resources they need in order to provide high-quality care in the era of accountability—or, to put it simply, we seek to help you spend more time on patients, and less time on paperwork.

ARTHUR E. JONGSMA, JR.
Grand Rapids, Michigan

ACKNOWLEDGMENTS

We would like to thank Jen Byrne, Dr. Jongsma's assistant, for her persistent attention to the detail of compiling this manuscript in preparation for submission to the publisher. She kept track of countless revisions to every chapter and pulled multiple files together at the end of this project with her usual efficiency and thoroughness.

The supportive staff at John Wiley and Sons deserve our thanks also. Peggy Alexander, Cris Wojdylo, Judi Knott, and David Bernstein provide the professional skills that keep the Practice Planner series as a best-selling resource for mental health practitioners.

The Psychopharmacology Treatment Planner

INTRODUCTION

Since the early 1960s, formalized treatment planning has gradually become a vital aspect of the entire health-care delivery system, whether it is treatment related to physical health, mental health, child welfare, or substance abuse. What started in the medical sector in the 1960s spread into the mental health sector in the 1970s as clinics, psychiatric hospitals, agencies, and so on began to seek accreditation from bodies such as the Joint Commission on Accreditation of Healthcare Organizations (JCAHO) to qualify for third-party reimbursements. For most treatment providers to achieve accreditation, they had to begin developing and strengthening their documentation skills. Previously, most mental health and substance abuse treatment providers had, at best, a bare-bones plan that looked similar for most of the individuals they treated. Patients were often uncertain about what they were trying to attain in mental health treatment. Goals were vague, objectives were nonexistent, and interventions were applied equally to all patients. Outcome data were not measurable, and neither the treatment provider nor the patient knew exactly when treatment was complete. The initial development of rudimentary treatment plans made inroads toward addressing some of these issues.

With the advent of managed care in the 1980s, treatment planning has taken on even more importance. Managed care systems *insist* that clinicians move rapidly from assessment of the problem to the formulation and implementation of a treatment plan. The goal of most managed care companies is to expedite the treatment process by prompting the patient and treatment provider to focus on identifying and changing behavioral problems as quickly as possible. Treatment plans must be specific as to the problems and interventions, individualized to meet the patient's needs and goals, with measurable milestones that can be used to chart the patient's progress. Pressure from third-party payers, accrediting agencies, and other outside parties has therefore increased the need for clinicians to produce effective, high-quality treatment plans in a short time frame. However, many mental health providers have little experience in treatment plan development. Our purpose in writing this book is to clarify, simplify, and accelerate the treatment planning process.

TREATMENT PLAN UTILITY

Detailed written treatment plans benefit not only the patient, physician, therapist, treatment team, insurance community, and treatment agency, but also the overall mental health profession. A written plan stipulates the issues that are the focus of the treatment process. It is very easy for both provider and patient to lose sight of what the issues were that brought the patient into treatment. The treatment plan is a guide that structures the focus of the therapeutic contract. Since issues can change as treatment progresses, the treatment plan must be viewed as a dynamic document that can and must be updated to reflect any major change of problem, definition, goal, objective, or intervention.

Patients and treatment providers benefit from the treatment plan that focuses on outcomes. Behaviorally stated, measurable objectives clearly focus the treatment endeavor. Patients no longer wonder what the treatment is trying to accomplish. Clear objectives also allow the patient to channel effort into specific changes that will lead to long-term problem resolution. Treatment is not a vague contract to take medication or talk honestly and openly about emotions and cognitions until the patient feels better. Both the patient and treatment provider concentrate on specifically stated objectives using specific interventions.

Treatment plans aid providers by forcing them to think analytically and critically about therapeutic interventions that are best suited for objective attainment for the patient. Therapists were traditionally trained to "follow the patient," but now a formalized plan guides the treatment process. The treatment provider gives advance attention to the technique, approach, assignment, or cathartic target that forms the basis for interventions.

Clinicians benefit when clear documentation of treatment provides a measure of added protection from possible patient litigation. The first line of defense against malpractice allegations is a complete clinical record detailing the treatment process. A written, individualized, formal treatment plan that is the guideline for the therapeutic process that has been reviewed and signed by the patient and that is coupled with problem-oriented progress notes is a powerful defense against exaggerated or false claims.

A well-crafted treatment plan that clearly stipulates presenting problems and intervention strategies facilitates the treatment process carried out by team members in inpatient, residential, or intensive outpatient settings. Good communication between team members about what approach is being implemented and who is responsible for each intervention is critical. Team meetings to discuss patient treatment used to be the only source of interaction between providers; often, therapeutic conclusions or assignments were not recorded. Now, a thorough treatment plan stipulates in writing the details of objectives and the varied interventions (pharmacologic, milieu, group therapy, didactic, recreational, individual therapy, etc.) and who will implement them.

Treatment agencies or institutions are looking for ways to increase the quality and uniformity of the documentation in the clinical record. A standardized, written treatment plan with problem definitions, goals, objectives, and interventions in every patient's file enhances uniformity of documentation, easing the task of record reviewers inside and outside the agency. Outside reviewers, such as JCAHO, insist on documentation that clearly outlines assessment, treatment, progress, and discharge status.

The demand for accountability from third-party payers and health maintenance organizations (HMOs) is partially satisfied by a written treatment plan and complete progress notes. More and more managed care systems are requiring a structured therapeutic contract that has measurable objectives and explicit interventions. Clinicians are held accountable to those outside the treatment process.

The mental health profession benefits from the use of more precise, measurable objectives to evaluate success in mental health treatment. With the advent of detailed treatment plans, outcome data can be more easily collected for interventions that are effective in achieving specific goals.

DEVELOPING A TREATMENT PLAN

The process of developing a treatment plan involves a logical series of steps that build on one another much like constructing a house. The foundation of any effective treatment plan is the data gathered in a thorough biopsychosocial assessment. As the patient presents himself or herself for treatment, the clinician must sensitively listen to and understand what the patient struggles with in terms of family of origin issues, current stressors, emotional status, social network, physical health, coping skills, interpersonal conflicts, self-esteem, and so on. Assessment data may be gathered from a social history, physical exam, clinical interview, psychological testing, or contact with a patient's significant others. The integration of the data by the clinician or the multidisciplinary treatment team members is critical for understanding the patient, as is an awareness of the basis of the patient's struggle. We have identified six specific steps for developing an effective treatment plan based on the assessment data.

Step One: Problem Selection

Although the patient may discuss a variety of issues during the assessment, the clinician must determine the most significant problems on which to focus the treatment process. Usually a *primary* problem will surface, although *secondary* problems may also be evident. *Other* problems may have to be set aside as not urgent enough to require treatment at this time. An effective treatment plan can only deal with a few selected problems or the treatment will lose its direction. This *Planner* offers 28 problems from which to select those that most accurately represent your patient's presenting issues.

As the problems to be selected become clear to the clinician or the treatment team, it is important to include opinions from the patient as to his or her prioritization of issues for which help is being sought. A patient's motivation to participate in and cooperate with the treatment process depends, to some extent, on the degree to which treatment addresses his or her greatest needs.

Step Two: Problem Definition

Each individual patient presents with unique nuances as to how a problem behaviorally reveals itself in his or her life. Therefore, each problem that is selected for treatment focus requires a specific definition about how it is evidenced in the particular patient. The symptom pattern should be associated with diagnostic criteria and codes such as those found in the *Diagnostic and Statistical Manual IV (DSM-IV)* or the *International Classification of Diseases*. The *Planner,* following the pattern established by *DSM-IV,* offers behaviorally specific definition statements to choose from or to serve as a model for your own personally crafted statements. You will find several behavior symptoms or syndromes listed that may characterize one of the 28 presenting problems.

Step Three: Goal Development

The next step in treatment plan development is that of setting broad goals for the resolution of the target problem. These statements need not be crafted in measurable terms but can be global, long-term goals that indicate a desired positive outcome to the treatment procedures. The *Planner* suggests several possible goal statements for each problem, but one statement is all that is required in a treatment plan.

Step Four: Objective Construction

In contrast to long-term goals, objectives must be stated in behaviorally measurable language. It must be clear when the patient has achieved the established objectives; therefore, vague, subjective objectives are not acceptable. Review agencies (e.g., JCAHO), HMOs, and managed care organizations insist that psychiatric treatment outcomes be measurable. The objectives presented in this *Planner* meet this demand for accountability. Numerous alternatives are presented to allow construction of a variety of treatment plan possibilities for the same presenting problem. The clinician must exercise professional judgment as to which objectives are most appropriate for a given patient.

Each objective should be developed as a step toward attaining the broad treatment goal. In essence, objectives can be thought of as a series of steps that, when completed, will result in the achievement of the long-term goal. There should be at least two objectives for each problem, but the clinician may construct as many as are necessary for goal achievement. Target attainment dates should be listed for each objective. New objectives should be added to the plan as the individual's treatment progresses. When all the necessary objectives have been achieved, the patient should have resolved the target problem successfully.

Step Five: Intervention Creation

Interventions are the actions of the clinician designed to help the patient complete the objectives. There should be at least one intervention for every objective. If the patient does not accomplish the objective after the initial intervention, new interventions should be added to the plan.

Interventions should be selected on the basis of the patient's needs and the treatment provider's full therapeutic repertoire. This *Planner* contains interventions from a broad range of therapeutic approaches, including pharmacologic interventions as well as other therapeutic interventions (e.g., psychotherapy, substance abuse treatment, physical or occupational therapy). Other interventions may be written by the provider to reflect his or her own training and experience. The addition of new problems, definitions, goals, objectives, and interventions to those found in the *Planner* is encouraged because doing so adds to the database for future reference and use.

Some suggested interventions listed in the *Planner* refer to specific books that can be assigned to the patient. Appendix B contains a full reference list of self-help or patient education materials. The books are arranged under each problem for which they are appropriate. When a book is used as part of an intervention plan, it should be reviewed with the patient after it is read, enhancing the application of the content of the book to the specific patient's circumstances. For further information about self-help books, mental health professionals may wish to consult *The Authoritative Guide to Self-Help Books* (2003) by Santrock, Minnett, and Campbell (available from The Guilford Press, New York, NY).

Assigning an intervention to a specific provider is most relevant if the patient is being treated by a team in an inpatient, residential, or intensive outpatient setting. Within these settings, personnel other than the primary clinician may be responsible for implementing a specific intervention. Review agencies require that the responsible provider's name be stipulated for every intervention.

Step Six: Diagnosis Determination

The determination of an appropriate diagnosis is based on an evaluation of the patient's complete clinical presentation. The clinician must compare the behavioral, cognitive, emotional, and interpersonal symptoms that the patient presents to the criteria for diagnosis of a mental illness condition as described in *DSM-IV*. The issue of differential diagnosis is admittedly a difficult one that research has shown to have rather low interrater reliability. Mental health professionals are often trained to think more in terms of maladaptive behavior than disease labels. In spite of these factors, diagnosis is a reality that exists in the world of mental health care, and it is a necessity for third-party reimbursement. (However, recently, managed care agencies are more interested in behavioral indices that are exhibited by the patient than the actual diagnosis.) It is the clinician's thorough knowledge of *DSM-IV* criteria and a complete understanding of the patient assessment data that contribute to the most reliable, valid diagnosis. An accurate assessment of behavioral indicators will also contribute to more effective treatment planning.

HOW TO USE THIS PLANNER

Our experience has taught us that learning the skills of effective treatment plan writing can be a tedious and difficult process for many clinicians. It is more stressful to try to develop this expertise when under the pressure of increased patient load and short time frames placed on clinicians today by managed care systems. The documentation demands can be overwhelming when we must move quickly from assessment to treatment plan to progress notes. In the process, we must be very specific about how and when objectives can be achieved, and how progress is exhibited in each patient. *The Psychopharmacology Treatment Planner* was developed as a tool to aid clinicians in writing a treatment plan in a rapid manner that is clear, specific, and highly individualized according to the following progression:

1. Choose one presenting problem (Step One) you have identified through your assessment process. Locate the corresponding page number for that problem in the *Planner's* table of contents.
2. Select two or three of the listed behavioral definitions (Step Two) and record them in the appropriate section on your treatment plan form. Feel free to add your own defining statement if you determine that your patient's behavioral manifestation of the identified problem is not listed. (Note that while our design for treatment planning is vertical, it will work equally well on plan forms formatted horizontally.)
3. Select a single long-term goal (Step Three) and again write the selection, exactly as it is written in the *Planner* or in some appropriately modified form, in the corresponding area of your own form.
4. Review the listed objectives for this problem and select the ones that you judge to be clinically indicated for your patient (Step Four). Remember, it is recommended that you select at least two objectives for each problem. Add a target date or the number of sessions allocated for the attainment of each objective.
5. Choose relevant interventions (Step Five). The *Planner* offers suggested interventions related to each objective in the parentheses following the objective statement. Select the medication intervention that you believe is most appropriate for the patient. A chart of commonly used psychiatric medications with their indications and dosages can be found in Appendix A. Also, just as with definitions, goals, and objectives, there is space allowed for you to enter your own interventions into the *Planner.* This allows you to refer to these entries when you create a plan around this problem in the future. You will have to assign responsibility to a specific person for implementation of each intervention if the treatment is being carried out by a multidisciplinary team.
6. Several *DSM-IV* diagnoses are listed at the end of each chapter that are commonly associated with a patient who has this problem. These diagnoses are meant to be suggestions for clinical consideration. Select a diagnosis listed or assign a more appropriate choice from the *DSM-IV* (Step Six).

To accommodate those practitioners who tend to plan treatment in terms of diagnostic labels rather than presenting problems, Appendix C lists all of the *DSM-IV* diagnoses that have been presented in the various presenting problem chapters as suggestions for consideration. Each diagnosis is followed by the presenting problem that has been associated with that diagnosis. Providers may look up the presenting problems for a selected diagnosis to review definitions, goals, objectives and interventions that may be appropriate for their patients with that diagnosis.

Congratulations! You should now have a complete, individualized treatment plan that is ready for immediate implementation and presentation to the patient. It should resemble the format of the "Sample Standard Treatment Plan" on page 9.

A FINAL NOTE

One important aspect of effective treatment planning is that each plan should be tailored to the individual patient's problems and needs. Treatment plans should not be mass-produced, even if patients have similar problems. The individual's strengths and weaknesses, unique stressors, social network, family circumstances, and symptom patterns *must* be considered in developing a treatment strategy. Drawing upon our own years of clinical experience, we have put together a variety of treatment choices. These statements can be combined in thousands of permutations to develop detailed treatment plans. Relying on their own good judgment, clinicians can easily select the statements that are appropriate for the individuals they are treating. In addition, we encourage readers to add their own definitions, goals, objectives, and interventions to the existing samples. It is our hope that *The Psychopharmacology Treatment Planner* will promote effective, creative treatment planning—a process that will ultimately benefit the patient, the clinician, and the mental health community.

SAMPLE TREATMENT PLAN

PROBLEM: ANGER MANAGEMENT

Definitions: Overreaction of hostility to insignificant irritants.
Use of verbally abusive language.
History of explosive aggressive outbursts out of proportion
to any precipitating stressors leading to assaults or destruction of property.

Goals: Take the appropriate medication and dose and/or participate
in psychotherapy to decrease overall intensity and frequency of angry feelings and outbursts.

OBJECTIVES

1. Describe the nature and history of anger expression and note its impact on daily life. (5/20/03)

2. Patient and/or significant other to describe any current or past violent threats or actions. (5/27/03)

INTERVENTIONS

1. Explore the patient's dysfunctional pattern of anger expression (e.g., physical violence, destructive acts, overreaction to irritants, challenging authority figures, problems with legal system) and how it affects his/her daily life.

2. Assist the patient in identifying specific targets of and causes for anger.

1. Assess the patient's potential for violence and determine the presence of current and past threats or acts of aggression.

2. Arrange for hospitalization, as necessary, when the patient is judged to be harmful to self or others or unable to care for his/her basic needs.

3. Pursue treatment for concurrent medical problems that may contribute poor anger control. (6/05/03)

   1. Treat or refer the patient for treatment for any medical problem that may be contributing to poor anger control (e.g., acquired brain damage, elevated testosterone levels).

   2. Monitor the patient's progress in recovery from concomitant disorders and the impact of the recovery on his/her anger management.

4. Take prescribed medications responsibly at times ordered by the physician. (6/5/03)

   1. Prescribe to the patient a selective serotonin reuptake inhibitor (SSRI) (e.g., paroxetine [Paxil®], sertraline [Zoloft®], citalopram [Celexa™], escitalopram [Lexapro™], fluoxetine [Prozac®], or fluvoxamine [Luvox®]); strongly consider this in patients with concurrent depressive symptoms.

   2. Titrate the patient's medication to the minimum effective dose for treating his/her symptoms.

5. Report as to the effectiveness of medications and any side effects that develop. (7/05/03)

   1. Monitor the patient frequently for the development of side effects, response to medication, adherence to treatment, and abuse of medication (if he/she is taking benzodiazepines).

   2. Evaluate the patient after six weeks of therapy with an SSRI for his/her response to medication; determine if he/she has had a partial response or a full response to the medication.

6. Retain a significant improvement in anger management. (9/5/03)

   1. Maintain the patient on current medication indefinitely if he/she has shown an improvement in anger management.

Diagnosis: 312.34   Intermittent Explosive Disorder

ADJUSTMENT DISORDER WITH DEPRESSION OR ANXIETY

BEHAVIORAL DEFINITIONS

1. Depressive symptoms (e.g., sad mood, tearfulness, feelings of hope-lessness) that develop in response to an identifiable stressor (e.g., medical illness, marital problems, loss of a job, financial problems, conflicts about religion).
2. Anxiety symptoms (e.g., nervousness, worry, jitteriness) that develop in response to an identifiable stressor.
3. Symptoms cause distress beyond what would normally be expected.
4. Significant impairment in social and/or occupational functioning be-cause of the symptoms.

—. _____
   _____
—. _____
   _____
—. _____
   _____

LONG-TERM GOALS

1. Alleviate symptoms of stress-related depression through medication and/or psychotherapy.
2. Alleviate symptoms of stress-related anxiety through medication and/or psychotherapy.
3. Stabilize anxiety and/or depression levels while increasing ability to function on a daily basis.

4. Learn and demonstrate strategies to deal with dysphoric and/or anxious moods.
5. Effectively cope with the full variety of life's stressors.

—. _____

_____

—. _____

_____

—. _____

_____

SHORT-TERM OBJECTIVES

THERAPEUTIC INTERVENTIONS

1. Describe the signs and symptoms of an adjustment disorder that are experienced and note their impact on daily life. (1, 2, 3)

1. Explore the adjustment disorder symptoms that are experienced by the patient (e.g., excessive worry about a current stressor, sad mood, decreased sleep, reduced appetite).

2. Determine what stressors are present and the time course of symptoms in relation to the stressors.

3. Gather information from the patient about the impact of the symptoms on daily life (e.g., impaired social or occupational functioning, neglect of routine chores).

2. Describe other symptoms or disorders that may also be present. (4, 5)

4. Assess the patient for comorbid disorders (e.g., see the Personality Disorder, Psychosis, and Panic Disorder chapters in this *Planner*).

5. Gather detailed personal and family history information regarding the patient's substance abuse and its potential contribution to the adjustment disorder;

refer the patient for in-depth substance abuse treatment, if indicated (see the Chemical Dependence chapters in this *Planner*).

3. Verbalize any current suicidal thoughts and any history of suicidal behavior. (6, 7, 8)

6. Explore the patient's current and past suicidal thoughts and suicidal behavior; check for family history of suicide (see interventions designed for Suicidal Ideation in this *Planner*).

7. Administer to the patient an objective assessment instrument for assessing suicidality (e.g., the Beck Scale for Suicidal Ideation); evaluate the results and give feedback to the patient.

8. Arrange for hospitalization when the patient is judged to be harmful to himself/herself or others or unable to care for his/her basic needs.

4. Outline a complete and accurate medical and psychiatric history, including treatment received and its effectiveness. (9, 10)

9. Explore the patient's history of previous treatment for any psychiatric disorder and the success of, as well as tolerance for, that treatment.

10. Assess the patient for the presence of other medical problems and the medications used to treat them.

5. Cooperate with a physical examination and laboratory tests. (11, 12)

11. Perform a complete physical and neurological examination on the patient and send his/her blood and/or urine for analysis to assess any medical problem that may contribute to the adjustment disorder (e.g., cancer, diabetes, hypertension, cardiovascular disease).

12. Provide feedback to the patient regarding the results and

6. Pursue treatment for concurrent medical problems that
may contribute to depressive
and anxiety symptoms.
(13, 14)

7. Complete psychological
testing and other questionnaires
for measuring depressive and
anxiety symptoms. (15)

8. Express an understanding of
possible causes for adjustment disorder and the relationship between substance abuse
and adjustment disorder.
(16, 17)

9. Verbalize an understanding
of treatment options, expected
results from medication, and
potential side effects.
(18, 19)

implications of the physical
examination and laboratory
test results.

13. Treat or refer the patient for
treatment for any medical problem that may be causing or contributing to the adjustment
disorder.

14. Monitor the patient's progress in
recovery from concomitant disorders and the impact on his/her
mood.

15. Administer objective instruments
to assess the patient's depressive
and anxiety symptoms (e.g., Beck
Depression Inventory [BDI],
Hamilton Depression Rating Scale
[HDRS], Montgomery Asberg
Depression Rating Scale
[MADRS], Hamilton Anxiety
Rating Scale [HARS]); evaluate
the results and give him/her
feedback.

16. Emphasize the negative and
dangerous impact of substance
abuse on adjustment disorder
symptoms.

17. Educate the patient on the possible contributing factors (e.g.,
stressful life events, maladaptive
coping skills) and signs of adjustment disorder.

18. Discuss appropriate treatment
options with the patient
including medication and
psychotherapy.

19. Educate the patient on psychotropic medication treatment including the expected results,
potential side effects, and dosing
strategies.

10. Participate in psychotherapy sessions as planned with the therapist. (20, 21)

20. Assess the patient for potential benefit from psychotherapy and refer him/her to a psychotherapist, if necessary.

21. Monitor the patient's response to psychotherapy; assess his/her ability to verbalize a basis for progress in recovery from the adjustment disorder (e.g., improved mood, reduced anxiety, increased ability to cope with adversity, improved social and occupational functioning).

11. Verbalize any symptoms of anxiety that are experienced. (22, 23)

22. Explore the adjustment disorder symptoms that are experienced by the patient (e.g., excessive worry about a current stressor, sad mood, decreased sleep, reduced appetite).

23. Determine if the patient has debilitating symptoms of anxiety (e.g., worry, nervousness, reduced sleep) that interfere with his/her functioning.

12. Take prescribed antianxiety or hypnotic medications responsibly at times ordered by the physician. (24, 25, 26, 27)

24. Prescribe to the patient an anxiolytic or hypnotic agent (e.g., zolpidem [Ambien®], zaleplon [Sonata®], lorazepam [Ativan®], flurazepam [Dalmane®], triazolam [Halcion®], diazepam [Valium®], chloral hydrate [Noctec®], estazolam [ProSom®], temazepam [Restoril®]) to help the patient with sleep (see the Sleep Disturbance chapter in this *Planner*).

25. Consider the use of a long-acting benzodiazepine (e.g., clonazepam [Klonopin®], diazepam [Valium®]) to help alleviate excessive daytime anxiety.

26. Avoid the use of benzodiazepines and other hypnotics if the patient has a history of substance abuse; use an alternative medication (e.g., hydroxyzine [Atarax®, Vistaril®], diphenhydramine [Benadryl®], trazodone [Desyrel®]) for the patient.

27. Instruct the patient to minimize his/her use of medication and take it only when symptoms become intolerable.

13. Report as to the effectiveness of the antianxiety medication and any side effects that develop. (28, 29)

28. Titrate the medication every two to three days, as tolerated, until the patient's symptoms are controlled or the maximum dose is reached.

29. Monitor the patient frequently for the development of side effects, response to medication, adherence to treatment, and abuse of the medication.

14. Verbalize any depressive symptoms that are experienced. (30, 31)

30. Explore the adjustment disorder symptoms that are experienced by the patient (e.g., excessive worry about a current stressor, sad mood, decreased sleep, reduced appetite).

31. Determine if the patient has debilitating depressive symptoms (e.g., sad mood, tearfulness, decreased appetite) in response to a chronic stressor (e.g., chronic medical illness, ongoing financial or legal problems).

15. Adhere to the SSRI antidepressant medication as prescribed by the physician. (32, 33)

32. Consider prescribing a selective serotonin reuptake inhibitor (SSRI) (e.g., fluoxetine [Prozac®], sertraline [Zoloft®], paroxetine [Paxil®], citalopram [Celexa™], escitalopram

[Lexapro™]) to help treat the patient's depressive symptoms (see the Depression chapter in this *Planner*).

33. Titrate the patient's SSRI antidepressant medication to the minimum effective dose for treating the patient's symptoms.

16. Report as to the effectiveness of the SSRI antidepressant medication and any side effects that develop. (34, 35, 36)

34. Monitor the patient frequently for the development of side effects, response to the SSRI medication, and adherence to treatment.

35. Increase the dose of the SSRI antidepressant every four to six weeks, as tolerated, until the patient has a satisfactory response or the maximum dose is reached.

36. Repeat administration of objective rating instruments for assessment of the patient's depression and anxiety; evaluate the results and give him/her feedback.

17. Retain a remission or significant reduction in depressive and/or anxiety symptoms. (37, 38, 39)

37. Maintain the patient on current medication until the stressor(s) resolve and/or the patient develops better coping skills to reduce his/her depression or anxiety without medication.

38. Continue antidepressant treatment indefinitely if he/she has had previous episodes of adjustment disorder and has shown limited or no progress in developing adequate coping skills to effectively deal with adversity.

39. Reduce medications gradually over several days to weeks; monitor closely for recurrence of symptoms and/or withdrawal.

—. _____   —. _____
   _____   _____

—. _____   —. _____
   _____   _____

—. _____   —. _____
   _____   _____

DIAGNOSTIC SUGGESTIONS:

Axis I:	309.0	Adjustment Disorder with Depressed Mood
	309.24	Adjustment Disorder with Anxiety
	309.28	Adjustment Disorder with Mixed Anxiety and Depressed Mood
	309.3	Adjustment Disorder with Disturbance of Conduct
	309.4	Adjustment Disorder with Mixed Disturbance of Conduct and Emotions
	309.9	Adjustment Disorder Unspecified
	296.xx	Major Depression
	309.81	Posttraumatic Stress Disorder
	308.3	Acute Stress Disorder
	V62.82	Bereavement
	305.00	Alcohol Abuse
	305.60	Cocaine Abuse

_____   _____

_____   _____

Axis II: 301.83   Borderline Personality Disorder

_____   _____

_____   _____

ANGER MANAGEMENT

BEHAVIORAL DEFINITIONS

1. History of explosive, aggressive outbursts out of proportion to any precipitating stressors leading to assaults or destruction of property.
2. Overreaction of hostility to insignificant irritants.
3. Swift and harsh judgment statements made to or about others.
4. Body language of tense muscles (e.g., clenched fist or jaw, glaring looks, or refusal to make eye contact).
5. Use of passive-aggressive patterns (e.g., social withdrawal due to anger, lack of complete or timely compliance in following directions or rules, complaining about authority figures behind their backs, or non-participation in meeting expected behavioral norms).
6. Consistent pattern of challenging or disrespectful treatment of authority figures.
7. Use of verbally abusive language.

—. _____
   _____
—. _____
   _____
—. _____
   _____

LONG-TERM GOALS

1. Take the appropriate medication and dose and/or participate in psychotherapy to decrease overall intensity and frequency of angry feelings and outbursts.
2. Increase the ability to recognize and appropriately express angry feelings as they occur.

3. Develop an awareness of current angry behaviors, clarifying origins of and alternatives to aggressive anger.
4. Come to an awareness and acceptance of angry feelings while developing better control and more serenity.
5. Express angry feelings in constructive ways that enhance daily functioning.

—. _____
_____
—. _____
_____
—. _____
_____

SHORT-TERM OBJECTIVES

THERAPEUTIC INTERVENTIONS

1. Describe the nature and history of anger expression and note its impact on daily life. (1, 2)

1. Explore the patient's dysfunctional pattern of anger expression (e.g., physical violence, destructive acts, overreaction to irritants, challenging authority figures, problems with legal system) and how it affects his/her daily life.

2. Assist the patient in identifying specific targets of and causes for anger.

2. Describe other symptoms or disorders that may also be present. (3, 4, 5)

3. Assess the patient for symptoms of depression, hypomania/mania, posttraumatic stress disorder or psychosis (see relevant chapters in this *Planner*).

4. Assess the patient's intellectual capacity and determine if he/she has mental retardation (see the Cognitive Deficits—Developmental Delay chapter in this *Planner*).

5. Gather detailed personal and family history information regarding substance abuse and its interaction with the mismanagement of anger; refer the patient for in-depth substance abuse treatment, if indicated (see the Chemical Dependence chapters in this *Planner*).

3. Patient and/or significant other describe any current or past violent threats or actions. (6, 7)

6. Assess the patient's potential for violence and determine the presence of current and past threats or acts of aggression.

7. Arrange for hospitalization, as necessary, when the patient is judged to be harmful to self or others or unable to care for his/her basic needs.

4. Outline a complete and accurate medical and psychiatric history, including treatment received and its effectiveness. (8, 9)

8. Explore the patient's history of previous treatment for anger management and the success of, as well as his/her tolerance for, that treatment.

9. Assess the patient for the presence of other medical problems and the medications used to treat them.

5. Cooperate with a physical examination and laboratory tests. (10, 11)

10. Perform a complete physical and neurological examination on the patient and send his/her blood and/or urine for analysis to rule out organic contributors (e.g., acquired brain injury, elevated testosterone levels) to poor anger control.

11. Provide feedback to the patient regarding the results and implications of the physical examination and laboratory test results.

6. Complete psychological testing and other

12. Administer objective anger rating instruments to the patient

questionnaires for assessing anger expression. (12)

(e.g., Anger, Irritability, and Assault Questionnaire [AIAQ], Buss-Durkee Hostility Inventory [BDHI], State-Trait Anger Expression Inventory [STAXI]); evaluate the results and give him/her feedback.

7. Pursue treatment for concurrent medical problems that may contribute poor anger control. (13, 14)

13. Treat or refer the patient for treatment for any medical problem that may be contributing to poor anger control (e.g., acquired brain damage, elevated testosterone levels).

14. Monitor the patient's progress in recovery from concomitant disorders and the impact of the recovery on his/her anger management.

8. Verbalize an understanding of the impact of substance abuse on anger control. (15)

15. Emphasize to the patient the negative and dangerous interaction of substance abuse with anger expression (e.g., increased impulsivity, physical violence, overreaction to irritants).

9. Express an understanding of treatment options, expected results from medication and potential side effects. (16, 17)

16. Discuss appropriate treatment options for anger management with the patient including medications and psychotherapy.

17. Educate the patient on medication treatment including expected results, potential side effects, and dosing strategies.

10. Participate in psychotherapy sessions as planned with the therapist. (18, 19)

18. Assess the patient for potential benefit from psychotherapy; refer him/her to a psychotherapist, if indicated.

19. Monitor the patient's response to psychotherapy; assess his/her ability to verbalize a basis for progress in anger management (e.g., increased ability to recognize anger, more appropriate

expressions of anger, reduction in violent behavior, sobriety).

11. Take prescribed medications responsibly at times ordered by the physician. (20, 21, 22)

20. Prescribe to the patient a selective serotonin reuptake inhibitor (SSRI) (e.g., paroxetine [Paxil®], sertraline [Zoloft®], citalopram [Celexa™], escitalopram [Lexapro™], fluoxetine [Prozac®], or fluvoxamine [Luvox®]); strongly consider this in patients with concurrent depressive symptoms.

21. Consider prescribing a long-acting benzodiazepine (e.g., clonazepam [Klonopin®], diazepam [Valium®]) if the patient has severe aggression (i.e., physical violence) requiring rapid treatment.

22. Titrate the patient's medication to the minimum effective dose for treating his/her symptoms.

12. Report as to the effectiveness of medications and any side effects that develop. (23, 24)

23. Monitor the patient frequently for the development of side effects, response to medication, adherence to treatment and abuse of medication (if he/she is taking benzodiazepines).

24. Evaluate the patient after six weeks of therapy with an SSRI for his/her response to medication; determine if he/she has had a partial response or a full response to the medication.

13. Cooperate with any changes in medication dose. (25)

25. Increase medication dose if the patient has had a partial response; titrate his/her dose every two weeks until the patient's symptoms are controlled or until the maximum dose is reached.

14. Adhere to changes in anti-depressant medication and

26. Prescribe an alternative anti-depressant (e.g., a second SSRI,

dose prescribed by the physician. (26, 27)

trazodone [Desyrel®], nefazodone [Serzone®], amitriptyline [Elavil®], imipramine [Tofranil®]) if the patient has an unsatisfactory response to an SSRI.

27. Titrate the antidepressant every two to four weeks, as tolerated, until the patient's symptoms are controlled or the maximum dose is reached.

15. Take additional medication to control symptoms of sympathetic outflow. (28, 29, 30)

28. Prescribe clonidine [Catapres®] or a β-blocker (e.g., propranolol [Inderal®], atenolol [Tenormin®]) if the patient has signs and/or symptoms of sympathetic stimulation (e.g., tachycardia, elevated blood pressure, muscle tension) preceding anger outbursts.

29. Titrate the medication every one to two weeks, as tolerated, until the patient's symptoms are controlled or the maximum dose is reached.

30. Monitor the patient's blood pressure during treatment with clonidine [Catapres®] or a β-blocker.

16. Express an understanding of the need for mood stabilizing medication and cooperate with the prescribed treatment. (31)

31. Consider adding a mood stabilizer (e.g., carbamazepine [Tegretol®], lithium [Eskalith®, Lithonate®], divalproex sodium [Depakote®], or lamotrigine [Lamictal®]) if the patient does not have a satisfactory response to other medications.

17. Cooperate with blood draws to monitor medication levels and adhere to any adjustments in medication dose. (32)

32. Measure medication blood levels in four to five days if the patient is taking lithium (Lithonate®, Eskalith®), divalproex sodium (Depakote®) or

carbamazepine (Tegretol®); adjust the dose to obtain therapeutic blood levels.

18. Report as to the effectiveness of the mood-stabilizing medication and any side effects that develop. (33)

33. Reassess the patient in one to two weeks for response to the mood-stabilizing medication, development of side effects, and adherence to treatment.

19. Take an atypical antipsychotic agent added to the medication regimen. (34, 35, 36)

34. Consider adding an atypical antipsychotic agent (e.g., risperidone [Risperdal®], olanzapine [Zyprexa®], ziprasidone [Geodon®], aripiprazole [Abilify™], quetiapine [Seroquel®], clozapine [Clozaril®]) if the patient does not have a satisfactory response to other medications.

35. Monitor the patient frequently for the development of side effects to the antipsychotic medication, response to the medication and adherence to treatment.

36. Titrate the patient's antipsychotic dose every two weeks until his/her symptoms are controlled or the maximum dose is reached.

20. Retain a significant improvement in anger management. (37)

37. Maintain the patient on current medication indefinitely if he/she has shown an improvement in anger management.

21. Read books on coping with anger and implement newly learned techniques. (38)

38. Recommend that the patient read books on coping with anger (e.g., *Of Course You're Angry* by Rosellini and Worden; *The Angry Book* by Rubin; *Anger Work Out Book* by Weisinger; *Forgive and Forget* by Smedes); process his/her implementation of

coping techniques, reinforcing success and redirecting for failure.

—. _____   —. _____
   _____   _____
—. _____   —. _____
   _____   _____
—. _____   —. _____
   _____   _____

DIAGNOSTIC SUGGESTIONS:

Axis I:

312.34	Intermittent Explosive Disorder
296.xx	Bipolar I Disorder
296.89	Bipolar II Disorder
296.xx	Major Depression
312.30	Impulse Control Disorder NOS
309.3	Adjustment Disorder with Disturbance of Conduct
312.8	Conduct Disorder
310.1	Personality Change Due to (Axis III Disorder)
309.81	Posttraumatic Stress Disorder
303.90	Alcohol Dependence
304.20	Cocaine Dependence

_____   _____

_____   _____

Axis II:

301.83	Borderline Personality Disorder
301.7	Antisocial Personality Disorder
301.81	Narcissistic Personality Disorder
301.0	Paranoid Personality Disorder
301.9	Personality Disorder NOS

_____   _____

_____   _____

ANTISOCIAL BEHAVIOR

BEHAVIORAL DEFINITIONS

1. An adolescent history of consistent rule breaking, lying, physical aggression, disrespect for others and their property, stealing, and/or substance abuse resulting in frequent confrontation with authority.
2. Consistent pattern of blaming others for life's failures, conflicts, painful circumstances versus taking personal responsibility for decisions and actions that have caused the negative consequences.
3. Refusal to follow rules with the attitude that they apply to others, not to him/her.
4. History of reckless behaviors that reflect a lack of regard for self or others and show a high need for excitement, having fun, and living on the edge.
5. Little regard for truth as reflected in a pattern of consistently lying to and/or conning others.
6. Pattern of sexual promiscuity: has never been totally monogamous in any relationship and does not take responsibility for children.
7. Pattern of interacting in an irritable, aggressive, and/or argumentative way with authority figures.
8. Experiences little or no remorse for causing pain to others.
9. Often initiates verbal or physical fights.
10. Failure to conform to social norms with respect to the law as shown by repeatedly performed antisocial acts for which he/she may or may not have been arrested (e.g., destroying property, stealing, or pursuing an illegal job).
11. Pattern of impulsive behaviors such as moving often, traveling with no goal, or quitting a job without having another.
12. Inability to maintain consistent employment.
13. Failure to function as a consistently concerned and responsible parent.

—__.__ _____

_____

—__.__ _____

_____

—__.__ _____

_____

LONG-TERM GOALS

1. Reduce the frequency and severity of antisocial behaviors through participation in psychotherapy and/or taking medication.
2. Develop and demonstrate a healthy sense of respect for social norms, the rights of others and the need for honesty.
3. Accept responsibility for own actions, including apologizing for hurts and not blaming others.
4. Improve method of relating to the world, especially authority figures; be more realistic, less defiant, and more socially sensitive.
5. Come to an understanding and acceptance of the need for limits and boundaries on behavior.
6. Maintain consistent employment and demonstrate financial and emotional responsibility for children.

—__.__ _____

_____

—__.__ _____

_____

—__.__ _____

_____

SHORT-TERM OBJECTIVES

THERAPEUTIC INTERVENTIONS

1. Describe the nature and history of the antisocial behavior and note its impact on daily life. (1, 2)

1. Explore the patient's pattern of antisocial behavior (e.g., physical violence, illegal acts, poor occupational functioning, lack of empathy and/or remorse) and how it affects his/her daily life.

2. Describe other symptoms or disorders that may also be present. (3, 4, 5)

3. Patient and/or significant other to describe any current or past suicidal thoughts/behavior as well as violent threats or actions. (6, 7, 8)

4. Outline a complete and accurate medical and

2. Explore the patient's history of conduct disorder symptoms he/she experienced as a child and/or adolescent.

3. Assess the patient for concurrent symptoms of depression, hypomania/mania, attention deficit/hyperactivity disorder, or psychosis (see relevant chapters in this *Planner*).

4. Assess the patient's intellectual capacity and determine if he/she has mental retardation (see the Cognitive Deficits—Developmental Delay chapter in this *Planner*).

5. Gather detailed personal and family history information regarding substance abuse and its interaction with antisocial behavior; refer the patient for in-depth substance abuse treatment, if indicated (see the Chemical Dependence chapters in this *Planner*).

6. Explore the patient's current and past suicidal thoughts and suicidal behavior; ask about family history of suicide (see the Suicidal Ideation chapter in this *Planner*).

7. Assess the patient's potential for violence and determine the presence of current and past threats or acts of aggression.

8. Arrange for hospitalization, as necessary, when the patient is judged to be harmful to self or others or unable to care for his/her basic needs.

9. Explore the patient's history of previous treatment for antisocial

psychiatric history, including treatment received and its effectiveness. (9, 10)

5. Cooperate with a physical examination and laboratory tests. (11, 12)

6. Complete psychological testing and other questionnaires for assessing antisocial behavior. (13)

7. Pursue treatment for concurrent medical problems that may contribute to antisocial behavior. (14, 15)

8. Verbalize an understanding of the aspects of antisocial

behavior and the success of, as well as his/her tolerance for, that treatment.

10. Assess the patient for the presence of other medical problems and the medications used to treat them.

11. Perform a complete physical and neurological examination on the patient and send his/her blood and/or urine for analysis to rule out organic contributors (e.g., prefrontal cortex damage, elevated testosterone levels) to antisocial behavior.

12. Provide feedback to the patient regarding the results and implications of the physical examination and laboratory test results.

13. Administer objective antisocial behavior, impulsivity, and/or aggression rating instruments to the patient (e.g., Psychopathy Checklist Revised [PCL-R], Aggressive Acts Questionnaire [AAQ], Barratt Impulsiveness Scale-11 [BIS-11]); evaluate the results and give him/her feedback.

14. Treat or refer the patient for treatment for any medical problem that may be contributing to antisocial behavior (e.g., prefrontal cortex damage, elevated testosterone levels).

15. Monitor the patient's progress in recovery from concomitant disorders and the impact of the recovery on his/her antisocial behavior.

16. Educate the patient on the unsociable and/or illegal

behavior and its relationship with other psychiatric disorders and substance abuse. (16, 17, 18)

9. Express an understanding of treatment options, expected results from medication, and potential side effects. (19, 20)

10. Participate in psychotherapy sessions as planned with the therapist. (21, 22)

11. Take prescribed medications responsibly at times ordered by the physician. (23, 24, 25)

behaviors he/she may display, as well as consequences for that behavior.

17. Teach the patient to recognize symptoms of other disorders (e.g., depression, hypomania/mania) that are often concurrent with antisocial behavior.

18. Emphasize to the patient the negative and dangerous interaction of substance abuse with antisocial behavior (e.g., increased risk-taking behavior, impulsivity, disregard for social mores).

19. Discuss appropriate treatment options for antisocial behavior with the patient including medications and behaviorally-oriented psychotherapy.

20. Educate the patient on medication treatment including expected results, potential side effects, and dosing strategies.

21. Assess the patient for potential benefit from psychotherapy; refer him/her to a psychotherapist, if indicated.

22. Monitor the patient's response to psychotherapy; assess his/her ability to verbalize a basis for progress in reduction of antisocial behavior (e.g., improvement in social and occupational functioning, increased responsibility for actions, reduction in violent behavior, sobriety).

23. Prescribe to the patient a selective serotonin reuptake inhibitor (SSRI) (e.g., paroxetine [Paxil®], sertraline [Zoloft®], citalopram

[Celexa™], escitalopram [Lexapro™], fluoxetine [Prozac®], or fluvoxamine [Luvox®]); strongly consider this in patients with concurrent depressive symptoms.

24. Consider prescribing a long-acting benzodiazepine (e.g., clonazepam [Klonopin®], diazepam [Valium®]) if the patient has severe aggression (i.e., physical violence) requiring rapid treatment.

25. Titrate the patient's medication to the minimum effective dose for treating his/her symptoms.

12. Report as to the effectiveness of medications and any side effects that develop. (26, 27, 28)

26. Monitor the patient frequently for the development of side effects, response to medication, adherence to treatment, and abuse of medication (if he/she is taking benzodiazepines).

27. Evaluate the patient after six weeks of therapy with an SSRI for his/her response to medication; determine if he/she has had a partial response or a full response to the treatment regimen.

28. Increase the medication dose if the patient has had a partial response; titrate his/her dose every two weeks until the patient's symptoms are controlled or until a maximum dose is reached.

13. Express an understanding of the need for mood-stabilizing medication and cooperate with the prescribed treatment. (29)

29. Consider adding a mood stabilizer (e.g., carbamazepine [Tegretol®], lithium [Eskalith®, Lithonate®], divalproex sodium [Depakote®], or lamotrigine [Lamictal®]) if the patient displays impulsive and/or

14. Cooperate with blood draws to monitor medication levels and adhere to any adjustments in medication dose. (30)

15. Report as to the effectiveness of the mood-stabilizing medication and any side effects that develop. (31)

16. Take an atypical antipsychotic agent added to the medication regimen. (32, 33, 34)

17. Adhere to the schedule for medication injections to control sexual aggression. (35)

18. Retain a significant reduction in antisocial behavior. (36)

aggressive behavior that is not controlled with an SSRI.

30. Measure medication blood levels in four to five days if the patient is taking lithium (Lithonate®, Eskalith®), divalproex sodium (Depakote®), or carbamazepine (Tegretol®); adjust the dose to obtain therapeutic blood levels.

31. Reassess the patient in one to two weeks for response to the mood-stabilizing medication, development of side effects and adherence to treatment.

32. Consider adding an atypical antipsychotic agent (e.g., risperidone [Risperdal®], olanzapine [Zyprexa®], ziprasidone [Geodon®], aripiprazole [Abilify™], quetiapine [Seroquel®], clozapine [Clozaril®]) if the patient does not have a satisfactory response to other medications.

33. Monitor the patient frequently for the development of side effects, response to medication, and adherence to treatment.

34. Titrate the patient's antipsychotic dose every two weeks until his/her symptoms are controlled or the maximum dose is reached.

35. Consider prescribing intramuscular medroxyprogesterone (Depo-Provera®) if the patient has a history of sexual violence or aggression.

36. Maintain the patient on current medication indefinitely if he/she has shown

an improvement in antisocial
behavior.

—. _____ —. _____

   _____   _____

—. _____ —. _____

   _____   _____

—. _____ —. _____

   _____   _____

DIAGNOSTIC SUGGESTIONS:

Axis I:	314.xx	Attention-Deficit/Hyperactivity Disorder
	296.xx	Bipolar I Disorder
	296.89	Bipolar II Disorder
	312.30	Impulse Control Disorder NOS
	295.xx	Schizophrenia
	309.3	Adjustment Disorder with Disturbance of Conduct
	312.8	Conduct Disorder
	303.90	Alcohol Dependence
	304.20	Cocaine Dependence
	304.80	Polysubstance Dependence
	_____	_____
	_____	_____
Axis II:	301.70	Antisocial Personality Disorder
	301.81	Narcissistic Personality Disorder
	_____	_____
	_____	_____

ANXIETY

BEHAVIORAL DEFINITIONS

1. Excessive and persistent daily worry about several life circumstances such as relationships, work, or school performance.
2. Difficulty controlling the worry.
3. Impaired functioning because of the worry (e.g., avoidance of anxiety-provoking situations).
4. Symptoms of motor tension such as restlessness, tiredness, shakiness, or muscle tension.
5. Symptoms of autonomic hyperactivity such as tremor, dry mouth, trouble swallowing, nausea, or diarrhea.
6. Difficulty concentrating.
7. Trouble falling or staying asleep.
8. Feelings of irritability.

—. _____

_____

—. _____

_____

—. _____

_____

LONG-TERM GOALS

1. Reduce overall frequency and intensity of the anxiety so that daily functioning is not impaired.
2. Take the appropriate medication and dose to control symptoms of anxiety.
3. Stabilize anxiety level while increasing ability to function on a daily basis.

4. Effectively cope with the full variety of life's anxieties.

—. _____

_____

—. _____

_____

—. _____

_____

SHORT-TERM OBJECTIVES

1. Describe the signs and symptoms of anxiety that are experienced and note their impact on daily life. (1, 2)

2. Describe other symptoms or disorders that may also be present. (3, 4, 5)

THERAPEUTIC INTERVENTIONS

1. Explore how anxiety is experienced by the patient and how it affects his/her daily life (e.g., frequent worrying, social withdrawal, tension, insomnia).

2. Determine the acuity and severity of the anxiety symptoms (e.g., extreme restlessness, suicidal thoughts) and the urgency with which they need to be controlled.

3. Assess the patient for comorbid disorders (e.g., depression or panic) (see the Depression and/or Phobia-Panic/Agoraphobia chapters in this *Planner*).

4. Gather detailed personal and family history information regarding substance abuse and its potential contribution to anxiety; refer the patient for in-depth substance abuse treatment, if indicated (see the Chemical Dependence chapters in this *Planner*).

5. Emphasize the negative and dangerous impact of substance abuse on anxiety.

3. Complete psychological testing and other questionnaires
for measuring level of anxiety.
(6)

4. Outline a complete and accurate medical and psychiatric
history, including treatment
received and its effectiveness.
(7, 8, 9)

5. Cooperate with a physical examination and laboratory tests.
(10, 11)

6. Pursue treatment for concurrent medical problems that
may contribute to anxiety
symptoms. (12, 13)

6. Administer an objective anxiety
assessment instrument to the
patient (e.g., Beck Anxiety
Inventory [BAI], Hamilton
Anxiety Rating Scale [HARS]);
evaluate the results and give
feedback to him/her.

7. Explore the patient's history of
previous treatment for anxiety
and the success of, as well as
his/her tolerance for, that
treatment.

8. Assess the patient for the presence of other medical problems
and what medications are used
to treat them.

9. Explore the patient's use of any
medication or other substance
that could produce or worsen
anxiety (i.e., caffeine, ephedrine,
pseudoephedrine, ampheta-
mines, bronchodilators, anticholinergics, corticosteroids).

10. Perform a complete physical and
neurological examination on the
patient and send his/her blood
and/or urine for analysis to rule
out an organic cause for anxiety.

11. Provide feedback to the patient
regarding the results and
implications of the physical
examination and laboratory test
results.

12. Treat or refer the patient for
treatment for any medical
problem that may be causing
or contributing to anxiety
symptoms (e.g., cardio-
vascular disease, pulmonary
disease, endocrine disorders,
pheochromocytoma, carcinoid
syndrome).

7. Express an understanding of the possible causes for anxiety and the relationships between anxiety, depression, and substance abuse. (14, 15, 16)

8. Express an understanding of treatment options, expected results from medication and potential side effects. (17, 18)

9. Take prescribed medications responsibly at times ordered by the physician. (19, 20, 21, 22, 23)

13. Monitor the patient's progress in recovery from concomitant disorders and the impact of the recovery on his/her anxiety.

14. Emphasize the negative and dangerous impact of substance abuse on anxiety.

15. Educate the patient on the possible causes (e.g., interpersonal conflicts, life stressors, genetic propensity, medical illness, medications) and signs of anxiety.

16. Ask the patient to identify what he/she believes may be contributing factors to his/her anxiety.

17. Discuss appropriate treatment options with the patient including medications and psychotherapy.

18. Educate the patient on psychotropic medication treatment including expected results, potential side effects, dependence liability, potential of benzodiazepines, and dosing strategies.

19. Prescribe a selective serotonin reuptake inhibitor (SSRI) with documented antianxiety properties (e.g., paroxetine [Paxil®]); strongly consider this strategy in patients with comorbid depression (see the Depression chapter in this *Planner*).

20. Prescribe a benzodiazepine (e.g., diazepam [Valium®], clonazepam [Klonopin®], oxazepam [Serax®]) if the patient needs urgent symptom relief or has been treated with

benzodiazepines previously and has no history of substance abuse.

21. Determine if the patient has somatic anxiety symptoms (e.g., muscle tension, dry mouth, nausea, and vomiting); consider the use of benzodiazepines in patients with these symptoms.

22. Consider using buspirone (BuSpar®) in patients that require less urgent symptom relief or in patients who have a history of substance abuse.

23. Determine if the patient has emotional symptoms of anxiety (e.g., interpersonal sensitivity, anger, or hostility); if any of these are present consider prescribing an antidepressant.

10. Report on the effectiveness of medications and any side effects that develop. (24, 25, 26)

24. Titrate the dose of benzodiazepines or buspirone (BuSpar®) every two to three days until anxiety symptoms are controlled or the maximum dose for the medication is reached.

25. Titrate the antidepressant medication to the minimum effective dose for treating the patient's anxiety.

26. Monitor the patient frequently for the development of side effects, response to medication, adherence to treatment, or withdrawal symptoms (if he/she takes benzodiazepines).

11. Participate in psychotherapy sessions as planned with therapist. (27, 28)

27. Assess the patient for potential benefit from psychotherapy and refer him/her to a psychotherapist, if necessary.

28. Monitor the patient's investment in and response to psychotherapy;

assess his/her ability to verbalize a basis for progress in anxiety recovery (e.g., reduction in worry, resolved conflicts, improved relationships, sobriety).

12. Attend follow-up appointments as scheduled by the physician. (29, 30, 31)

29. Reassess the patient who is taking a benzodiazepine or buspirone (BuSpar®) in two weeks; determine whether the medication is adequate, needs a dose increase, or another agent needs to be tried.

30. Reassess the patient who is taking an antidepressant in four weeks; determine whether the medication is adequate, needs a dose increase, or another agent needs to be tried.

31. Evaluate the patient at six weeks for his/her response to medication; determine if he/she has had a full response or partial response to the treatment regimen.

13. Report evidence of the degree of improvement in anxiety symptoms as well as any co-morbid disorders. (32, 33)

32. Repeat the administration of objective rating instruments to the patient for assessment of his/her anxiety severity, evaluate the results, and give him/her feedback.

33. Discuss other treatment options with the patient if he/she shows only a partial treatment response.

14. Adhere to augmentation of medication regimen. (34, 35, 36)

34. Increase medication dose if the patient has had a partial response; titrate his/her dose every two weeks until the maximum dose is reached.

35. Determine if the patient needs additional medication to augment current therapy; consider adding a medication from

15. Cooperate with changes in type of antianxiety medication prescribed. (37, 38, 39, 40, 41)

another class to the current treatment (e.g., antidepressants, benzodiazepines, buspirone [BuSpar®], or hydroxyzine [Vistaril®]).

36. Maximize augmentation medication as tolerated by the patient.

37. Consider changing the patient's medication to another agent if he/she has minimal or no response to the initial medication and the augmentation process; alternatives include an SSRI, tricyclic antidepressant (TCA) (e.g., imipramine [Tofranil®], amitriptyline [Elavil®], venlafaxine [Effexor®], nefazodone [Serzone®], hydroxyzine [Vistaril®], mirtazapine [Remeron®], or monoamine oxidase inhibitors [MAOIs]).

38. Complete a medical evaluation on the patient including an electrocardiogram, if necessary, before starting him/her on a TCA; gradually titrate dose of TCA as necessary to maximum effectiveness.

39. Educate the patient on dietary restrictions and ask him/her to try the restrictions before starting a MAOI.

40. Prescribe MAOI and titrate dose as necessary, monitoring for effectiveness and side effects as well as the patient's compliance with the dietary restrictions.

41. Titrate the dose of the alternative Anxiolytic medication every two or three days until minimum dose is reached for symptom

16. Retain a remission of anxiety symptoms with a minimum amount of medications. (42, 43)

17. Read books on coping with anxiety and implement newly learned techniques. (44)

control or until maximum dose for the medication is reached.

42. Maintain the patient on current medication for four to six months if he/she has shown a fully successful response; if he/she has had previous episodes of anxiety, consider continuing treatment indefinitely.

43. Taper benzodiazepines off slowly to avoid the patient experiencing withdrawal symptoms (e.g., rebound anxiety, tremor, nausea, elevated pulse or blood pressure).

44. Recommend that the patient read books on coping with anxiety (e.g., *Ten Days to Self Esteem!* by Burns; *Relaxation and Stress Reduction Workbook* by Davis, Eshelman, and McKay); process his/her implementation of coping techniques, reinforcing success and redirecting for failure

__. _____   __. _____
   _____   _____

__. _____   __. _____
   _____   _____

__. _____   __. _____
   _____   _____

__. _____   __. _____
   _____   _____

__. _____   __. _____
   _____   _____

__. _____   __. _____
   _____   _____

DIAGNOSTIC SUGGESTIONS:

Axis I:
300.02	Generalized Anxiety Disorder
293.89	Anxiety Disorder Due to (Axis III Disorder)
300.23	Social Phobia
300.01	Panic Disorder without Agoraphobia
300.21	Panic Disorder with Agoraphobia
300.29	Specific Phobia
309.81	Posttraumatic Stress Disorder
300.3	Obsessive-Compulsive Disorder
308.3	Acute Stress Disorder
291.8	Alcohol-Induced Mood Disorder
292.89	Substance-Induced Anxiety Disorder
296.2x	Major Depressive Disorder, Single Episode
296.3x	Major Depressive Disorder, Recurrent
309.24	Adjustment Disorder with Anxiety

_____   _____

_____   _____

Axis II:

_____   _____

_____   _____

ATTENTION DEFICIT/HYPERACTIVITY DISORDER (ADHD)—ADULT

BEHAVIORAL DEFINITIONS

1. Childhood history of attention deficit/hyperactivity disorder (ADHD) that was either diagnosed or later concluded from the symptoms of behavioral problems at school, impulsivity, over-excitability, temper outbursts, and lacking concentration.
2. Unable to concentrate or pay attention to subjects of low interest, even when those things are important.
3. Easily distracted and drawn from the task at hand.
4. Restless and fidgety; unable to be sedentary for more than a short time.
5. Impulsive; has an easily observable pattern of acting first, thinking later.
6. Rapid mood swings and mood lability within short spans of time.
7. Disorganized in most areas of life.
8. Starts many projects but rarely finishes any.
9. Has a quick temper.
10. Exhibits low stress tolerance; is easily frustrated, hassled, or upset.
11. Chronic low self-esteem.
12. Tendency toward cngaging in addictive behaviors (e.g., alcohol/drug abuse, gambling) due to impulsivity and restlessness.
13. Impairment in social and occupational functioning because of inattention and related behaviors.

—. _____
   _____
—. _____
   _____
—. _____
   _____

LONG-TERM GOALS

1. Accept ADHD as a chronic issue requiring continuing medication treatment.
2. Reduce impulsive actions while increasing concentration and focus on low-interest activities.
3. Reduce ADHD behavioral interference in daily life.
4. Sustain attention and concentration for consistently longer periods of time.
5. Achieve a satisfactory level of balance, structure, and intimacy in personal life.

__. _____

_____

_____

__. _____

_____

__. _____

_____

SHORT-TERM OBJECTIVES

THERAPEUTIC INTERVENTIONS

1. Describe the nature and history of the attention deficit symptoms and note their impact on daily life. (1, 2)

1. Explore what symptoms are experienced by the patient (e.g., distractibility, inability to complete tasks, quick temper, restlessness) and how they affect his/her daily life.

2. Explore the patient's history of ADHD symptoms he/she experienced as a child.

2. Describe other symptoms or disorders that may also be present. (3, 4, 5)

3. Evaluate the patient for any symptoms that would suggest a diagnosis of hypomania/mania rather than ADHD (e.g., decreased sleep, rapid speech, expansive mood, depression cycling).

4. Assess the patient for concurrent symptoms of depression, mania or antisocial

behavior (see Depression, Hypomania/Mania, and Antisocial Behavior chapters in this *Planner*).

5. Gather detailed personal and family history information regarding substance abuse and its interaction with ADHD; refer the patient for in-depth substance abuse treatment, if indicated (see the Chemical Dependence chapters in this *Planner*).

3. Outline a complete and accurate medical and psychiatric history, including treatment received and its effectiveness. (6, 7)

6. Explore the patient's history of previous treatment for ADHD and the success of, as well as his/her tolerance for, that treatment.

7. Assess the patient for the presence of other medical problems and the medications used to treat them.

4. Cooperate with a physical examination and laboratory tests. (8, 9)

8. Perform a complete physical and neurological examination on the patient and send his/her blood and/or urine for analysis to rule out organic contributors to ADHD.

9. Provide feedback to the patient regarding the results and implications of the physical examination and laboratory test results.

5. Complete psychological testing and other questionnaires for assessing the symptoms of ADHD. (10)

10. Administer an objective ADHD rating instrument to the patient (e.g., Copeland Symptom Checklist for Adult ADHD, Brown Adult ADD Scale); evaluate the results and give him/her feedback.

6. Pursue treatment for concurrent medical problems that may contribute to ADHD symptoms. (11, 12)

11. Treat or refer the patient for treatment for any medical problem that may be contributing to ADHD (e.g., thyroid disease, seizures, sleep apnea,

intoxication, hearing deficits, vitamin B12 deficiency, head injury, heavy metal poisoning).

12. Monitor the patient's progress in recovery from concomitant disorders and the impact of the recovery on his/her ADHD symptoms.

7. Verbalize an understanding of the possible causes for ADHD and its relationship with other psychiatric disorders and substance abuse. (13, 14, 15)

13. Educate the patient on the possible causes (e.g., genetic propensity, brain metabolism abnormalities, neurotransmitter abnormalities) and signs of ADHD.

14. Teach the patient to recognize symptoms of other disorders (e.g., depression, hypomania/mania) that are often comorbid with ADHD.

15. Emphasize to the patient the negative and dangerous impact of substance abuse on ADHD.

8. Express an understanding of treatment options, expected results from medication, and potential side effects. (16, 17)

16. Discuss appropriate treatment options for ADHD with the patient including medications and psychotherapy.

17. Educate the patient on stimulant medication treatment including expected results, potential side effects, and dosing strategies.

9. Take prescribed medications responsibly at times ordered by the physician. (18, 19)

18. Prescribe to the patient a long-acting stimulant (i.e., sustained-release methylphenidate [Concerta®, Ritalin-LA®, Metadate CD®] or sustained-release amphetamine [Adderall® XR]); do not use in patients with a history of cocaine or amphetamine abuse.

19. Consider prescribing a non-stimulant agent (i.e., atomoxetine

[Strattera®], bupropion [Wellbutrin®], venlafaxine [Effexor®], imipramine [Tofranil®], desipramine [Norpramin®]) if the patient has a history of cocaine or amphetamine abuse.

10. Comply with changes in medication dosing as recommended by the physician. (20, 21)

20. Titrate stimulants every two to three days until symptoms are controlled or maximum dose is reached.

21. Titrate nonstimulants every two to four weeks until the patient's symptoms are controlled or maximum dose is reached.

11. Identify times of the day when the medication is less effective. (22, 23, 24)

22. Evaluate the patient for periods of the day (especially early morning or late afternoon) when symptoms are poorly controlled.

23. Recommend the patient keep a journal to document symptom severity throughout the day.

24. Consider adding a short-acting stimulant (i.e., methylphenidate [Ritalin®] or amphetamine [Adderall®]) to "jump start" the patient in the morning or provide a boost at other times of symptom worsening.

12. Participate in psychotherapy sessions as planned with the therapist. (25, 26)

25. Assess the patient for potential benefit from psychotherapy; refer him/her to a psychotherapist if necessary.

26. Monitor the patient's response to psychotherapy; assess his/her ability to verbalize a basis for progress in ADHD symptom reduction (e.g., improvement in social and occupational functioning, increased focus on tasks, sobriety).

13. Report on the effectiveness of medications and any side effects that develop. (27, 28, 29)

14. Express an understanding of additional treatment options and cooperate with the prescribed treatment. (30, 31, 32, 33)

27. Monitor the patient for any possible medication abuse or development of side effects from stimulants (e.g., insomnia, anxiety, poor appetite, feeling jittery); decrease the dose, terminate the prescription, or change the scheduled times for taking the medication as necessary.

28. Monitor blood pressure if the patient is treated with stimulants.

29. Repeat administration of objective rating instruments for assessment of the patient's ADHD; evaluate the results and give him/her feedback.

30. Discuss alternative treatments if the patient does not obtain full symptom relief or cannot tolerate or control his/her use of stimulants.

31. Prescribe an alternative medication (i.e., atomoxetine [Strattera®], bupropion [Wellbutrin®], clonidine [Catapres®], buspirone [BuSpar®], modafinil [Provigil®]) to augment or replace stimulant therapy.

32. Consider prescribing an antidepressant medication (e.g., bupropion [Wellbutrin®], venlafaxine [Effexor®], imipramine [Tofranil®], desipramine [Norpramin®], fluoxetine [Prozac®], sertraline [Zoloft®], paroxetine [Paxil®]) to augment current therapy; strongly consider this if the patient has comorbid depression.

33. Titrate the alternative medication as appropriate until symptoms are

controlled or maximum dose is reached.

15. Verbalize an understanding of risks associated with pemoline treatment and cooperate with necessary blood work. (34, 35)

34. Consider using pemoline (Cylert®) if the patient has failed to improve with the use of other medications.

35. Educate the patient on the risk of hepatotoxicity with acute liver failure that is associated with pemoline treatment; closely monitor hepatic transaminases during treatment.

16. Retain a significant reduction in ADHD symptoms. (36)

36. Maintain the patient on current medication if he/she has shown a satisfactory improvement in ADHD symptoms.

17. Read books on ADHD to learn more about the disorder. (37)

37. Recommend the patient read books on ADHD (e.g., *Driven to Distraction* by Hallowell and Raty; *The Hyperactive Child, Adolescent and Adult* by Wender; *Putting in the Brakes* by Quinn and Stern; *You Mean I'm Not Lazy, Stupid or Crazy* by Kelly and Ramundo) to gain a better understanding of the disorder.

__. _____   __. _____
    _____   _____

__. _____   __. _____
    _____   _____

__. _____   __. _____
    _____   _____

__. _____   __. _____
    _____   _____

__. _____   __. _____
    _____   _____

DIAGNOSTIC SUGGESTIONS:

Axis I:

314.00	Attention-Deficit/Hyperactivity Disorder, Predominately Inattentive Type
314.01	Attention-Deficit/Hyperactivity Disorder, Predominately Hyperactivity-Impulsive Type
314.9	Attention-Deficit/Hyperactivity Disorder NOS
296.xx	Bipolar I Disorder
296.89	Bipolar II Disorder
301.13	Cyclothymic Disorder
296.80	Bipolar Disorder NOS
312.30	Impulse Control Disorder
303.90	Alcohol Dependence
305.00	Alcohol Abuse
304.20	Cocaine Dependence
305.60	Cocaine Abuse
304.40	Amphetamine Dependence
305.70	Amphetamine Abuse
304.30	Cannabis Dependence
305.20	Cannabis Abuse

_____   _____

_____   _____

Axis II: 301.70   Antisocial Personality Disorder

_____   _____

_____   _____

BORDERLINE PERSONALITY

BEHAVIORAL DEFINITIONS

1. Under minor stress displays extreme emotional reactivity (e.g., anger, depression, anxiety) that usually does not last more than a few hours to a few days.
2. A pattern of intense, chaotic interpersonal relationships.
3. Marked identity disturbance.
4. Impulsive behavior that is potentially self-damaging.
5. Recurrent suicidal gestures, threats, or self-mutilative behavior.
6. Chronic feelings of emptiness and boredom.
7. Severe mood lability.
8. Frequent eruptions of intense, inappropriate anger.
9. Easily feels that others are treating him/her unfairly or that they can't be trusted.
10. Analyzes most issues in simple terms of right and wrong (e.g., black/white, trustworthy/deceitful) without regard for extenuating circumstances or complex situations.
11. Becomes very anxious with any hint of perceived abandonment in a relationship.

—. _____

_____

—. _____

_____

—. _____

_____

LONG-TERM GOALS

1. Reduce the frequency and severity of mood swings and self-damaging behaviors through medication and/or psychotherapy.
2. Develop the ability to control impulses.
3. Learn and demonstrate strategies to deal with dysphoric moods.
4. Replace dichotomous thinking with the ability to tolerate ambiguity and complexity in people and issues.
5. Learn and demonstrate anger management skills.
6. Learn and practice interpersonal relationship skills.

—. _____

   _____

—. _____

   _____

—. _____

   _____

SHORT-TERM OBJECTIVES

1. Describe the signs and symptoms associated with borderline personality and note their impact on daily life. (1)

2. Describe other symptoms or disorders that may also be present. (2, 3)

THERAPEUTIC INTERVENTIONS

1. Explore the symptoms that are experienced by the patient (e.g., mood swings, dysphoric mood, anxiety, chaotic relationships, self-damaging behavior, transient psychotic episodes) and how they affect his/her daily life.

2. Assess the patient for concurrent symptoms of depression, hypomania/ mania, anxiety or psychosis (see the relevant chapters in this *Planner*).

3. Gather detailed personal and family history information regarding substance abuse and its interaction with antisocial behavior; refer the patient for in-depth substance abuse treatment, if indicated (see the Chemical

3. Patient and/or significant other describe any current or past suicidal thoughts/behavior as well as violent threats or actions. (4, 5, 6, 7)

4. Outline a complete and accurate medical and psychiatric history, including treatment received and its effectiveness. (8, 9)

5. Cooperate with a physical cxamination and laboratory tests. (10, 11)

Dependence chapters in this *Planner*).

4. Explore the patient's current and past suicidal thoughts and suicidal behavior; ask about family history of suicide (see the Suicidal Ideation chapter in this *Planner*).

5. Assess the patient's potential for violence and determine the presence of current and past threats or acts of aggression.

6. Arrange for hospitalization, as necessary, when the patient is judged to be harmful to self or others or unable to care for his/her basic needs.

7. Reinforce with the patient his/her responsibility for any suicidal behavior that he/she may display.

8. Explore the patient's history of previous treatment for symptoms associated with borderline personality and the success of, as well as his/her tolerance for, that treatment.

9. Assess the patient for the presence of other medical problems and the medications used to treat them.

10. Perform a complete physical and neurological examination on the patient and send his/her blood and/or urine for analysis to rule out organic contributors (e.g., prefrontal cortex damage, endocrine disease) to symptoms of borderline personality.

11. Provide feedback to the patient regarding the results and implications of the physical

6. Complete psychological testing and other questionnaires for assessing symptoms assocated with borderline personality. (12)

7. Pursue treatment for concurrent medical problems that may complicate the treatment of borderline personality. (13, 14)

8. Verbalize an understanding of the aspects of borderline personality and its relationship with other psychiatric disorders and substance abuse. (15, 16, 17)

examination and laboratory test results.

12. Administer to the patient objective rating instruments to measure depression, suicidality, impulsivity and/or aggression (e.g., Hamilton Depression Rating Scale [HDRS], Beck's Scale for Suicide Ideation [SSI], Aggressive Acts Questionnaire [AAQ], Barratt Impulsiveness Scale-11 [BIS-11]); evaluate the results and give him/her feedback.

13. Treat or refer the patient for treatment of any medical problem that may complicate the treatment of borderline personality (e.g., prefrontal cortex damage, hypertension, diabetes, thyroid disease).

14. Monitor the patient's progress in recovering from concomitant disorders and the impact of the recovery on his/her maladaptive behavior.

15. Educate the patient on the impulsive, emotionally reactive, self-destructive, and/or illegal behaviors he/she may display, as well as consequences for that behavior.

16. Teach the patient to recognize symptoms of other disorders (e.g., depression, anxiety, psychosis) that are often concurrent with borderline personality.

17. Emphasize to the patient the negative and dangerous impact of substance abuse on symptoms associated with borderline personality.

9. Express an understanding of treatment options, expected results from medication, and potential side effects. (18, 19, 20, 21)

18. Discuss appropriate treatment options for borderline personality with the patient including medications and psychotherapy.

19. Educate the patient on medication treatment including expected results, potential side effects, and dosing strategies.

20. Educate the patient on his/her responsibility for taking medications as prescribed and the potential consequences of overdosing.

21. Refer the patient to an advocacy group for patients with borderline personality disorder (e.g., Treatment and Research Advancements [TARA]).

10. Participate in psychotherapy sessions as planned with the therapist. (22, 23)

22. Assess the patient for potential benefit from psychotherapy; refer him/her to a psychotherapist, if necessary.

23. Monitor the patient's response to psychotherapy; assess his/her ability to verbalize a basis for progress in reduction of maladaptive behavior (e.g., improvement in social and occupational functioning, reduction in self-damaging behavior, improvement in coping skills used during adversity, sobriety).

11. Take prescribed medications responsibly at times ordered by the physician. (24, 25, 26)

24. Prescribe to the patient a selective serotonin reuptake inhibitor (SSRI) (e.g., paroxetine [Paxil®], sertraline [Zoloft®], citalopram [Celexa™], escitalopram [Lexapro™], fluoxetine [Prozac®], or fluvoxamine [Luvox®]); strongly consider this in patients with rapid mood

swings and/or depressive symptoms.

25. Avoid the use of medications that have a high lethality potential if overdosed (i.e., tricyclic antidepressants [TCAs]).

26. Titrate the patient's medication to the minimum effective dose for treating his/her symptoms.

12. Report as to the effectiveness of SSRI medications and any side effects that develop. (27, 28)

27. Monitor the patient frequently for the development of side effects, response to medication, and adherence to treatment.

28. Evaluate the patient after six weeks of therapy with an SSRI for his/her response to medication; determine if he/she has had a partial response or a full response to the treatment regimen.

13. Cooperate with increases in dose or changes in medication. (29, 30, 31)

29. Increase medication dose if the patient has had a partial response; titrate his/her dose every two weeks until the patient's symptoms are controlled or the maximum dose is reached.

30. Prescribe a different SSRI if the patient does not have a satisfactory response to the first SSRI; titrate the dose until the patient's symptoms are controlled or the maximum dose is reached.

31. Consider prescribing an anxiolytic (e.g., clonazepam [Klonopin®], buspirone [BuSpar®], hydroxyzine [Vistaril®, Atarax®]) if the patient experiences acute or reactive anxiety to stressors; avoid the use of short-acting benzodiazepines (e.g., alprazolam [Xanax®]), which could cause disinhibition.

14. Express an understanding of the need for mood-stabilizing medication and cooperate with the prescribed treatment. (32, 33)

15. Cooperate with blood tests to monitor medication levels and adhere to any adjustments in medication dose. (34)

16. Report on the effectiveness of the mood-stabilizing medication and any side effects that develop. (35, 36)

17. Take an atypical antipsychotic added to the medication regimen. (37, 38, 39, 40)

32. Determine if the patient displays impulsive behavior or rapid mood swings that are not controlled with an SSRI.

33. Consider adding a mood stabilizer (e.g., carbamazepine [Tegretol®], lithium [Eskalith®, Lithonate®], divalproex sodium [Depakote®], or lamotrigine [Lamictal®]).

34. Measure medication blood levels in four to five days if the patient is taking lithium (Lithonate®, Eskalith®), divalproex sodium (Depakote®), or carbamazepine (Tegretol®); adjust the dose to obtain therapeutic blood levels.

35. Reassess the patient in one to two weeks for response to medication, development of side effects, and adherence to treatment.

36. Repeat administration of objective rating instruments for assessment of the patient's mood stability, impulsivity and suicidality; evaluate the results and give him/her feedback.

37. Determine if the patient has periods of transient psychosis or self-mutilative behavior that is not controlled with other medications.

38. Prescribe a low dose of an atypical antipsychotic agent (e.g., risperidone [Risperdal®], olanzapine [Zyprexa®], ziprasidone [Geodon®], aripiprazole [Abilify™], quetiapine [Seroquel®], or clozapine [Clozaril®]).

39. Monitor the patient frequently for the development of side effects, response to medication, and adherence to treatment.

40. Titrate the patient's antipsychotic dose every two weeks until his/her symptoms are controlled or the maximum dose is reached.

18. Retain a significant reduction in symptoms of borderline personality. (41)

41. Maintain the patient on current medication if he/she has shown improvement in signs and symptoms of borderline personality.

__. _____

_____

__. _____

_____

__. _____

_____

__. _____

_____

DIAGNOSTIC SUGGESTIONS:

Axis I:	296.xx	Major Depressive Disorder
	300.4	Dysthymic Disorder
	301.13	Cyclothymic Disorder
	296.xx	Bipolar I Disorder
	296.89	Bipolar II Disorder
	307.1	Anorexia Nervosa
	307.51	Bulimia Nervosa
	295.xx	Schizophrenia
	303.90	Alcohol Dependence
	304.20	Cocaine Dependence
	304.80	Polysubstance Dependence
	_____	_____
	_____	_____
Axis II:	301.83	Borderline Personality Disorder
	301.9	Personality Disorder NOS
	_____	_____
	_____	_____

CHEMICAL DEPENDENCE—RELAPSE PREVENTION

BEHAVIORAL DEFINITIONS

1. Inability to abstain from mood-altering drugs after receiving treatment for substance abuse.
2. Inability to stay sober even though attending Alcoholics Anonymous (AA) or another support group or rehabilitation program meetings regularly.
3. Relapse into abuse of mood-altering substances after a substantial period of sobriety.
4. Chronic pattern of periods of sobriety (6 months or more) followed by a relapse, then reestablishing sobriety.

—. _____
   _____
—. _____
   _____
—. _____
   _____

LONG-TERM GOALS

1. Take appropriate medication and dose to aid in maintaining sobriety indefinitely.
2. Acquire the necessary skills to maintain long-term sobriety from all mood-altering substances and live a life free of chemicals.
3. Develop an increased awareness of relapse triggers and the coping strategies to effectively deal with them.

4. Achieve a quality of life that is substance free on a continuing basis.

—. _____

_____

—. _____

_____

—. _____

_____

SHORT-TERM OBJECTIVES

1. Describe the amount, frequency, and history of substance abuse. (1, 2)

2. Describe symptoms of withdrawal and/or symptoms of other disorders that may also be present. (3, 4)

3. Complete psychological testing and other questionnaires

THERAPEUTIC INTERVENTIONS

1. Gather detailed personal history information regarding substance abuse, including types of substance used, amount and pattern of use, signs and symptoms of use, and negative consequences (i.e., social, legal, relational, and vocational).

2. Gather detailed family history information regarding substance abuse.

3. Assess the patient for the presence of withdrawal symptoms that need to be treated pharmacologically (e.g., tachycardia, tremor, anxiety, seizures, nausea, insomnia, sweating) (see the Chemical Dependence—Withdrawal chapter in this *Planner*).

4. Assess the patient for concurrent mental disorders and recommended treatment as needed (see the Depression, Mania/Hypomania, Anxiety, and/or Psychoticism chapters in this *Planner*).

5. Administer objective addiction severity rating instruments to the

for measuring the severity of addiction. (5)

patient (e.g., Addiction Severity Index [ASI], Alcohol Dependence Scale [ADS], University of Rhode Island Change Assessment [URICA]); evaluate the results and give him/her feedback.

4. Outline a complete and accurate medical and psychiatric history, including treatment received and its effectiveness. (6, 7)

6. Explore the patient's history of previous treatment for chemical dependence or other psychiatric disorder and the success of, as well as his/her tolerance for and follow-through with, that treatment.

7. Assess the patient for the presence of other medical problems and what medications are used to treat them.

5. Cooperate with a physical examination and laboratory tests. (8, 9, 10)

8. Perform a complete physical and neurological examination on the patient and send his/her blood and/or urine for analysis to assess his/her current state of health.

9. Provide feedback to the patient regarding the results and implications of the physical examination and laboratory test results.

10. Perform regular urine screens for illicit drugs (e.g., cocaine, cannabis, opioids, amphetamine, phencyclidine) and prescription drugs with abuse potential (e.g., opioids, benzodiazepines, barbiturates).

6. Pursue treatment for concurrent medical or psychiatric problems that may complicate chemical dependence recovery. (11, 12)

11. Treat or refer the patient for treatment for any medical or psychiatric problem that may complicate recovery from chemical dependence (e.g., diabetes, hypertension, cardiac disease, liver disease, depression, anxiety, psychosis).

12. Monitor the patient's progress in recovery from concomitant disorders and the impact of the recovery on his/her chemical dependence.

7. Verbalize an understanding of the possible contributing factors for chemical dependence and the relationship between chemical dependence and other psychiatric disorders. (13, 14)

13. Educate the patient on the possible contributing factors to chemical dependence relapse (e.g., genetic propensity, environmental dynamics, medical illness, psychiatric illness, pain avoidance).

14. Emphasize to the patient the negative and dangerous impact of substance abuse on other psychiatric disorders.

8. Participate in psychotherapy sessions and/or alcohol and drug treatment programs as planned with the therapist. (15, 16, 17, 18)

15. Educate the patient and/or significant others on the potential benefits of psychotherapy and alcohol and drug abuse treatment programs.

16. Refer the patient to a psychotherapist and/or a structured alcohol and drug abuse treatment program (e.g., Alcoholics Anonymous [AA], Narcotics Anonymous [NA], Cocaine Anonymous [CA], a residential treatment facility, or other inpatient or outpatient treatment facility,) if necessary.

17. Refer the patient's significant other(s) to a support group for families of chemically dependent individuals (e.g., Alateen, Al-Anon), if necessary.

18. Monitor the patient's investment in and response to psychotherapy and/or alcohol and drug abuse treatment; assess his/her ability to verbalize a basis for progress in chemical

9. Express an understanding of medication treatment options for alcohol relapse prevention, expected results from medication, and potential side effects. (19, 20)

10. Take prescribed medications for alcohol relapse prevention responsibly at times ordered by the physician. (21, 22)

11. Cooperate with changes in type and/or dose of medication dose. (23, 24, 25)

dependence recovery (e.g., acceptance of chemical dependence, ability to identify triggers, improved coping skills for dealing with triggers).

19. Educate the patient on pharmacologic treatment options for alcohol relapse prevention, including expected results, potential side effects, and dosing strategies.

20. Educate the patient on disulfiram (Antabuse) and the risks associated with alcohol ingestion while taking it (e.g., flushing, feeling warm, increased heart rate, palpitations, nausea, sweating); inform the patient that the symptoms last approximately 30 minutes and are usually self-limiting but that the possibility of a life-threatening reaction exists.

21. Prescribe disulfiram (Antabuse) for the patient who is willing to take the medication and understands the risks; monitor results.

22. Seek the involvement of the patient's significant other(s) to help encourage the patient to take the disulfiram on a daily basis.

23. Consider challenging the patient with a dose of alcohol to test the effectiveness of the disulfiram; increase the dose, as necessary, until the maximum dose is reached.

24. Prescribe a medication with the potential to reduce the patient's craving for alcohol (e.g., a selective serotonin reuptake

inhibitor [SSRI], naltrexone [ReVia®]).

25. Titrate the dose of naltrexone every two to three days or the dose of the SSRI every two to four weeks until alcohol craving is controlled or the maximum dose is reached.

12. Express an understanding of medication treatment options for opioid relapse prevention, expected results from medication, and potential side effects. (26, 27)

26. Educate the patient on treatment options for opioid relapse prevention, including expected results, potential side effects, and dosing strategies.

27. Educate the patient on the guidelines for methadone maintenance therapy (e.g., abstinence from all substances of abuse, daily visits to the treatment center) and the possibility of life-long treatment with methadone.

13. Take prescribed medications for opioid relapse prevention responsibly at times ordered by the physician. (28, 29, 30, 31)

28. Prescribe methadone (Dolophine®, Methadose®) for the patient who is willing to take the medication and understands the guidelines for methadone maintenance therapy; refer the patient to a methadone maintenance treatment program, if necessary.

29. Titrate the dose of methadone every two days until the patient is free from withdrawal symptoms and cravings.

30. Consider the use of levacetylmethadol (L-α-acetylmethadol, LAAM) for patients who are not able or willing to visit the treatment center on a daily basis.

31. Titrate the dose of LAAM every two days until the target dose of 100 mg every other day is reached; inform the patient that

the full effect of LAAM may not be felt for two weeks.

14. Express an understanding of alternative opioid abuse treatment options and cooperate with the treatment. (32, 33)

32. Consider the use of an alternative medication for opioid relapse prevention (e.g., buprenorphine [Buprenex®, Subutex®, Suboxone®], naltrexone [ReVia®]) for patients who are highly motivated to stay sober and are unwilling or unable to take methadone or LAAM.

33. Titrate the dose every two to three days until withdrawal symptoms and cravings are controlled or the maximum dose is reached.

15. Express an understanding of medication treatment options for cocaine relapse prevention. (34)

34. Educate the patient on treatment options for cocaine relapse prevention, including expected results, potential side effects, and dosing strategies.

16. Take prescribed medications for cocaine relapse prevention responsibly at times ordered by the physician. (35, 36, 37)

35. Prescribe selective serotonin reuptake inhibitor (SSRI) (e.g., paroxetine [Paxil®], sertraline [Zoloft®], citalopram [Celexa™], escitalopram [Lexapro™], fluoxetine [Prozac®]); strongly consider this strategy for patients with comorbid depression or anxiety.

36. Titrate the SSRI every two to four weeks until cravings are controlled or the maximum dose is reached.

37. Consider bupropion (Wellbutrin®) as an alternative for patients who do not respond to an SSRI; avoid use of bupropion in patients with a concurrent anxiety or seizure disorder.

17. Retain a remission in chemical dependence. (38, 39)

38. Maintain the patient on current medication indefinitely if he/she has shown a fully successful response or significant reduction in substance use.

39. Taper the medication slowly over several months if the patient decides he/she no longer wants to take it; monitor him/her closely for withdrawal symptoms and increased craving during the taper period.

18. Read books on coping with chemical dependence and implement newly learned techniques. (40)

40. Recommend that the patient read books on coping with chemical dependence (e.g., *Many Roads, One Journey: Moving Beyond the 12 Steps* by Kasl-Davis; *Stage II Recovery* by Larsen; *Ten Days to Self Esteem!* by Burns; *The Staying Sober Workbook* by Gorski); process his/her implementation of coping techniques, reinforcing success and redirecting for failure.

—. _____   —. _____
     _____   _____

—. _____   —. _____
     _____   _____

—. _____   —. _____
     _____   _____

—. _____   —. _____
     _____   _____

—. _____   —. _____
     _____   _____

—. _____   —. _____
     _____   _____

DIAGNOSTIC SUGGESTIONS:

Axis I:	303.90	Alcohol Dependence
	305.00	Alcohol Abuse
	304.20	Cocaine Dependence
	305.60	Cocaine Abuse
	304.00	Opioid Dependence
	305.50	Opioid Abuse
	304.80	Polysubstance Dependence
	304.10	Sedative, Hypnotic or Anxiolytic Dependence
	305.40	Sedative, Hypnotic or Anxiolytic Abuse
	291.2	Alcohol-Induced Persisting Dementia
	291.8	Alcohol-Induced Mood Disorder
	292.84	Substance-Induced Mood Disorder
	296.xx	Major Depression
	296.xx	Bipolar I Disorder
	296.89	Bipolar II Disorder
	295.xx	Schizophrenia
	_____	_____
	_____	_____
Axis II:	301.70	Antisocial Personality Disorder
	_____	_____
	_____	_____

CHEMICAL DEPENDENCE— WITHDRAWAL

BEHAVIORAL DEFINITIONS

1. Consistent use of alcohol or other mood-altering drugs until high, intoxicated, or passed out.
2. Physical symptoms, such as shaking, seizures, nausea, headaches, sweating, anxiety, insomnia, and/or depression, when withdrawing from the substance.
3. Amnesiac blackouts occurred when abusing alcohol.
4. Blood work reflecting the results of a pattern of heavy substance use, for example, elevated liver enzymes.
5. Continued drug and/or alcohol use despite experiencing persistent and recurring physical, legal, vocational, social, or relationship problems that are directly caused by the use of the substance.
6. Increased tolerance for the drug evidenced by the need to use more to become intoxicated or to attain the desired effect.
7. Inability to stop or cut down use of the mood-altering drug once started, despite the verbalized desire to do so and the negative consequences continued use brings.
8. Denial that chemical dependence is a problem despite direct feedback from spouse, relatives, friends, and/or employers that the use of substance is negatively affecting them and others.
9. Suspension of important social, recreational, or occupational activities because they interfere with using drugs.
10. Large time investment in activities to obtain or use the substance or to recover from its effects.
11. Consumption of the substance in greater amounts and for longer periods than intended.
12. Continued use of a mood-altering chemical after being told by a physician that it is causing health problems.

—. _____
   _____
—. _____
   _____
—. _____
   _____

LONG-TERM GOALS

1. Withdraw from mood-altering substance, stabilize physically and emotionally, and establish a supportive recovery plan.
2. Accept chemical dependence and begin to actively participate in a recovery program.
3. Establish a sustained recovery, free from the use of all mood-altering substances.
4. Establish and maintain total abstinence while increasing knowledge of the disease and the process of recovery.
5. Improve quality of life by maintaining an ongoing abstinence from all mood-altering chemicals.

—. _____
   _____
—. _____
   _____
—. _____
   _____

SHORT-TERM OBJECTIVES

1. Describe the amount, frequency, and history of substance abuse. (1, 2, 3)

THERAPEUTIC INTERVENTIONS

1. Gather detailed personal history information regarding substance abuse, including types of substance used, amount and pattern of use, signs and symptoms of use, and negative consequences (i.e., social, legal, relational, and vocational).

2. Explore what signs and symptoms of withdrawal are experienced by the patient (e.g., tachycardia, tremor, anxiety, seizures, nausea, insomnia, sweating) and how he/she manages these symptoms (i.e., using more substance to reduce the symptoms).

3. Gather detailed family history information regarding substance abuse.

2. Describe other symptoms or disorders that may also be present. (4)

4. Assess the patient for concurrent mental disorders and recommend treatment, as needed (see the Depression, Mania/Hypomania, Anxiety, and/or Psychoticism chapters in this *Planner*).

3. Patient and/or significant other(s) to describe any current or past suicidal thoughts/behavior as well as violent threats or actions. (5, 6, 7)

5. Explore the patient's current and past suicidal thoughts and suicidal behavior; ask about family history of suicide (see the Suicidal Ideation chapter in this *Planner*).

6. Assess the patient's potential for violence and determine the presence of current and past threats or acts of aggression.

7. Arrange for hospitalization, as necessary, when the patient is judged to be harmful to self or others or unable to care for his/her basic needs.

4. Complete psychological testing and other questionnaires for measuring the severity of addiction and withdrawal symptoms. (8)

8. Administer objective addiction and withdrawal severity rating instruments to the patient (e.g., Addiction Severity Index [ASI], Clinical Institute Withdrawal Assessment for Alcohol [CIWA-Ar]); evaluate the results and give him/her feedback.

5. Outline a complete and accurate medical and psychiatric history, including treatment received and its effectiveness. (9, 10)

9. Explore the patient's history of previous treatment for chemical dependence or other psychiatric disorder and the success of, as well as his/her tolerance for and follow-through with, that treatment.

10. Assess the patient for the presence of other medical problems and the medications used to treat them.

6. Cooperate with a physical examination and laboratory tests. (11, 12, 13)

11. Perform a complete physical and neurological examination on the patient and send his/her blood and/or urine for analysis to rule out organic contributors to withdrawal symptoms.

12. Provide feedback to the patient regarding the results and implications of the physical examination and laboratory test results.

13. Perform regular urine screens for illicit drugs (e.g., cocaine, cannabis, opioids, amphetamine, phencyclidine) and prescription drugs with abuse potential (e.g., opioids, benzodiazepines, barbiturates).

7. Pursue treatment for concurrent medical problems that may contribute to withdrawal symptoms. (14, 15)

14. Treat or refer the patient for treatment for any medical problem that may be contributing to withdrawal symptoms (e.g., malnutrition, dehydration, electrolyte imbalance, infection).

15. Monitor the patient's recovery progress from concomitant disorders and the impact of the recovery on his/her withdrawal symptoms.

8. Verbalize an understanding of the possible contributing factors for chemical dependence and the relationship between

16. Educate the patient on the possible contributing factors to chemical dependence (e.g., genetic propensity, environmental

chemical dependence and other psychiatric disorders. (16, 17, 18)

dynamics, medical illness, psychiatric illness, pain avoidance).

17. Educate the patient on the signs and symptoms of substance withdrawal (e.g., tachycardia, tremor, anxiety, seizures, nausea, insomnia, sweating).

18. Emphasize to the patient the negative and dangerous impact of substance abuse on other psychiatric disorders.

9. Express an understanding of the potential risks of substance withdrawal. (19)

19. Educate the patient on the potential risks of withdrawal from alcohol, sedatives, hypnotics, or anxiolytics (e.g., seizures, delirium tremens, death), from opiates (e.g., anxiety, restlessness, achy feelings, muscle cramps), and from cocaine (e.g., transient mood symptoms, suicidal ideation/attempts), as appropriate.

10. Cooperate with the recommended treatment for detoxification. (20, 21, 22)

20. Assess the severity and stage of withdrawal (i.e., mild, moderate, severe or delirium tremens [for alcohol, sedative, hypnotic or anxiolytic withdrawal]).

21. Discuss appropriate withdrawal treatment options with the patient (e.g., medication, close monitoring without medication) if he/she is experiencing mild or moderate withdrawal symptoms.

22. Arrange for an inpatient detoxification if the patient is experiencing severe withdrawal symptoms (e.g., seizures, tachycardia, significantly elevated blood pressure) or delirium tremens (e.g., confusion, hallucinations, severe agitation).

11. Verbalize the type and amount of alcohol, sedatives, hypnotics, and/or anxiolytics used. (23)

12. Take prescribed medications responsibly at times ordered by the physician. (24, 25, 26)

13. Report on the effectiveness of medications used to control withdrawal symptoms. (27, 28, 29, 30)

23. Determine if the patient is withdrawing from alcohol, sedatives, hypnotics, or anxiolytics and the amount he/she used over the past 24 hours.

24. Prescribe vitamins (e.g., multivitamin, thiamine, folate) and give fluids intravenously or encourage the patient to drink plenty of fluids; strongly consider this for patients with alcohol dependence.

25. Prescribe a long-acting benzodiazepine (e.g., diazepam [Valium®], clonazepam [Klonopin®], or chlordiazepoxide [Librium®]) to stabilize agitation if the patient's liver function is not impaired.

26. Prescribe a benzodiazepine without active metabolites (e.g., oxazepam [Serax®], lorazepam [Ativan®]) to stabilize agitation if the patient has impaired liver function.

27. Titrate the dose of medication until the patient's withdrawal symptoms are eliminated.

28. Taper the benzodiazepine as tolerated by the patient over three to five days; slow the taper if he/she experiences withdrawal symptoms when the dose is decreased.

29. Monitor the patient's vital signs frequently during the withdrawal period.

30. Provide additional doses of benzodiazepine if the patient experiences break-through

withdrawal symptoms during the taper.

14. Cooperate with symptom-triggered strategies for detoxification. (31, 32)

31. Consider using a symptom-triggered benzodiazepine dosing strategy if the patient is treated as an inpatient under close medical observation; scheduled doses of medication are not necessary with this strategy.

32. Assess the patient's withdrawal using the CIWA-Ar every 30 to 60 minutes and give the patient a dose of medication if the CIWA-Ar score is 8 or higher; continue until the patient's withdrawal is complete.

15. Take additional prescribed medications to alleviate physical complications related to alcohol withdrawal. (33, 34)

33. Consider prescribing an anticonvulsant (e.g., carbamazepine [Tegretol®], divalproex sodium [Depakote®], phenobarbital) if the patient experiences withdrawal seizures.

34. Add a β-blocker (e.g., atenolol [Tenormin®], propranolol [Inderal®]) if the patient has autonomic symptoms (tachycardia, hypertension, sweating) or cardiac arrhythmias associated with the withdrawal; consider using clonidine (Catapres®) for treating withdrawal-emergent hypertension.

16. Verbalize the type and amount of opioids used. (35)

35. Determine if the patient is withdrawing from opioids and the amount taken in the past 24 hours.

17. Take prescribed medications responsibly at times ordered by the physician for opioid withdrawal treatment. (36, 37)

36. Prescribe a medication with opioid receptor agonist activity (e.g., methadone [Dolophine®, Methadose®], buprenorphine [Buprenex®, Subutex®, Suboxone®]); use caution when

prescribing buprenorphine if the patient has recently taken an opioid agonist.

37. Titrate the dose of the opioid agonist until the patient's withdrawal symptoms are controlled.

18. Report as to the effectiveness of medications used to control withdrawal symptoms. (38, 39)

38. Monitor the patient for vital sign fluctuations and other withdrawal symptoms frequently during the detoxification period.

39. Taper the medication over several days to weeks as tolerated by the patient.

19. Take clonidine responsibly at times ordered by the physician for opioid withdrawal treatment. (40, 41, 42)

40. Prescribe clonidine [Catapres®] to control the patient's withdrawal symptoms if opioid agonists are unavailable or inappropriate.

41. Titrate the clonidine dose, as tolerated by the patient, until the withdrawal symptoms are controlled; a clonidine patch (Catapres® TTS) may be used in place of oral clonidine.

42. Taper the oral clonidine over five to ten days as tolerated by the patient; taper the clonidine patch over several weeks as tolerated by the patient.

20. Express an understanding of additional treatment options for opioid withdrawal and cooperate with the treatment. (43, 44)

43. Consider the addition of naltrexone [ReVia®] to the oral clonidine if a rapid detoxification is desired.

44. Taper the clonidine dose and increase the naltrexone dose on a daily basis over three to five days as tolerated by the patient.

21. Retain a remission in substance abuse. (45)

45. Treat or refer the patient for ongoing treatment of chemical dependence (see the Chemical

Dependence—Relapse
Prevention chapter in this
Planner).

—. _____   —. _____
_____   _____
—. _____   —. _____
_____   _____
—. _____   —. _____
_____   _____

DIAGNOSTIC SUGGESTIONS:

Axis I:	303.90	Alcohol Dependence
	291.80	Alcohol Withdrawal
	304.20	Cocaine Dependence
	292.0	Cocaine Withdrawal
	304.00	Opioid Dependence
	292.0	Opioid Withdrawal
	304.80	Polysubstance Dependence
	304.10	Sedative, Hypnotic or Anxiolytic Dependence
	292.0	Sedative, Hypnotic or Anxiolytic Withdrawal
	291.2	Alcohol-Induced Persisting Dementia
	291.8	Alcohol-Induced Mood Disorder
	292.84	Substance-Induced Mood Disorder
	296.xx	Major Depression
	296.xx	Bipolar I Disorder
	296.89	Bipolar II Disorder
	295.xx	Schizophrenia

_____ _____

_____ _____

Axis II:	301.7	Antisocial Personality Disorder

_____ _____

_____ _____

CHRONIC FATIGUE SYNDROME

BEHAVIORAL DEFINITIONS

1. Chronic feeling of being physically tired or fatigued that is not due to ongoing exertion.
2. Fatigue is not substantially alleviated after a period of rest.
3. Memory impairment.
4. Poor concentration.
5. Tender lymph nodes.
6. Pain in muscles or joints.
7. Headaches.
8. Unrefreshing sleep.
9. A sense of malaise or bodily discomfort after exertion.
10. Feelings of dysphoria.
11. Symptoms associated with chronic fatigue have an identifiable time of onset.

—. _____

_____

—. _____

_____

—. _____

_____

LONG-TERM GOALS

1. Take the appropriate medication and dose and/or participate in psychotherapy to alleviate fatigue and return to previous level of functioning.
2. Improve other symptoms associated with fatigue that have a detrimental effect on daily living.

3. Increase levels of activity to enhance quality of life.
4. Prevent relapse and recurrence of chronic fatigue signs and symptoms.

__. _____

_____

__. _____

_____

__. _____

_____

SHORT-TERM OBJECTIVES

THERAPEUTIC INTERVENTIONS

1. Describe the signs and symptoms of fatigue that are experienced and note their impact on daily life. (1, 2)

1. Explore how fatigue is experienced by the patient and how it affects his/her daily life (e.g., poor energy, social withdrawal, unrefreshing sleep, muscle and joint pains).

2. Gather information from the patient about level of functioning prior to the onset of fatigue symptoms.

2. Describe other symptoms or disorders that may also be present. (3, 4)

3. Assess the patient for comorbid disorders (e.g., see the Depression and Anxiety chapters in this *Planner*).

4. Gather detailed personal and family history information regarding substance and/or alcohol abuse and its potential contribution to fatigue; refer the patient for in-depth substance abuse treatment, if indicated (see the Chemical Dependence chapters in this *Planner*).

3. Verbalize any current suicidal thoughts and any history of suicidal behavior. (5, 6)

5. Explore the patient's current and past suicidal thoughts and suicidal behavior; check for family history

of suicide (see the Suicidal Ideation chapter in this *Planner*).

6. Arrange for hospitalization, as necessary, when the patient is judged to be harmful to himself/ herself or others or unable to care for his/her basic needs.

4. Outline a complete and accurate medical and psychiatric history, including treatment received and its effectiveness. (7, 8)

7. Explore the patient's history of previous treatment for chronic fatigue and the success and tolerance of that treatment.

8. Assess the patient for the presence of other medical problems and medications used to treat them.

5. Cooperate with a physical examination and laboratory tests. (9, 10)

9. Perform a complete physical and neurological examination on the patient and send his/her blood and/or urine for analysis to rule out an organic cause for fatigue (e.g., infection, severe obesity, cancer, neurologic disease, endocrine disease, obstructive sleep apnea).

10. Provide feedback to the patient regarding the results and implications of the physical examination and laboratory test results.

6. Pursue treatment for concurrent medical problems that may contribute to chronic fatigue symptoms. (11, 12, 13)

11. Treat or refer the patient for treatment for any medical problem that may be causing or contributing to chronic fatigue symptoms (e.g., infection, severe obesity, cancer, neurologic disease, endocrine disease, obstructive sleep apnea).

12. Refer the patient to a rheumatologist for a complete evaluation and treatment of potential autoimmune disorder (e.g., systemic lupus erythematosus

[SLE], rheumatoid arthritis, fibromyalgia).

13. Monitor the patient's progress in recovery from concomitant disorders and the impact on his/her fatigue.

7. Complete psychological test-ing and other questionnaires for assessing chronic fatigue. (14)

14. Administer to the patient an objective assessment instrument for measuring fatigue and its impact on functioning (e.g., General Health Survey—Short Form (SF-36), Karnofsky Scale, Chalder Fatigue Scale); evaluate the results and give him/her feedback.

8. Verbalize an understanding of the impact of substance abuse on chronic fatigue. (15)

15. Emphasize to the patient the negative and dangerous interac-tion of substance abuse with chronic fatigue (e.g., worsened mood, increased anxiety, decreased energy).

9. Express an understanding of treatment options, expected results, and potential side effects of medication. (16)

16. Discuss appropriate treatment options with the patient includ-ing medications, psychotherapy, and exercise.

10. Participate in an exercise program as planned with an exercise physiologist. (17, 18)

17. Refer the patient to an exercise physiologist for planning and implementation of a gradually progressive, aerobic exercise program.

18. Monitor the patient's invest-ment in and response to exercise (e.g., follow-through, increased energy, improved sense of well-being).

11. Participate in psychotherapy sessions as planned with therapist. (19, 20)

19. Assess the patient for potential benefit from psychotherapy and refer to a psychotherapist, if necessary.

20. Monitor the patient's investment in and response to psychotherapy;

assess his/her ability to verbalize a basis for progress in recovery from chronic fatigue (e.g., increased daily activity, improved coping mechanisms, assuming more responsibilities, improved mood).

12. Take prescribed medications responsibly at times ordered by physician. (21, 22)

21. Prescribe to the patient a selective serotonin reuptake inhibitor (SSRI) (e.g., paroxetine [Paxil®], sertraline [Zoloft®], citalopram [Celexa™], escitalopram [Lexapro™], fluoxetine [Prozac®], or fluvoxamine [Luvox®]).

22. Titrate the patient's SSRI medication to the minimum effective dose for treating his/her symptoms.

13. Report as to the effectiveness of SSRI medications and any side effects that develop. (23, 24, 25)

23. Monitor the patient frequently for the development of side effects, response to medication, and adherence to treatment.

24. Evaluate the patient after four weeks of therapy with an SSRI for his/her response to medication; determine if he/she has had a partial response or a full response to the medication.

25. Repeat administration of objective rating instruments to the patient for assessment of his/her fatigue symptoms; evaluate the results and give him/her feedback.

14. Cooperate with changes in type of medication prescribed as well as additional medical tests and dietary restrictions. (26, 27, 28, 29)

26. Prescribe an alternative antidepressant agent (e.g., venlafaxine [Effexor®], mirtazapine [Remeron®], bupropion [Wellbutrin®], nefazodone [Serzone®], tricyclic antidepressant [TCA], or monoamine oxidase inhibitor

[MAOI]) if the patient has an unsatisfactory response to an SSRI.

27. Complete a medical evaluation on the patient including an electrocardiogram, if necessary, before starting him/her on a TCA.

28. Educate the patient on dietary restrictions and ask him/her to try the restrictions before starting an MAOI.

29. Titrate the alternative antidepressant every two to four weeks, as tolerated, until the patient's symptoms are controlled or the maximum dose is reached.

15. Adhere to the injection schedule for magnesium as ordered by the physician. (30)

30. Consider prescribing weekly magnesium sulphate injections if the patient has an unsatisfactory response to other treatments.

16. Retain a significant improvement in fatigue symptoms. (31, 32)

31. Maintain the patient on current medication for at least 12 months if he/she has shown a complete recovery from fatigue symptoms; if the patient has only a partial response, maintain him/her on the current dose of medication indefinitely.

32. Taper medications off slowly over several months; closely monitor for recurrence of symptoms.

17. Read books on coping with chronic fatigue. (33)

33. Recommend that the patient read books on coping with chronic fatigue (e.g., *From Fatigued to Fantastic!* by Teitelbaum; *Chronic Fatigue Syndrome, Fibromyalgia, and Other Invisible Illnesses* by Berne and Bennett); process

his/her implementation of coping techniques, reinforcing success and redirecting for failure.

—. _____   —. _____
    _____   _____

—. _____   —. _____
    _____   _____

—. _____   —. _____
    _____   _____

DIAGNOSTIC SUGGESTIONS:

Axis I: 296.xx   Major Depressive Disorder
               296.xx   Major Depressive Disorder with Atypical Features
               293.83   Mood Disorder Due to (Axis III Disorder)
               300.4   Dysthymic Disorder
               296.89   Bipolar II Disorder
               305.00   Hypochondriasis
               305.40   Alcohol Abuse
               305.40   Sedative, Hypnotic, or Anxiolytic Abuse
               305.60   Cocaine Abuse
               V65.2   Malingering

               _____   _____

               _____   _____

Axis II: 301.6   Dependent Personality Disorder
               301.9   Personality Disorder NOS

               _____   _____

               _____   _____

CHRONIC PAIN

BEHAVIORAL DEFINITIONS

1. Experiences pain beyond the normal healing process (six months or more) that significantly limits physical activities.
2. Complains of generalized pain in many joints, muscles, and bones that debilitates normal functioning.
3. Overuse or use of increased amounts of medication with little, if any, pain relief.
4. Experiences tension, migraine, cluster, or chronic daily headaches.
5. Experiences back or neck pain, interstitial cystitis, diabetic neuropathy, or fibromyalgia.
6. Intermittent pain of rheumatoid arthritis or irritable bowel syndrome.
7. Decreased or stopped activities (e.g., work, household chores, socializing, exercise, sex, or other pleasurable activities) because of pain.
8. Experiences an increase in physical symptoms (e.g., fatigue, night sweats, insomnia, muscle tension, body aches, decreased concentration, or decreased memory).
9. Exhibits signs and symptoms of depression.
10. Makes statements like "I can't do what I used to do," "No one understands me," "Why me?" "When will this go away?" and "I can't go on."

—. _____
_____
—. _____
_____
—. _____
_____

LONG-TERM GOALS

1. Establish control of the pain such that medications needed to relieve pain on a daily basis are at a minimum.
2. Acquire and utilize the necessary pain management skills.
3. Regulate pain to maximize daily functioning and return to productive employment.
4. Find relief from pain and build renewed contentment and joy in performing activities of everyday life.
5. Find an escape route from the pain.
6. "Make peace with chronic pain and move on" (Hunter).
7. Lessen daily suffering from pain.
8. Regain control over life.

—. _____

_____

—. _____

_____

—. _____

_____

SHORT-TERM OBJECTIVES	THERAPEUTIC INTERVENTIONS
1. Describe the symptoms of pain that are experienced and note their impact on daily life. (1, 2)	1. Gather a history and current status of the patient's chronic pain, including its location, intensity, and nature (e.g., sharp, aching, burning, throbbing).
	2. Explore how pain affects the patient's daily life (e.g. insomnia, difficulty performing activities of daily living, inability to function at work or do chores at home, decrease in pleasurable activities).
2. Identify current and past strategies (both healthy and maladaptive) used to control pain. (3, 4)	3. Explore the patient's history of previous treatment for chronic pain and the success and tolerability of that treatment.

4. Determine how the patient is currently handling the pain (e.g., medications, behavioral modification); evaluate if the patient is over-using medications or displaying maladaptive behaviors.

3. Describe other symptoms or disorders that may also be present. (5, 6)

5. Assess the patient for comorbid disorders such as depression or anxiety (see the Depression and Anxiety chapters in this *Planner*).

6. Gather detailed personal and family history information regarding substance (e.g., opioids) and/or alcohol abuse and its role in the patient's pain syndrome; refer him/her for in-depth substance abuse treatment, if indicated (see the Chemical Dependence chapters in this *Planner*).

4. Verbalize any current suicidal thoughts and any history of suicidal behavior. (7, 8)

7. Explore the patient's current and past suicidal thoughts and suicidal behavior; check for family history of suicide (see the Suicidal Ideation chapter in this *Planner,* if necessary).

8. Arrange for hospitalization, as necessary, when the patient is judged to be harmful to self or unable to care for his/her basic needs.

5. Outline a complete and accurate medical and psychiatric history, including treatment received and its effectiveness. (9, 10)

9. Assess the patient for the presence of other medical problems and medications used to treat them; obtain reports from other treating physicians.

10. Determine if the patient has a history of mental illness and identify any medications used to treat it.

6. Cooperate with a physical examination and laboratory tests. (11, 12, 13)

11. Perform a complete physical and neurological examination on the patient and send his/her blood and/or urine for analysis to evaluate any causes for pain.

12. Make a determination as to whether the patient's pain is nociceptive or neuropathic in origin.

13. Provide feedback to the patient regarding the results and implications of the physical examination and laboratory test results.

7. Pursue treatment for concurrent medical problems that may contribute to pain symptoms. (14, 15)

14. Treat or refer the patient for treatment of any medical problem that may be causing or contributing to the pain syndrome (e.g., arthritis, diabetes, autoimmune disease, post-herpetic neuralgia, degenerative disk disease).

15. Monitor the patient's progress in recovery from concomitant disorders and the impact on his/her pain perception.

8. Complete psychological testing and other questionnaires for measuring pain and its effect on functioning. (16)

16. Administer objective pain assessment instruments to the patient (e.g., visual analog scales, McGill Pain Questionnaire [MPQ], West Haven-Yale Multidimensional Pain Inventory [WHYMPI]); evaluate the results and give feedback to him/her.

9. Verbalize an understanding of the relationship between pain and depression. (17)

17. Educate the patient on the relationship between pain and depression and the difficulties of treating one if the other is present.

10. Verbalize an understanding of treatment options, expected

18. Discuss appropriate treatment options with the patient (e.g.,

results from medication, and potential side effects. (18, 19)

11. Take prescribed medications responsibly at times ordered by physician. (20, 21, 22)

12. Verbalize an understanding of the potential for addiction to particular pain medications. (23)

13. Cooperate with changes in medications used to treat pain and/or depression. (24, 25, 26)

medications, psychotherapy, occupational therapy, massage therapy, relaxation techniques, biofeedback); refer to the appropriate specialists, if indicated.

19. Educate the patient on medications used to treat pain including expected results, potential side effects, and dosing strategies.

20. Treat or refer the patient for treatment with non-opioid analgesics (e.g., nonsteroidal antiinflammatory drugs [NSAIDS], COX-II inhibitors) and/or opioid analgesics (e.g., morphine, hydrocodone [Vicodin®, Lortab®], oxycodone [Percocet®], fentanyl [Duragesic®]); strongly consider this strategy for patients with nociceptive pain.

21. Titrate the dose every one to three days until the patient's pain is controlled or maximum dose is reached.

22. Consider prescribing another analgesic from a different class if the patient's pain is not well controlled after maximizing the dose of other analgesics.

23. Discuss with the patient the dependence liability potential of long-term treatment with opioid pain medications.

24. Prescribe a selective serotonin reuptake inhibitor (SSRI) (i.e., fluoxetine [Prozac®], paroxetine [Paxil®], sertraline [Zoloft®], escitalopram [Lexapro™], citalopram [Celexa™]) if the patient's pain is not controlled with analgesics;

strongly consider this strategy for patients with comorbid depression.

25. Prescribe an antidepressant agent that has both noradrenergic and serotonergic activity (e.g., venlafaxine [Effexor®], amitriptyline [Elavil®], nortriptyline [Pamelor®], imipramine [Tofranil®], desipramine [Norpramin®]) if the pain is neuropathic.

26. Complete a medical evaluation on the patient including an electrocardiogram (ECG), if necessary, before starting him/her on a tricyclic antidepressant (TCA) (e.g., amitriptyline [Elavil®], imipramine [Tofranil®], desipramine [Norpramin®]).

14. Participate in psychotherapy and other forms of therapy. (18, 27, 28)

18. Discuss appropriate treatment options with the patient (e.g., medications, psychotherapy, occupational therapy, massage therapy, relaxation techniques, biofeedback); refer to these specialists, if indicated.

27. Work closely with other clinicians that are involved with the patient's treatment for chronic pain; coordinate treatment plans among the various disciplines.

28. Monitor the patient's investment in and response to psychotherapy and other treatment modalities; assess his/her ability to verbalize a basis for progress in recovery from pain (e.g., healthier cognitions, improved tolerance for pain, increased functionality, improvements in mood).

15. Report evidence of improvement in pain symptoms as well as any comorbid disorders. (29)

16. Attend follow-up appointments as scheduled by the physician and adhere to changes in medication dose. (30, 31)

17. Adhere to changes in medication used to treat chronic pain and/or augment current treatment. (32, 33, 34, 35)

29. Repeat objective measures for assessing the patient's pain on a regular basis to monitor improvement.

30. Increase the patient's medication every two weeks if he/she has limited improvement in pain; continue until maximum dose is reached or pain is controlled.

31. Monitor the patient frequently for development of side effects, response to medication, and adherence to treatment.

32. Consider changing the patient's medication to another antidepressant agent that has noradrenergic activity (e.g., venlafaxine [Effexor®], amitriptyline [Elavil®], imipramine [Tofranil®], desipramine [Norpramin®]) if he/she does not respond to an SSRI.

33. Monitor the patient for his/her response to and tolerance of medication; titrate the dose every two weeks, as tolerated, until pain is controlled or maximum dose is reached.

34. Consider the use of topical agents such as transdermal lidocaine (Lidoderm) or capsaicin cream (Zostrix, Capsaicin-P) if the patient suffers from postherpetic neuralgia.

35. Prescribe an anticonvulsant medication (e.g., gabapentin [Neurontin®], lamotrigine [Lamictal®], topiramate [Topamax®], carbamazepine [Tegretol®], phenytoin [Dilantin®]) if the patient continues to have pain despite

18. Cooperate with blood draws and changes in anticonvulsant dosing. (36, 37)

36. Monitor the patient's blood levels of carbamazepine and phenytoin four to five days after starting the medication or increasing the dose to obtain a therapeutic blood level.

    maximized antidepressant therapy.

37. Titrate the anticonvulsant every four to five days until the patient's pain is improved or maximum dose is reached.

19. Retain a remission or significant reduction in pain symptoms with a minimum amount of medications. (38)

38. Maintain the patient on current medication indefinitely if the patient's pain is controlled and underlying cause for the pain persists.

20. Read books on coping with chronic pain. (39)

39. Recommend that the patient read books on coping with pain (e.g. *The Culture of Pain* by Morris; *Making Peace with Chronic Pain* by Hunter; *The Mind/Body Effect* by Benson; *Managing Pain before It Manages You* by Caudill; *The Feeling Good Handbook* by Burns); process his/her implementation of coping techniques, reinforcing success and redirecting for failure.

21. Verbalize any current suicidal thoughts and any history of suicidal behavior. (40, 41)

40. Explore the patient's current and past suicidal thoughts and suicidal behavior; ask about family history of suicide (see interventions designed for Suicidal Ideation in this *Planner,* if necessary).

41. Arrange for hospitalization, as necessary, when the patient is judged to be harmful to self or unable to care for his/her basic needs.

—. _____   —. _____
   _____   _____
—. _____   —. _____
   _____   _____
—. _____   —. _____
   _____   _____

DIAGNOSTIC SUGGESTIONS:

Axis I: 307.89   Pain Disorder Associated with Both Psycho-
                          logical Factors and an Axis III Disorder
                307.80   Pain Disorder Associated with Psychological
                          Factors
                300.81   Somatization Disorder
                300.11   Conversion Disorder
                296.3x   Major Depressive Disorder, Recurrent
                300.4   Dysthymic Disorder
                300.02   Generalized Anxiety Disorder
                300.3   Obsessive-Compulsive Disorder
                302.70   Sexual Dysfunction NOS
                304.00   Opioid Dependence
                304.10   Sedative, Hypnotic or Anxiolytic Dependence
                303.90   Alcohol Dependence
                304.80   Polysubstance Dependence

                _____   _____

                _____   _____

Axis II: 301.6   Dependent Personality Disorder
                301.9   Personality Disorder NOS

                _____   _____

                _____   _____

COGNITIVE DEFICITS—DEMENTIA

BEHAVIORAL DEFINITIONS

1. Cognitive impairment represents a significant decline from a previous level of functioning.
2. Concrete thinking or impaired abstract thinking.
3. Lack of insight into the consequences of impaired judgment or behavior.
4. Short-term and/or long-term memory deficits.
5. Difficulty following complex or sequential directions.
6. Loss of orientation to time, person, and/or place.
7. Distractibility in attention.
8. Impulsive behavior that violates social mores.
9. Speech and language impairment.
10. Impairment in performing simple motor tasks (e.g., buttoning a shirt, combing hair, feeding oneself).
11. Significant impairment in social and occupational functioning.

—. _____

_____

—. _____

_____

—. _____

_____

LONG-TERM GOALS

1. Take the appropriate medication and dose to slow the progression of cognitive impairment.
2. Control disruptive behaviors associated with cognitive decline.

3. Cooperate with an assessment as to the degree and cause of cognitive impairment.
4. Develop alternative coping strategies to compensate for cognitive limitations.

—. _____

_____

—. _____

_____

—. _____

_____

SHORT-TERM OBJECTIVES

THERAPEUTIC INTERVENTIONS

1. Describe the nature and history of cognitive deficits. (1, 2)

2. Describe other symptoms or disorders that may also be present. (3, 4)

1. Explore the patient's signs and symptoms of cognitive impairment (e.g., memory, coordination, speech and language, executive function, orientation, attention) and how they affect his/her daily life.

2. Determine the time course (e.g., gradual onset over months to years, acute onset, step-wise progression) and severity of the cognitive deficits.

3. Assess the patient for comorbid disorders (e.g., see the Depression, Mania, Psychosis chapters in this *Planner*) that may contribute to his/her cognitive deficit symptom pattern.

4. Gather detailed personal and family history information regarding the patient's substance abuse and its potential interaction with the cognitive deficits; refer the patient for in-depth substance abuse treatment, if indicated

3. Patient or significant other(s) describe any current or past suicidal thoughts/behavior as well as violent threats or actions. (5, 6, 7)

(see the Chemical Dependence chapters in this *Planner*).

5. Explore the patient's current and past suicidal thoughts and suicidal behavior; ask about family history of suicide (see the Suicidal Ideation chapter in this *Planner*).

6. Assess the patient's potential for violence and determine the presence of current and past threats or acts of aggression.

7. Arrange for hospitalization, as necessary, when the patient is judged to be harmful to self or others or unable to care for his/her basic needs.

4. Complete psychological testing and other questionnaires for measuring the severity of dementia. (8)

8. Administer objective instruments to assess the patient's cognitive deficits (e.g., Mini Mental State Exam [MMSE], Alzheimer's Disease Assessment Scale [ADAS], Neuropsychiatric Inventory); evaluate the results and give him/her feedback.

5. Outline a complete and accurate medical and psychiatric history, including treatment received and its effectiveness. (9, 10)

9. Explore the patient's history of previous treatment for dementia and the success of, as well as his/her tolerance for, that treatment.

10. Assess the patient for the presence of other medical problems and what medications are used to treat them.

6. Cooperate with a physical examination and laboratory tests. (11, 12, 13)

11. Perform a complete physical and neurological examination on the patient and send his/her blood and/or urine for analysis to rule out organic causes

and/or contributors to cognitive decline (e.g., vitamin deficiency, infection, endocrine disease, cerebrovascular disease, autoimmune disease, acquired brain injury, chronic and heavy alcohol use).

12. Obtain radiologic studies (i.e., head computed tomography [CT] scan or magnetic resonance imaging [MRI]) of the patient, if necessary, to assess for any acquired brain injury that may account for the cognitive deficit symptoms.

13. Provide feedback to the patient and family regarding the results and implications of the physical examination and laboratory test results.

7. Pursue treatment for concurrent medical problems that may contribute to cognitive deficits. (14, 15)

14. Treat or refer the patient for treatment of any medical problem that may be causing and/or contributing to cognitive deficits (e.g., vitamin deficiency, infection, endocrine disease, cerebrovascular disease, autoimmune disease, acquired brain injury).

15. Monitor the patient's progress in recovery from concomitant disorders and the impact of the recovery on his/her cognition.

8. Express an understanding of dementia, including the signs and symptoms, prognosis, and possible causes and contributing factors to cognitive deficits. (16, 17, 18)

16. Educate the patient and significant others on the signs, symptoms, and prognosis of dementia.

17. Educate the patient and significant others on the possible causes for dementia (e.g., genetic propensity,

neurologic illness, psychiatric illness, chronic substance abuse).

18. Emphasize the negative and dangerous impact of substance abuse on cognitive functioning.

9. Verbalize an understanding of the treatment options for dementia and expected results from treatment. (19)

19. Discuss appropriate treatment options (e.g., medications, psychosocial therapy, occupational therapy, physical therapy) and the expected results of treatment with the patient and significant others.

10. Participate in therapy sessions as planned with the therapist. (20, 21)

20. Assess the patient for potential benefit from psychosocial (e.g., day treatment), occupational and/or physical therapy; refer him/her to a specialist in each of these areas, if necessary.

21. Monitor the patient's response to therapy; assess his/her ability to verbalize and/or demonstrate a basis for progress in coping with cognitive deficits (e.g., improvement in social and occupational functioning, improvement performing activities of daily living [ADLs], development of memory loss coping strategies).

11. Express an understanding of medication treatment options, expected results and potential side effects. (22)

22. Educate the patient and or significant others on psychotropic medication treatment, including the expected results, potential side effects, and dosing strategies.

12. Take prescribed medications responsibly at times ordered by the physician. (23)

23. Prescribe an acetylcholinesterase inhibitor (e.g., donepezil [Aricept®], rivastigmine [Exelon®], galantamine [Reminyl®], tacrine

13. Report as to the effectiveness of medications and any side effects that develop. (24, 25, 26)

14. Attend follow-up appointments as scheduled by the physician and adhere to any adjustments in medication dose. (27)

15. Cooperate with a change in the type and dose of medication that is prescribed. (28, 29)

16. Adhere to the hormone replacement therapy as prescribed by the physician. (30)

17. Patient and caretakers report on the presence of behavioral disturbances and psychosis. (31)

[Cognex®]); initial dosing should be in the minimum dosing range.

24. Monitor the patient frequently for the development of side effects, response to medication, and adherence to treatment.

25. Reassess the patient who is taking an acetylcholinesterase inhibitor at four weeks; determine whether the medication is adequate or needs a dose increase.

26. Repeat administration of objective rating instruments for assessment of the patient's cognition; evaluate the results and give him/her feedback.

27. Increase the acetylcholinesterase inhibitor dose every three to four weeks, as tolerated, until the patient shows improvement in cognition or the maximum dose is reached.

28. Consider prescribing an alternative medication (i.e., selegiline [Eldepryl®] or ginkgo biloba) that has shown efficacy in improving cognition.

29. Titrate the medication every three to four weeks, as tolerated, until the patient's cognition improves or maximum dose is reached.

30. Consider prescribing hormone replacement therapy for females who are postmenopausal.

31. Assess the patient for the presence of behavioral disturbances (e.g., combativeness with ADLs, verbal and/or physical threats,

striking out) and/or psychotic symptoms (e.g., hallucinations, delusions, paranoia).

18. Take antipsychotic medication as prescribed by the physician. (32, 33)

32. Prescribe a low dose of an atypical antipsychotic agent (e.g., risperidone [Risperdal®], olanzapine [Zyprexa®], ziprasidone [Geodon®], aripiprazole [Abilify™], or quetiapine [Seroquel®]).

33. Titrate the patient's anti-psychotic dose every three to four days, as tolerated, until his/her behavioral symptoms are controlled or the maximum dose is reached.

19. Cooperate with the addition of a mood stabilizer, blood draws, and adjustments in medication dose. (34, 35, 36)

34. Consider the addition of a mood stabilizer (e.g., divalproex sodium [Depakote®] or carba-mazepine [Tegretol®]) if the patient's behavioral symptoms are not controlled with an antipsychotic medication.

35. Measure blood levels of the mood stabilizer in four to five days; adjust the dose as neces-sary to obtain therapeutic blood levels.

36. Monitor the patient closely for side effects from the medication (e.g., over sedation, unsteady gait, increased confusion); reduce the medication dose if necessary.

20. Retain a remission or signifi-cant reduction in disruptive behavior and/or psychotic symptoms with a minimum amount of medications. (37)

37. Maintain the patient on current medication indefinitely if he/she has shown a significant reduc-tion in disruptive behavior and/or psychotic symptoms.

—. _____   —. _____
    _____   _____
—. _____   —. _____
    _____   _____
—. _____   . _____
    _____   _____

DIAGNOSTIC SUGGESTIONS:

Axis I:

290.xx	Dementia of the Alzheimer's Type
290.4x	Vascular Dementia
290.10	Dementia Due to Pick's Disease
294.1	Dementia Due to (Axis III Disorder)
291.2	Alcohol-Induced Persisting Dementia
294.8	Dementia NOS
294.0	Amnestic Disorder Due to (Axis III Disorder)
294.8	Amnestic Disorder NOS
294.9	Cognitive Disorder NOS
296.xx	Major Depressive Disorder
295.xx	Schizophrenia
303.90	Alcohol Dependence

_____   _____
_____   _____

Axis II:

_____   _____
_____   _____

COGNITIVE DEFICITS— DEVELOPMENTAL DISORDER

BEHAVIORAL DEFINITIONS

1. Cognitive impairment has been present since childhood and does not represent a decline from a previous level of functioning.
2. Intelligence quotient (IQ) below 70.
3. Concrete thinking or impaired abstract thinking.
4. Lack of insight into the consequences of behavior or impaired judgment.
5. Short-term and/or long-term memory deficits.
6. Difficulty following complex or sequential directions.
7. Loss of orientation to time, person, and/or place.
8. Distractibility in attention.
9. Impulsive behavior that violates social mores.
10. Speech and language impairment.
11. Significant impairment in social and occupational functioning.

—. _____
   _____
—. _____
   _____
—. _____
   _____

LONG-TERM GOALS

1. Take the appropriate medication and dose to control disruptive behaviors (e.g., self-injurious behavior, aggression, tics, stereotypies) and/or psychotic symptoms.

2. Cooperate with an assessment to determine the degree and cause of cognitive impairment.
3. Develop alternative coping strategies to compensate for cognitive limitations.

—. _____

_____

—. _____

_____

—. _____

_____

SHORT-TERM OBJECTIVES

THERAPEUTIC INTERVENTIONS

1. Parents and the patient describe the nature and history of the cognitive deficits. (1, 2, 3)

2. Describe other symptoms or disorders that may also be present. (4, 5)

1. Explore the patient's signs and symptoms of cognitive impairment (e.g., memory, coordination, speech and language, executive function, orientation, attention) and how they affect his/her daily life; gather history from significant others as to the patient's functioning.

2. Determine if the patient displays repetitive and rhythmic self-injurious behavior (e.g., banging head, hitting or biting himself/herself), psychotic symptoms (e.g., hallucinations, delusions, paranoia), tics, or stereotypies.

3. Explore the patient's developmental and educational history (e.g., development of motor and language skills, school performance, attendance in special education classes).

4. Assess the patient for comorbid disorders (e.g., see the Depression, Mania, Anxiety, Obsessive-Compulsive Disorder

chapters in this *Planner*) that may require treatment in addition to symptoms related to cognitive deficits.

5. Gather detailed personal and family history information regarding the patient's substance abuse and its potential interaction with the cognitive deficits; refer him/her for in-depth substance abuse treatment, if indicated (see the Chemical Dependence chapters in this *Planner*).

3. Patient or significant other describe any current or past suicidal thoughts/behavior as well as violent threats or actions. (6, 7, 8)

6. Explore the patient's current and past suicidal thoughts and suicidal behavior; ask about a family history of suicide (see the Suicidal Ideation chapter in this *Planner*).

7. Assess the patient's potential for violence and determine the presence of current and past threats or acts of aggression.

8. Arrange for hospitalization, as necessary, when the patient is judged to be harmful to self or others or unable to care for his/her basic needs.

4. Complete psychological testing and other questionnaires for measuring the severity of cognitive deficits and behavioral disturbances. (9)

9. Administer objective instruments to assess the patient's cognitive deficits and behavioral disturbances (e.g., Mini Mental State Exam [MMSE], Wechsler Adult Intelligence Scale–Revised [WAIS-R], Overt Aggression Scale–Modified [OAS-M]); evaluate the results and give him/her feedback.

5. Parents and the patient outline a complete and accurate medical and psychiatric

10. Inquire of the parents and/or the patient about prenatal, perinatal, or early-life exposure insults

history, including treatment received and its effectiveness. (10, 11, 12)

(e.g., in utero infections or teratogens, central nervous system infections, abuse, neglect, malnutrition) that could cause cognitive deficits.

11. Explore the patient's history of previous treatment for cognitive deficits and the success of, as well as his/her tolerance for, that treatment.

12. Assess the patient for the presence of other medical problems and the medications used to treat them.

6. Cooperate with a physical examination and laboratory tests. (13, 14, 15)

13. Perform a complete physical and neurological examination on the patient and send his/her blood and/or urine for analysis to rule out organic causes of developmental delay (e.g., genetic and/or chromosomal disorders, metabolic disorders, congenital malformations).

14. Obtain radiologic studies (i.e., head computed tomography [CT] scan or magnetic resonance imaging [MRI]) of the patient, if necessary, to assess for an acquired brain injury that may account for the cognitive deficit symptoms.

15. Provide feedback to the patient and parents regarding the results and implications of the physical examination and laboratory test results.

7. Pursue treatment for concurrent medical problems that may contribute to cognitive deficits. (16, 17)

16. Treat or refer the patient for treatment for any medical problem that may be causing and/or contributing to developmental delay (e.g., malnutrition, metabolic disorders, infection).

17. Monitor the patient's progress in recovery from concomitant disorders and the impact of the recovery on his/her cognition.

8. Parents and the patient, if possible, express an understanding of developmental delay, including the signs and symptoms, prognosis, and possible causes and contributing factors to cognitive deficits. (18, 19)

18. Educate the patient and/or significant others on the possible causes for developmental delay (e.g., genetic disorders, prenatal or perinatal infection, teratogen exposure, head trauma).

19. Emphasize the negative and dangerous impact of substance abuse on cognitive functioning.

9. Parents and the patient, if possible, verbalize an understanding of the treatment options and expected results from treatment. (20)

20. Discuss appropriate treatment options (e.g., medications, psychosocial therapy, occupational therapy, physical therapy, vocational training) and expected results of treatment with the patient and/or significant others.

10. Participate in therapy sessions as planned with the therapist. (21, 22)

21. Assess the patient for potential benefit from psychosocial therapy (e.g., day treatment), vocational training, occupational, and/or physical therapy; refer him/her to a specialist in each of these areas, if necessary.

22. Monitor the patient's response to therapy; assess his/her ability to verbalize and/or demonstrate a basis for progress in coping with cognitive deficits (e.g., improvement in social and occupational functioning, increased ability to performing activities of daily living, development of memory loss coping strategies).

11. Parents and the patient, if possible, express an understanding of medication treatment options, expected results, and potential side effects. (23, 24)

23. Discuss appropriate medication treatment options with the patient and/or significant others.

24. Educate the patient and/or significant others on psychotropic

12. Take medications prescribed for controlling self-injurious or aggressive behavior as ordered by the physician. (25, 26)

13. Report as to the effectiveness of SSRI medications and any side effects that develop. (27, 28)

14. Adhere to the augmenting medication regimen as prescribed by the physician. (29, 30, 31)

medication treatment including expected results, potential side effects, and dosing strategies.

25. Determine if the patient displays self-injurious or aggressive behavior.

26. Prescribe to the patient a selective serotonin reuptake inhibitor (SSRI) (e.g., paroxetine [Paxil®], sertraline [Zoloft®], citalopram [Celexa™], escitalopram [Lexapro™], fluoxetine [Prozac®], or fluvoxamine [Luvox®]).

27. Monitor the patient frequently for the development of side effects, response to SSRI medication, and adherence to treatment.

28. Increase the medication dose every three to four weeks, as tolerated, until the patient has a satisfactory response or the maximum dose is reached.

29. Consider the addition of an augmentation medication (e.g., clonidine [Catapres®], divalproex sodium [Depakote®], carbamazepine [Tegretol®], naltrexone [ReVia®]) if the patient has only a partial response to an SSRI.

30. Monitor the blood level of divalproex sodium (Depakote®) or carbamazepine (Tegretol®) four to five days after starting the medication or increasing the dose.

31. Titrate the dose of the augmenting medication every four to five days as tolerated.

15. Parents and the patient, if possible, report the presence of disruptive behaviors or psychotic symptoms that are not controlled by the current medication. (32)

16. Take antipsychotic medication as prescribed by the physician. (33, 34, 35)

17. Cooperate with any changes in the prescribed anti-psychotic regimen. (36)

18. Parents and the patient, if possible, verbalize an under-standing of treatment with clozapine (Clozaril) for refract-tory symptoms and cooperate with treatment guidelines. (37, 38, 39)

32. Determine if the patient displays self-injurious or aggressive behavior that is not controlled by other medications, psychotic symptoms, (e.g., hallucinations, delusions, paranoia), tics, or stereotypes.

33. Prescribe an atypical antipsy-chotic agent (e.g., risperidone [Risperdal®], olanzapine [Zyprexa®], ziprasidone [Geodon®], aripiprazole [Abilify™], quetiapine [Seroquel®], clozapine [Clozaril®]) if the patient does not have a satisfactory response to other medications.

34. Monitor the patient frequently for the development of side effects, response to the antipsychotic medication and adherence to treatment.

35. Titrate the patient's antipsy-chotic dose every two weeks until his/her symptoms are con-trolled or the maximum dose is reached.

36. Switch the patient's medication to another atypical antipsychotic agent if patient has no response or a partial response; give each individual atypical antipsychotic a full trial, if necessary.

37. Consider prescribing clozapine (Clozaril®) if the patient has had a poor response to all other atypical antipsychotics.

38. Educate the patient and/or significant others on the potential risks and side effects of clozapine (Clozaril®) (e.g., agranulocytosis, weight gain, elevated blood glucose, sedation).

39. Perform a full medical evaluation and check baseline laboratory values, including a complete blood count, prior to starting clozapine (Clozaril®) therapy; follow published guidelines for prescribing clozapine.

19. Retain a remission or significant reduction in disruptive behavior and/or psychotic symptoms with a minimum amount of medications. (40)

40. Maintain the patient on current medication indefinitely if he/she has shown a significant reduction in disruptive behavior and/or psychotic symptoms.

__. _____

_____

__. _____

_____

__. _____

_____

__. _____

_____

__. _____

_____

__. _____

_____

DIAGNOSTIC SUGGESTIONS:

Axis I:

299.00	Autistic Disorder
299.80	Rett's Disorder
299.80	Asperger's Disorder
299.80	Pervasive Developmental Disorder NOS
315.31	Expressive Language Disorder
315.31	Mixed Receptive-Expressive Language Disorder
315.4	Developmental Coordination Disorder

_____ _____

_____ _____

Axis II:

317	Mild Mental Retardation
318.0	Moderate Mental Retardation
318.1	Severe Mental Retardation
318.2	Profound Mental Retardation
319	Mental Retardation, Severity Unspecified

_____ _____

_____ _____

DEPRESSION

BEHAVIORAL DEFINITIONS

1. Sad mood.
2. Depressed affect.
3. Diminished interest in or enjoyment of activities.
4. Psychomotor agitation or retardation.
5. Loss of appetite.
6. Sleeplessness or hypersomnia.
7. Lack of energy.
8. Poor concentration and indecisiveness.
9. Impairment of memory.
10. Social withdrawal.
11. Feelings of hopelessness, worthlessness, or inappropriate guilt.
12. Low self-esteem.
13. Unexplained crying spells.
14. Diurnal mood variation—feeling most depressed in the morning and somewhat better later in the day.
15. Irritability and/or anger attacks.
16. Suicidal thoughts and/or gestures.
17. Mood-related hallucinations or delusions.
18. History of recurrent or chronic depression for which antidepressant medication has been taken, hospitalization, outpatient treatment, or a course of electroconvulsive therapy has been ordered.

__. _____
    _____
__. _____
    _____
__. _____
    _____

LONG-TERM GOALS

1. Alleviate depressed mood and return to previous level of functioning.
2. Develop the ability to recognize, accept, and cope with feelings of depression.
3. Take the appropriate medication and dose to control symptoms of depression.
4. Cooperate with ongoing psychotherapy to prevent relapse.
5. Prevent relapse and recurrence of depressive signs and symptoms.

—. _____

   _____

—. _____

   _____

—. _____

   _____

SHORT-TERM OBJECTIVES

1. Describe the signs and symptoms of depression that are experienced and note their impact on daily life. (1, 2)

2. Describe other symptoms or disorders that may also be present. (3, 4)

THERAPEUTIC INTERVENTIONS

1. Explore how depression is experienced by the patient and how it affects his/her daily life (e.g., insomnia or hypersomnia, loss of interest, social withdrawal, poor energy, indecisiveness).

2. Ask the patient about the presence of mood-congruent delusions or hallucinations.

3. Assess the patient for comorbid disorders (e.g., anxiety, panic, or obsessive-compulsive disorder) (see the Anxiety, Phobia-Panic/ Agoraphobia, or Obsessive-Compulsive Disorder chapters in this *Planner* if one or more are present).

4. Gather detailed personal and family history information regarding substance and/or alcohol

abuse and its potential contribution to depression; refer the patient for in-depth substance abuse treatment, if indicated (see the Chemical Dependence chapters in this *Planner*).

3. Verbalize any current suicidal thoughts and any history of suicidal behavior. (5, 6, 7)

5. Explore the patient's current and past suicidal thoughts and suicidal behavior; check for family history of suicide (see interventions designed for Suicidal Ideation in this *Planner,* if necessary).

6. Arrange for hospitalization, as necessary, when the patient is judged to be harmful to himself/herself or others or unable to care for his/her basic needs.

7. Administer to the patient the Beck Scale for Suicidal Ideation or other objective assessment instrument; evaluate results and give feedback to the patient.

4. Outline a complete and accurate medical and psychiatric history, including treatment received and its effectiveness. (8, 9)

8. Explore the patient's history of previous treatment for depression and the success and tolerability of that treatment.

9. Assess the patient for the presence of other medical problems and medications used to treat them.

5. Cooperate with a physical examination and laboratory tests. (10, 11)

10. Perform a complete physical and neurological examination on the patient and send his/her blood and/or urine for analysis to rule out an organic cause for depression.

11. Provide feedback to the patient regarding the results and implications of the physical examination and laboratory test results.

6. Pursue treatment for concurrent medical problems that may contribute to depressive symptoms. (12, 13)

7. Complete psychological testing and other questionnaires for measuring level of depression. (14)

8. Express an understanding of the possible causes for depression and the relationship between substance abuse and depression. (15, 16)

9. Express an understanding of treatment options, expected results from medication, and potential side effects. (17, 18, 19)

12. Treat or refer the patient for treatment for any medical problem that may be causing or contributing to depressive symptoms (e.g., cardiovascular disease, neurologic disorders, cancer, endocrinologic disorders, infectious disease, or nutritional deficiencies).

13. Monitor the patient's progress in recovery from concomitant disorders and the impact on his/her mood.

14. Administer to the patient an objective assessment instrument for measuring his/her level of depression (e.g., Beck Depression Inventory [BDI], Hamilton Depression Rating Scale [HDRS], Zung Self-Rating Depression Scale); evaluate the results and give him/her feedback.

15. Educate the patient on the possible causes for (e.g., biochemical imbalance, cognitive distortions, life stressors, early life trauma, grief issues, genetic propensity) and signs of depression; emphasize the negative and dangerous impact of substance abuse on depression.

16. Ask the patient to identify what he/she believes may be contributing factors to his/her depression.

17. Discuss appropriate treatment options with the patient including medications, combination pharmacotherapy, electroconvulsive therapy, and psychotherapy.

18. Educate the patient on psycho-tropic medication treatment including expected results, potential side effects, and dosing strategies.

19. Discuss electroconvulsive ther-apy with the patient who has not responded well to medications; refer him/her for a course of treatment, if indicated.

10. Take prescribed medications responsibly at times ordered by the physician. (20, 21)

20. Prescribe a first-line antidepres-sant agent (e.g., a selective sero-tonin reuptake inhibitor [SSRI]), dosing as appropriate for the patient's age, health, and concurrent medications.

21. Treat the patient's coexisting psychotic symptoms using a low dose of an atypical antipsychotic medication (e.g., olanzapine [Zyprexa®], quetiapine [Sero-quel®], risperidone [Risper-dal®], aripiprazole [Abilify™], or ziprasidone [Geodon®]).

11. Report as to the effectiveness of medications and any side effects that develop. (22, 23, 24, 25)

22. Titrate the patient's medication to minimum effective dose for treating his/her depression.

23. Monitor the patient frequently for development of side effects, response to medication, adher-ence to treatment, and develop-ment of manic or hypomanic symptoms.

24. Consider changing the patient's medication to another antide-pressant agent in a different class if he/she has minimal or no response to the initial medica-tion. Alternatives include venla-faxine (Effexor®), mirtazapine (Remeron®), bupropion (Wellbutrin®), nefazodone

(Serzone®), tricyclic antidepressant (TCA), or monoamine
oxidase inhibitor (MAOI).

25. Monitor the patient for his/her
response to and tolerance of
medication increases.

12. Participate in psychotherapy
sessions as planned with the
therapist. (26, 27)

26. Assess the patient for potential
benefit from psychotherapy and
refer to a psychotherapist, if
necessary.

27. Monitor the patient's investment
in and response to psychotherapy; assess his/her ability to
verbalize a basis for progress in
depression recovery (e.g.,
healthier cognitions, resolved
conflicts, improved relationships, sobriety).

13. Attend follow-up appointments as scheduled by the
physician. (28, 29)

28. Reassess the patient in four
weeks for his/her response to
medication; determine whether
the medication is adequate,
needs a dose increase, or another
agent needs to be tried.

29. Evaluate the patient at six weeks
for his/her response to medication; determine if he/she has had
a full response or partial response to the treatment regimen.

14. Report evidence of improvement in depressive symptoms
as well as any comorbid
disorders. (30, 31, 32, 33)

30. Repeat administration of objective instruments to the patient
for assessment of his/her
depression severity; evaluate the
results and give him/her
feedback.

31. Discontinue the patient's
antipsychotic medication one to
two months after his/her
psychosis has resolved and the
depression has remitted; monitor
closely for relapse.

32. Maintain the patient on current medication for nine to twelve months if he/she has shown a fully successful response; if he/she has had previous episodes of depression, consider continuing treatment indefinitely.

33. Switch the patient to a different antidepressant in another class if he/she has shown only a partially successful medication response.

15. State no longer having thoughts of self-harm. (34, 35, 36)

34. Explore the patient's current and past suicidal thoughts and suicidal behavior check for family history of suicide (see the interventions designed for Suicidal Ideation in this *Planner* if present).

35. Administer to the patient the Beck Depression Inventory, Hamilton Depression Rating Scale, the Beck Scale for Suicidal Ideation, or other objective assessment instrument; evaluate the results and give him/her feedback.

36. Assess and monitor the patient's suicide potential on a continuing basis until depression is substantially diminished.

16. Verbalize the signs and symptoms of depression and how to gauge their severity. (15, 37)

15. Educate the patient on the possible causes for (e.g., biochemical imbalance, cognitive distortions, life stressors, early life trauma, grief issues, genetic propensity) and signs of depression; emphasize the negative and dangerous impact of substance abuse on depression.

37. Teach the patient how to monitor changes in his/her mood and

mental status (e.g., sociability, sleep, appetite or energy changes, irritability, disinterest, concentration loss).

17. Adhere to changes in medication dosing or augmentation. (38, 39, 40, 41, 42)

38. Discuss other treatment options with the patient if he/she shows only a partial treatment response.

39. Increase medication dose if the patient has had a partial response; titrate his/her dose every two weeks until the maximum dose is reached.

40. Determine if the patient needs additional medication to augment current antidepressant therapy. Lithium or thyroid hormone supplementation should be considered.

41. Maximize augmentation medication as tolerated by the patient.

42. Prescribe an alternative augmentation medication such as an atypical antipsychotic (e.g. olanzapine [Zyprexa®], risperidone [Risperdal®], ziprasidone [Geodon®], aripiprazole [Abilify™], or quetiapine [Seroquel®]) or a second antidepressant in another class if other augmentation strategies fail.

18. Cooperate with changes in type of antidepressant medication prescribed. (24, 43)

24. Consider changing to another antidepressant agent in a different class if the patient has minimal or no response to the initial medication. Alternatives include venlafaxine (Effexor®), mirtazapine (Remeron®), bupropion (Wellbutrin®), nefazodone (Serzone®), tricyclic antidepressant (TCA), or

19. Follow dietary restrictions and other monitoring tests for treatment with monoamine oxidase inhibitors (MAOIs). (44, 45, 46)

20. Read books on coping with depression. (47)

monoamine oxidase inhibitor (MAOI).

43. Complete medical evaluation on the patient including an electrocardiogram, if necessary, before starting him/her on a TCA; gradually titrate dose of TCA as necessary to maximum effectiveness.

44. Educate the patient on dietary restrictions and ask him/her to try the restrictions before starting a MAOI.

45. Measure platelet MAO activity, if available, before treatment with an MAOI.

46. Prescribe MAOI and titrate dose as necessary, monitoring for effectiveness and side-effects as well as the patient's compliance with the dietary restrictions; monitor MAO inhibition during treatment to target 85% inhibition.

47. Recommend that the patient read books on coping with depression (e.g., *The Feeling Good Handbook* by Burns; *What to say when Talking to Yourself* by Helmstetter; *Talking to Yourself* by Butler); process his/her implementation of coping techniques, reinforcing success and redirecting for failure.

__. _____   __. _____
    _____   _____
__. _____   __. _____
    _____   _____
__. _____   __. _____
    _____   _____

DIAGNOSTIC SUGGESTIONS:

Axis I:
296.2x	Major Depressive Disorder, Single Episode
296.3x	Major Depressive Disorder, Recurrent
300.4	Dysthymic Disorder
296.xx	Bipolar I Disorder
296.89	Bipolar II Disorder
301.13	Cyclothymic Disorder
309.0	Adjustment Disorder with Depressed Mood
295.70	Schizoaffective Disorder
291.8	Alcohol-Induced Mood Disorder
292.84	Substance-Induced Mood Disorder
293.83	Mood Disorder Due to (Axis III Disorder)
V62.82	Bereavement

_____ _____

_____ _____

Axis II:

_____ _____

_____ _____

DISSOCIATION

BEHAVIORAL DEFINITIONS

1. The existence of two or more distinct personalities or personality-states that recurrently take full control of behavior.
2. An episode of sudden inability to remember important personal information that is more than just ordinary forgetfulness.
3. Persistent or recurrent experiences of depersonalization, feeling as if detached from or outside of one's mental processes or body during which reality testing remains intact.
4. Persistent or recurrent experience of derealization, feeling as if one is automated or in a dream.
5. Depersonalization sufficiently severe and persistent as to cause marked distress in daily life.
6. Suddenly and unexpectedly traveling away from home or work with an inability to remember one's past.
7. Assumption of a new identity or displaying confusion about personal identity.

__. _____

_____

__. _____

_____

__. _____

_____

LONG-TERM GOALS

1. Reduce the frequency and duration of dissociative episodes through psychotherapy and medication.
2. Resolve the emotional trauma that underlies the dissociative disturbance.

3. Reduce the level of daily distress caused by dissociative disturbances.
4. Regain full memory.
5. Begin the process of integrating the various personalities.

—. _____
   _____

—. _____
   _____

—. _____
   _____

SHORT-TERM OBJECTIVES

THERAPEUTIC INTERVENTIONS

1. Describe the signs and symptoms of dissociation that are experienced and note their impact on daily life. (1)

1. Explore what dissociation symptoms are experienced by the patient and how it affects his/her daily life (e.g., no memory for recent events, recurrent feelings of depersonalization, performing dangerous acts during dissociation).

2. Describe other symptoms or disorders that may also be present. (2, 3)

2. Assess the patient for comorbid disorders (e.g., see the Post-traumatic Stress Disorder (PTSD), Depression, and/or Anxiety chapters in this *Planner*).

3. Gather detailed personal and family history information regarding the patient's substance abuse and its potential contribution to dissociation; refer the patient for in-depth substance abuse treatment, if indicated (see the Chemical Dependence chapters in this *Planner*).

3. Verbalize any current suicidal thoughts and any history of suicidal behavior. (4, 5)

4. Explore the patient's current and past suicidal thoughts and suicidal behavior; ask about a

4. Outline a complete and accurate medical and psychiatric history, including treatment received and its effectiveness. (6, 7)

5. Complete psychological testing and other questionnaires for measuring dissociation. (8)

6. Express an understanding of possible causes for dissociation and the relationship between substance abuse and dissociation. (9, 10)

7. Verbalize an understanding of treatment options, expected results from medication, and potential side effects. (11, 12, 13)

family history of suicide (see the Suicidal Ideation chapter in this *Planner*).

5. Arrange for hospitalization, as necessary, when the patient is judged to be harmful to self or unable to care for his/her basic needs.

6. Explore the patient's history of previous treatment for dissociation or depersonalization and the success of, as well as tolerance for, that treatment.

7. Assess the patient for the presence of other medical problems and medications used to treat them.

8. Administer objective instruments to assess the patient's dissociation severity and frequency (e.g., Dissociative Experiences Scale [DES], Dissociative Disorders Interview Schedule [DDIS]); evaluate the results and give him/her feedback.

9. Emphasize the negative and dangerous impact of substance abuse on dissociation.

10. Educate the patient on the possible contributing factors (e.g., stressful life events, history of abuse, or other traumatic experience) and signs of dissociation.

11. Discuss appropriate treatment options with the patient including medication, psychotherapy, and hypnosis.

12. Educate the patient on psychotropic medication treatment including the expected results,

8. Participate in psychotherapy sessions as planned with the therapist. (14, 15)

9. Take prescribed medications responsibly at times ordered by physician. (16)

10. Attend follow-up appointments and report as to the effectiveness of SSRI medications and any side effects that develop. (17, 18, 19)

potential side effects, and dosing strategies.

13. Inform the patient that medication is likely to provide only partial control of symptoms.

14. Assess the patient for potential benefit from psychotherapy and refer to a psychotherapist, if necessary.

15. Monitor the patient's response to psychotherapy; assess his/her ability to verbalize a basis for progress in recovery from dissociations (e.g., decreased frequency and duration of dissociations, reduction in distress caused by dissociations).

16. Prescribe to the patient a selective serotonin reuptake inhibitor (SSRI) (e.g., paroxetine [Paxil®], sertraline [Zoloft®], citalopram [Celexa™], escitalopram [Lexapro™], fluoxetine [Prozac®]); strongly consider this strategy for patients with depressive or anxiety symptoms.

17. Monitor the patient frequently for development of side effects, response to SSRI medication, and adherence to treatment.

18. Titrate the patient's SSRI medication every two to four weeks until the patient's symptoms are controlled or the maximum dose for the medication is reached.

19. Repeat administration of objective measures of the patient's dissociation severity; evaluate the results and give him/her feedback.

11. Adhere to changes in medication regimen or other recommended therapy. (20, 21, 22)

20. Consider the use of a low-dose atypical antipsychotic medication (i.e., olanzapine [Zyprexa®], quetiapine [Seroquel®], risperidone [Risperdal®], ziprasidone [Geodon®], or aripiprazole [Abilify™]) if the patient's dissociation symptoms are not controlled with an SSRI.

21. Titrate the patient's antipsychotic medication every two to four weeks until the patient's symptoms are controlled or the maximum dose for the medication is reached.

22. Prescribe an alternative treatment (i.e., clonazepam [Klonopin®], dextroamphetamine [Adderall®], or methamphetamine [Desoxyn®]) for severe dissociation or depersonalization that does not respond to other therapies.

12. Cooperate with a drug-assisted interview. (23)

23. Perform a drug-assisted interview using amobarbital (Amytal®) or thiopental (Pentothal®) if the patient has dissociative amnesia or other intransigent dissociation.

13. Retain a remission or significant reduction in dissociative symptoms. (24)

24. Consider maintaining the patient on medication indefinitely if he/she has response to medication and his/her side effects from the medication are tolerable.

__. _____

__. _____

__. _____

__. _____

__. _____

__. _____

DIAGNOSTIC SUGGESTIONS:

Axis I:

300.14	Dissociative Identity Disorder
300.12	Dissociative Amnesia
300.13	Dissociative Fugue
300.6	Depersonalization Disorder
300.15	Dissociative Disorder NOS
309.81	Posttraumatic Stress Disorder
303.90	Alcohol Dependence
304.30	Cannabis Dependence
304.50	Hallucinogen Dependence
304.90	Phencyclidine Dependence

_____   _____

_____   _____

Axis II: 301.83   Borderline Personality Disorder

_____   _____

_____   _____

EATING DISORDER

BEHAVIORAL DEFINITIONS

1. Chronic, rapid consumption of large quantities of high-carbohydrate food (binge eating).
2. Feeling a lack of control over eating during an eating binge.
3. Self-induced vomiting and/or abuse of laxatives due to fear of weight gain.
4. Extreme weight loss with refusal to maintain a minimal healthy weight.
5. Amenorrhea in females.
6. Very limited ingestion of food and high frequency of secret self-induced vomiting, inappropriate use of laxatives and/or excessive strenuous exercise.
7. Persistent preoccupation with body image related to grossly inaccurate assessment of self as overweight.
8. Intense, irrational fear of becoming overweight.
9. Escalating fluid and electrolyte imbalance resulting from the eating disorder.
10. Strong denial of seeing self as emaciated even when severely under recommended weight.

—. _____
   _____
—. _____
   _____
—. _____
   _____

LONG-TERM GOALS

1. Take the appropriate medication and dose and/or participate in psychotherapy to re-establish normal eating patterns.
2. Restore body weight, balanced fluid and electrolytes, and a realistic perception of body size.
3. Terminate pattern of binge eating and purging behavior with a return to normal eating of enough nutritious foods to maintain a healthy weight.
4. Gain sufficient insight into the cognitive and emotional struggle to allow termination of the eating disorder and responsible maintenance of nutritional food intake.
5. Change the definition of the self so that it does not focus on weight, size, and shape as the primary criteria for self-acceptance.
6. Restructure the distorted thoughts, beliefs, and values that contribute to eating-disorder development.

—. _____

_____

—. _____

_____

—. _____

_____

SHORT-TERM OBJECTIVES	THERAPEUTIC INTERVENTIONS
1. Describe patterns of eating, purging, and exercise. (1, 2, 3)	1. Explore what abnormal patterns of eating are exhibited by the patient (e.g., eating too little food, eating too much food, binge eating, food hoarding).
	2. Determine the type and frequency of purging behaviors (e.g., self-induced vomiting, laxative abuse) or excessive use of appetite suppressants by the patient to control caloric intake and weight.
	3. Explore a history of too vigorous and too frequent exercise in an effort to control weight.

2. Describe other symptoms or disorders that may also be present. (4, 5)

4. Assess the patient for comorbid disorders (e.g., depression, anxiety, personality disorder) (see the relevant chapters in this *Planner*).

5. Gather detailed personal and family history information regarding substance abuse and its potential interaction with eating disorders; refer the patient for in-depth substance abuse treatment, if indicated (see the Chemical Dependence chapters in this *Planner*).

3. Outline a complete and accurate medical and psychiatric history, including treatment received and its effectiveness. (6, 7)

6. Explore the patient's history of previous treatment for an eating disorder and the level of success of, as well as his/her tolerance for, that treatment.

7. Assess the patient for the presence of other medical problems and what medications are used to treat them.

4. Cooperate with physical and dental examinations and laboratory tests. (8, 9, 10, 11)

8. Perform a complete physical and neurological examination on the patient and send his/her blood and/or urine for analysis to evaluate nutrition and electrolyte status.

9. Arrange for hospitalization, as necessary, when the patient is judged to be harmful to self (e.g., not eating for a prolonged period of time, severely underweight) or in need of acute medical care (e.g., electrolyte abnormalities, metabolic acidosis, or alkalosis).

10. Refer the patient to a dentist for a complete dental exam.

11. Provide feedback to the patient regarding the results and

implications of the physical examination and laboratory test results.

5. Pursue treatment for concurrent medical problems that may contribute to anorexia or bulimia symptoms. (12, 13)

12. Treat or refer the patient for treatment for any medical problem that may be contributing to anorexia or bulimia symptoms (e.g., cancer, gastrointestinal disease, infection, endocrine disorders, autoimmune disease).

13. Monitor the patient's progress in recovery from concomitant disorders and the impact of the recovery on his/her eating disorder symptoms.

6. Complete psychological testing and other questionnaires for assessing eating disorders. (14)

14. Administer an objective eating disorder assessment instrument to the patient (e.g., Eating Disorder Inventory [EDI, EDI-2], Body Shape Questionnaire [BSQ], Three Factor Eating Questionnaire [TFEQ]); evaluate the results and give him/her feedback.

7. Verbalize an understanding of the possible contributing factors to eating disorders and the relationship between eating disorders and depression. (15, 16)

15. Educate the patient on the possible contributing factors to (e.g., neurotransmitter abnormalities, social factors, history of childhood abuse) and signs of eating disorders.

16. Educate the patient on the signs and symptoms of depression and how it affects eating disorders.

8. Follow dietary recommendations designed to help establish a healthy weight. (17, 18, 19)

17. Establish healthy weight goals for the patient per the Body Mass Index (BMI = weight in pounds × 703 ÷ height in inches ÷ height in inches); normal range is 20 to 24 and below 18.5 is seriously underweight according to the Metropolitan Height and Weight

Tables, Iowa Growth chart, or some other recognized standard.

18. Refer the patient to a dietitian who will help the patient outline a nutritionally balanced diet with enough calories to obtain a healthy weight.

19. Monitor the patient's weight on a regular basis.

9. Participate in psychotherapy sessions as planned with the therapist. (20, 21)

20. Assess the patient for potential benefit from psychotherapy and refer him/her to a psychotherapist, if necessary.

21. Monitor the patient's investment in and response to psychotherapy; assess his/her ability to verbalize a basis for progress in eating disorder recovery (e.g., reduction in binging and purging behavior, healthier image of himself/herself, maintenance of a healthy weight).

10. Express an understanding of medication treatment options, expected results, and potential side effects. (22, 23)

22. Discuss appropriate medication treatment options with the patient.

23. Educate the patient on psychotropic medication treatment including expected results, potential side effects, and dosing strategies.

11. Take prescribed SSRI medications responsibly at times ordered by the physician. (24, 25)

24. Prescribe to the patient a selective serotonin reuptake inhibitor (SSRI) (e.g., paroxetine [Paxil®], sertraline [Zoloft®], citalopram [Celexa™], escitalopram [Lexapro™], fluoxetine [Prozac®], fluvoxamine [Luvox®]).

25. Titrate the SSRI to the minimum effective dose for treating the patient's symptoms.

12. Report on the effectiveness of SSRI medications and any side effects that develop. (26, 27)

13. Cooperate with blood draws and changes in medication dose. (28, 29)

14. Attend follow-up appointments as scheduled by the physician. (30)

15. Report evidence of the degree of improvement in eating disorder symptoms. (31)

16. Cooperate with changes in type of medication prescribed as well as additional medical tests and dietary restrictions. (32, 33, 34, 35)

26. Monitor the patient frequently for the development of side effects, response to medication, and adherence to treatment.

27. Reassess the patient who is taking an antidepressant at two to three weeks; determine whether the medication is adequate or needs a dose increase.

28. Monitor plasma levels of the antidepressant to confirm adherence with the medication and to assess whether medication absorption is affected by purging.

29. Maximize the antidepressant dose as tolerated; allow for a full trial at the highest tolerated dose.

30. Evaluate the patient at six to twelve weeks for his/her response to medication; determine if he/she has had a full response or partial response to the treatment regimen.

31. Repeat administration of objective rating instruments for assessment of the patient's eating disorder symptoms; evaluate the results and give him/her feedback.

32. Consider changing the patient's medication to another agent if he/she has minimal or no response to the initial medication; alternatives include another SSRI, trazodone, a tricyclic antidepressant (TCA) (e.g., amitriptyline [Elavil®], imipramine [Tofranil®], desipramine [Norpramin®], nortriptyline [Pamelor®]), or a monoamine oxidase inhibitor

(MAOI) (e.g., phenelzine [Nardil®]).

33. Complete a medical evaluation on the patient including an electrocardiogram and measurement of electrolytes before starting him/her on a TCA.

34. Educate the patient on dietary restrictions and ask him/her to try the restrictions before starting an MAOI; closely monitor compliance with dietary restrictions during treatment.

35. Monitor plasma levels of the medication to confirm adequacy of the dose and adherence to the therapy; adjust the dose of medication as necessary.

17. Retain a remission of eating disorder symptoms and maintain a healthy body weight. (36, 37, 38)

36. Maintain the patient on current medication for at least 12 months if he/she has shown a fully successful response; if he/she has had previous eating disorder symptoms or demonstrates only a partial response, consider continuing treatment indefinitely.

37. Reduce medications gradually (i.e., approximately 25% of the dose every two months); monitor closely for recurrence of symptoms.

38. Refer the patient to a program that specializes in treating eating disorders if he/she does not have a full response to other therapies.

18. Read books on coping with an eating disorder and implement newly learned techniques. (39)

39. Recommend that the patient read books on coping with an eating disorder (e.g., *Body Traps* by Rodin; *Overcoming Binge Eating* by Fairburn; *Surviving*

an Eating Disorder by Seigel, Brisman, and Weinshel); process his/her implementation of coping techniques, reinforcing success and redirecting for failure.

—. _____   —. _____
   _____   _____
—. _____   —. _____
   _____   _____
—. _____   —. _____
   _____   _____

DIAGNOSTIC SUGGESTIONS:

Axis I: 307.1   Anorexia Nervosa
                   307.51   Bulimia Nervosa
                   307.50   Eating Disorder NOS
                   307.50   Binge Eating Disorder
                   307.50   Nocturnal Binge Eating Disorder
                   300.3   Obsessive-Compulsive Disorder
                   300.7   Body Dysmorphic Disorder
                   296.xx   Major Depressive Disorder

                   _____   _____
                   _____   _____

Axis II: 301.6   Dependent Personality Disorder
                   301.83   Borderline Personality Disorder

                   _____   _____
                   _____   _____

FEMALE SEXUAL DYSFUNCTION

BEHAVIORAL DEFINITIONS

1. Consistently very low desire for or no pleasurable anticipation of sexual activity.
2. Strong avoidance of and/or repulsion to any and all sexual contact in spite of a relationship of mutual caring and respect.
3. Recurrent lack of usual physiological response of sexual excitement and arousal (e.g., genital lubrication and swelling).
4. Consistent lack of subjective sense of enjoyment and pleasure during sexual activity.
5. Persistent delay in or absence of reaching orgasm after achieving arousal and in spite of sensitive sexual pleasuring by a caring partner.
6. Genital pain before, during, or after sexual intercourse.
7. Consistent or recurring involuntary spasm of the vagina that prohibits penetration for sexual intercourse.

—. _____
   _____

—. _____
   _____

—. _____
   _____

LONG-TERM GOALS

1. Take the appropriate medication and dose and/or participate in psychotherapy to alleviate symptoms of sexual dysfunction and return to previous level of functioning.
2. Increase desire for and enjoyment of sexual activity.

3. Attain and maintain physiological excitement response during sexual intercourse.
4. Reach orgasm within a reasonable amount of time, with intensity and focus given to sexual stimulation.
5. Eliminate pain and promote subjective pleasure before, during, and after sexual intercourse.
6. Eliminate vaginal spasms that prohibit penile penetration during sexual intercourse and achieve a sense of relaxed enjoyment of coital pleasure.

—. _____
_____

—. _____
_____

—. _____
_____

SHORT-TERM OBJECTIVES	THERAPEUTIC INTERVENTIONS
1. Describe the signs and symptoms of sexual dysfunction that are experienced and note their impact on daily life. (1, 2)	1. Explore what symptoms of sexual dysfunction are experienced by the patient and how it affects her daily life (e.g., low sexual desire, little or no physical sexual response, inability to have an orgasm, pain with intercourse, relationship difficulties with a mate).
	2. Explore with the patient any history of childhood physical or sexual abuse or sexual trauma as an adult (e.g., rape, sexual coercion).
2. Describe other symptoms or disorders that may also be present. (3, 4)	3. Assess the patient for comorbid psychiatric disorders (e.g., see the Depression or Anxiety chapters in this *Planner*) that may contribute to or result from the sexual dysfunction.

3. Outline a complete and accurate medical and psychiatric history, including treatment received and its effectiveness. (5, 6)

4. Gather detailed personal and family history information regarding the patient's substance and/or alcohol abuse and its potential contribution to sexual dysfunction; refer him/her for in-depth substance abuse treatment, if indicated (see the Chemical Dependence chapters in this *Planner*).

5. Explore the patient's history of previous treatment for sexual dysfunction and the success and tolerance of that treatment.

6. Assess the patient for the presence of other medical problems and medications used to treat them.

4. Cooperate with a physical examination and laboratory tests. (7, 8)

7. Perform or refer the patient for a complete physical, gynecological, and neurological examination and send her blood and/or urine for analysis to rule out an organic cause for sexual dysfunction (e.g., infection, hypertension, hypercholesterolemia, smoking, diabetes, neurological disorders, endocrine disease, history of radiation therapy).

8. Provide feedback to the patient regarding the results and implications of the physical examination and laboratory test results.

5. Pursue treatment for concurrent medical or psychiatric problems that may cause sexual dysfunction. (9, 10, 11)

9. Treat or refer the patient for treatment for any medical problem that may be causing sexual dysfunction (e.g., infection, hypertension, hypercholesterolemia, smoking, diabetes, neurological disorders, endocrine disease).

10. Treat the patient for any psychiatric disorder that may be causing sexual dysfunction (e.g., see the Depression or Anxiety chapters in this *Planner*).

11. Monitor the patient's progress in recovery from concomitant disorders and the impact on her sexual dysfunction.

6. Complete psychological testing and other questionnaires for assessing sexual dysfunction. (12)

12. Administer to the patient an objective assessment instrument for measuring female sexual dysfunction (e.g., Brief Index of Sexual Functioning for Women [BISF-W], Derogatis Interview for Sexual Functioning [DISF], Female Sexual Function Index [FSFI]); evaluate the results and give her feedback.

7. Verbalize an understanding of the impact of substance abuse on sexual dysfunction. (13)

13. Emphasize to the patient the negative and dangerous interaction of substance abuse with sexual functioning (e.g., decreased desire, reduced physical sexual response, decreased sensation during intercourse).

8. Express an understanding of treatment options, expected results, and potential side effects of medication. (14, 15)

14. Discuss appropriate treatment options with the patient, including medications and psychotherapy.

15. Educate the patient on medication treatment including the expected results, potential side effects, and dosing strategies.

9. Participate in psychotherapy sessions as planned with the therapist. (16, 17)

16. Assess the patient for potential benefit from psychotherapy and refer her to a psychotherapist, if necessary.

17. Monitor the patient's investment in and response to psychotherapy; assess her ability to

verbalize a basis for progress in recovery from sexual dysfunction (e.g., increased sexual desire, improved excitement response during sexual encounters, ability to reach orgasm, significantly reduced pain during intercourse).

10. Verbalize an understanding of the use of lubricants during sexual intercourse. (18, 19)

18. Recommend to the patient the use of a water-based lubricant (e.g., KY Jelly®, Astroglide®) during sexual intercourse if she has inadequate vaginal secretions during sexual arousal.

19. Educate the patient on the risk of condom failure if a nonwater-based lubricant (e.g., petroleum jelly [Vaseline®]) is used along with condoms.

11. Cooperate with blood draws to measure hormone levels. (20)

20. Measure the patient's hormone levels (e.g., estrogen, testosterone, prolactin [especially for patients taking an antipsychotic medication]).

12. Take hormone replacement medications as prescribed by the physician. (21, 22)

21. Prescribe hormone replacement therapy (HRT) to the patient if she has low hormone levels, is postmenopausal, or has had an oophorectomy.

22. Consider the use of estrogen cream (Estrace®) or vaginal estrogen inserts (Vagifem®) if the patient has vaginal atrophy.

13. Verbalize to the physician all medications and doses, as well as alcohol and illicit drugs, that are currently being taken. (23)

23. Determine if the patient is taking a substance could cause sexual dysfunction (e.g., antidepressant, antipsychotic, antihypertensive, anticholinergic, antihistamine, benzodiazepine, lithium, psychostimulant, alcohol, cannabis, opioid, barbiturate).

14. Refrain from the use of alcohol and illicit drugs as recommended by the physician. (24)

15. Adhere to any changes in medication as prescribed by the physician. (25, 26, 27, 28)

24. Emphasize to the patient that she refrain from the use of alcohol or other illicit substances if the sexual dysfunction occurs in the context of substance use.

25. Decrease the dose of medication that is thought to contribute to the sexual dysfunction if such a reduction does not adversely affect the patient.

26. Consider changing the patient's antidepressant to an alternative antidepressant without sexual side effects (e.g., mirtazapine [Remeron®], bupropion [Wellbutrin®], nefazodone [Serzone®]), if necessary.

27. Titrate the dose of the alternative medication to the minimum effective dose for treating depression, as tolerated by the patient.

28. Reduce the dose of the antidepressant medication that seems associated with the patient's sexual dysfunction slowly over weeks to months, as tolerated by the patient, until the medication is stopped.

16. Report on the effectiveness of the new medication and any side effects that develop. (29)

17. Cooperate with the addition| of any new medication as prescribed by the physician to help improve sexual functioning. (30, 31, 32, 33)

29. Monitor the patient closely for relapse or worsening of symptoms during the cross-titration of medications.

30. Consider the addition of a second antidepressant (e.g., mirtazapine [Remeron®], bupropion [Wellbutrin®], nefazodone [Serzone®]) or ginkgo biloba if the patient would be adversely affected by changing the current antidepressant medication.

31. Titrate the dose of the added medication every two to three weeks, as tolerated, until the patient has a satisfactory response or the maximum dose is reached.

32. Discuss with the patient the option of taking medication (e.g., sildenafil [Viagra®]) to help increase physical sexual response.

33. Prescribe to the patient the sexual response enhancing medication; educate the patient on the proper use of the medication to enhance sexual response (i.e., taking the medication one to two hours prior to a sexual encounter).

18. Verbalize an understanding of taking a "drug holiday" for temporary improvement in sexual side effects of medication. (34, 35)

34. Discuss with the patient the possibility of taking a "drug holiday" for one to two days if she is currently in remission from depressive symptoms.

35. Educate the patient on the importance of resuming the medication after the "drug holiday."

19. Cooperate with blood draws to measure prolactin levels and adhere to any changes in medication based on the results. (36, 37, 38)

36. Measure the patient's blood prolactin level, especially if she is taking an antipsychotic medication.

37. Consider reducing the dose of the antipsychotic or changing the patient to an antipsychotic with less D_2 dopamine receptor antagonism (e.g., quetiapine [Seroquel®], olanzapine [Zyprexa®], ziprasidone [Geodon®], aripiprazole [Abilify™]).

38. Monitor the patient closely for worsening psychotic symptoms during any change in medication.

20. Read books on enhancing sexuality and coping with sexual dysfunction. (39)

39. Recommend that the patient read books on sexuality and coping with sexual dysfunction (e.g., *Sexual Awareness* by McCarthy and McCarthy; *Becoming Orgasmic* by Heiman and Lopiccolo; *When a Woman's Body Says No to Sex* by Valins); process her implementation of coping techniques, reinforcing success and redirecting for failure.

__. _____   __. _____

_____   _____

__. _____   __. _____

_____   _____

__. _____   __. _____

_____   _____

DIAGNOSTIC SUGGESTIONS:

Axis I:	302.71	Hypoactive Sexual Desire Disorder
	302.79	Sexual Aversion Disorder
	302.72	Female Sexual Arousal Disorder
	302.73	Female Orgasmic Disorder
	302.76	Dyspareunia
	306.51	Vaginismus
	V61.21	Sexual Abuse of Child (995.5, victim)
	V61.1	Sexual Abuse of Adult (995.81, victim)
	625.8	Female Hypoactive Sexual Desire Disorder Due to (Axis III Disorder)
	302.70	Sexual Dysfunction NOS
	625.0	Female Dyspareunia Due to (Axis III Disorder)
	292.89	Substance-Induced Sexual Dysfunction
	296.xx	Major Depressive Disorder

_____ _____

_____ _____

Axis II: _____ _____

_____ _____

IMPULSE CONTROL DISORDER

BEHAVIORAL DEFINITIONS

1. A consistent pattern of acting before thinking that has resulted in numerous negative impacts on his/her life.
2. Failure to resist an impulse, desire, or temptation to perform some act that is harmful to self or others (e.g., pulling out own hair, setting fires, uncontrolled gambling).
3. Increasing anxiety or tension immediately preceding an impulsive act followed by a sense of relief, pleasure, or gratification after the act is completed.
4. Several episodes of loss of control of aggressive impulses out of proportion to the situation.
5. Over-reactivity to mildly aversive or pleasure-oriented stimulation.
6. Excessive shifting from one activity to another and rarely, if ever, completing anything that is started.
7. Difficulty organizing things or self without supervision.
8. Difficulty waiting for things (e.g., restlessness while standing in line, speaking out over others' voices in a group).

__. _____
_____
__. _____
_____
__. _____
_____

LONG-TERM GOALS

1. Take the appropriate medication and dose and/or participation in psychotherapy to decrease the frequency of impulsive acts.

2. Reduce the frequency of impulsive behavior and increase the frequency of behavior that is carefully thought out.
3. Reduce thoughts that trigger impulsive behavior and increase self-talk that controls behavior.
4. Learn to stop, think, listen, and plan before acting.

—. _____

_____

—. _____

_____

—. _____

_____

SHORT-TERM OBJECTIVES

THERAPEUTIC INTERVENTIONS

1. Describe the nature and history of impulsive acts and note their impact on daily life. (1, 2)

1. Explore the patient's history of impulsive behavior (e.g., physical violence, destructive acts, stealing, pulling out hair, setting fires, uncontrolled gambling) and how it affects his/her daily life.

2. Explore whether impulsive behavior is triggered by anxiety and maintained by anxiety relief rewards.

2. Describe other symptoms or disorders that may also be present. (3, 4, 5)

3. Assess the patient for symptoms of depression, hypomania/mania, posttraumatic stress disorder, obsessive-compulsive disorder, or psychosis (see the relevant chapters in this *Planner*).

4. Assess the patient's intellectual capacity and determine if he/she has mental retardation (see the Cognitive Deficits—Developmental Delay chapter in this *Planner*).

5. Gather detailed personal and family history information regarding substance abuse and its interaction with impulsive behavior; refer the patient for in-depth substance abuse treatment, if indicated (see the Chemical Dependence chapters in this *Planner*).

3. Patient and/or significant other(s) describe any current or past suicidal thoughts or behavior as well as violent threats or actions. (6, 7, 8)

6. Explore the patient's current and past suicidal thoughts and suicidal behavior; ask about family history of suicide (see the Suicidal Ideation chapter in this *Planner*).

7. Assess the patient's potential for violence and determine the presence of current and past threats or acts of aggression.

8. Arrange for hospitalization, as necessary, when the patient is judged to be harmful to self or others or unable to care for his/her basic needs.

4. Outline a complete and accurate medical and psychiatric history, including treatment received and its effectiveness. (9, 10)

9. Explore the patient's history of previous treatment for impulsive behavior and the success of, as well as his/her tolerance for, that treatment.

10. Assess the patient for the presence of other medical problems and the medications used to treat them.

5. Cooperate with a physical examination and laboratory tests. (11, 12)

11. Perform a complete physical and neurological examination on the patient and send his/her blood and/or urine for analysis to rule out organic contributors (e.g., acquired brain injury) to impulse dyscontrol.

12. Provide feedback to the patient regarding the results and implications of the physical

examination and laboratory test results.

6. Complete psychological testing and other questionnaires for assessing impulse control disorders. (13)

13. Administer objective impulse control disorder rating instruments to the patient (e.g., South Oaks Gambling Screen [SOGS], Massachusetts General Hospital Hairpulling Scale); evaluate the results and give him/her feedback.

7. Pursue treatment for concurrent medical problems that may contribute to poor impulse control. (14, 15)

14. Treat or refer the patient for treatment for any medical problem that may be contributing to poor impulse control (e.g., acquired brain damage).

15. Monitor the patient's progress in recovery from concomitant disorders and the impact of the recovery on his/her impulse control.

8. Verbalize an understanding of the impact of substance abuse on impulse control. (16)

16. Emphasize to the patient the negative and dangerous interaction of substance abuse with impulse control disorders (e.g., increased impulsivity, worsened anxiety).

9. Express an understanding of treatment options, expected results from medication, and potential side effects. (17, 18)

17. Discuss appropriate treatment options for impulse control with the patient including medications and psychotherapy.

18. Educate the patient on medication treatment including expected results, potential side effects, and dosing strategies.

10. Participate in psychotherapy sessions as planned with the therapist. (19, 20)

19. Assess the patient for potential benefit from psychotherapy; refer him/her to a psychotherapist, if indicated.

20. Monitor the patient's response to psychotherapy; assess his/her

ability to verbalize a basis for progress in impulse control (e.g., reduced frequency of impulsive behavior; improved ability to stop, think, listen, and plan before acting).

11. Take prescribed medications responsibly at times ordered by the physician. (21, 22)

21. Prescribe to the patient a selective serotonin reuptake inhibitor (SSRI) (e.g., paroxetine [Paxil®], sertraline [Zoloft®], citalopram [Celexa™], escitalopram [Lexapro™], fluoxetine [Prozac®], or fluvoxamine [Luvox®]).

22. Titrate the patient's medication to the minimum effective dose for treating his/her symptoms.

12. Report as to the effectiveness of SSRI medications and any side effects that develop. (23, 24, 25)

23. Monitor the patient frequently for the development of side effects, response to medication, adherence to treatment, and abuse of medication.

24. Evaluate the patient after four weeks of therapy with an SSRI for his/her response to medication; determine if he/she has had a partial response or a full response to the medication.

25. Repeat administration of objective rating instruments to the patient for assessment of his/her impulse control; evaluate the results and give him/her feedback.

13. Cooperate with any changes in medication dose. (26)

26. Increase medication dose if the patient has had a partial response; titrate his/her dose every two weeks until the patient's symptoms are controlled or maximum dose is reached.

14. Adhere to addition of mood-stabilizing medication prescribed by the physician. (27)

15. Cooperate with blood draws to monitor medication levels and adhere to any adjustments in medication dose. (28, 29)

16. Adhere to treatment with benzodiazepines to control severe symptoms of anxiety. (30, 31, 32)

17. Cooperate with any changes to an alternate anti-depressant medication and dose that is prescribed. (33, 34)

27. Augment the patient's anti-depressant with a mood stabilizer (e.g., carbamazepine [Tegretol®], lithium [Eskalith®, Lithonate®], divalproex sodium [Depakote®]) if the patient has only a partial response to the maximum antidepressant dose.

28. Measure mood-stabilizer blood levels in four to five days; adjust the dose, as necessary, to obtain therapeutic blood levels.

29. Reassess the patient in one to two weeks for response to the mood-stabilizing medication, development of side effects, and adherence to treatment.

30. Consider the addition of a benzodiazepine (e.g., clonazepam [Klonopin®], alprazolam [Xanax®]) if the patient has severe anxiety or tension in situations that lead to impulse dyscontrol; avoid this strategy in patients with a history of substance abuse.

31. Educate the patient on the dependence liability potential of benzodiazepines; monitor the patient closely for signs of benzodiazepine abuse.

32. Titrate the dose of benzodiazepine every two to three days, as tolerated, until the patient's anxiety is controlled or the maximum dose is reached.

33. Prescribe an alternative anti-depressant (e.g., venlafaxine [Effexor®], trazodone [Desyrel®], nefazodone [Serzone®], amitriptyline [Elavil®], imipramine

18. Cooperate with addition of medication and changes in dose used to augment current regimen. (27, 35, 36)

19. Retain a significant improvement in impulse control. (37, 38, 39)

[Tofranil®]) if the patient has an unsatisfactory response to an SSRI and mood stabilizer.

34. Titrate the antidepressant every two to four weeks, as tolerated, until the patient's symptoms are controlled or the maximum dose is reached.

27. Augment the patient's antidepressant with a mood stabilizer (e.g., carbamazepine [Tegretol®], lithium [Eskalith®, Lithonate®], divalproex sodium [Depakote®]) if the patient has only a partial response to the maximum antidepressant dose.

35. Consider prescribing an opioid receptor antagonist (e.g., naltrexone [ReVia®]), to the patient if other treatment options produce an unsatisfactory response.

36. Titrate the dose of naltrexone (ReVia®) every two to three days until impulsivity is improved or the maximum dose is reached.

37. Consider the addition of an atypical antipsychotic medication (e.g., risperidone [Risperdal®], olanzapine [Zyprexa®], ziprasidone [Geodon®], aririprazole [Abilify™], quetiapine [Seroquel®]), if the patient does not have an adequate response to other medications.

38. Maintain the patient on current medication for at least 12 months if he/she has shown a complete recovery from impulse dyscontrol; if the patient has

only a partial response, maintain him/her on the current dose of medication indefinitely.

39. Taper dose of medications slowly over several months; closely monitor for recurrence of symptoms.

—. _____   —. _____

_____   _____

—. _____   —. _____

_____   _____

—. _____   —. _____

_____   _____

DIAGNOSTIC SUGGESTIONS:

Axis I:	312.34	Intermittent Explosive Disorder
	312.32	Kleptomania
	312.31	Pathological Gambling
	312.39	Trichotillomania
	312.33	Pyromania
	312.30	Impulse Control Disorder NOS
	296.89	Bipolar II Disorder
	310.1	Personality Change Due to (Axis III Disorder)
	303.90	Alcohol Dependence
	304.20	Cocaine Dependence

_____   _____

_____   _____

Axis II:	301.83	Borderline Personality Disorder
	301.7	Antisocial Personality Disorder

_____   _____

_____   _____

MALE SEXUAL DYSFUNCTION

BEHAVIORAL DEFINITIONS

1. Consistently very low desire for or no pleasurable anticipation of sexual activity.
2. Strong avoidance of and/or repulsion to any and all sexual contact in spite of a relationship of mutual caring and respect.
3. Recurrent lack of usual physiological response of sexual excitement and arousal (e.g., attaining and/or maintaining an erection).
4. Consistent lack of subjective sense of enjoyment and pleasure during sexual activity.
5. Persistent delay in or absence of reaching orgasm after achieving arousal and in spite of sensitive sexual pleasuring by a caring partner.
6. Genital pain before, during, or after sexual intercourse.
7. Consistent or recurring premature ejaculation with minimal sexual stimulation.

—. _____

_____

—. _____

_____

—. _____

_____

LONG-TERM GOALS

1. Take the appropriate medication and dose and/or participate in psychotherapy to alleviate symptoms of sexual dysfunction and return to previous level of functioning.
2. Increase desire for and enjoyment of sexual activity.

3. Attain and maintain physiological excitement response during sexual intercourse.
4. Reach orgasm within a reasonable amount of time, with intensity and focus given to sexual stimulation.
5. Eliminate pain and promote subjective pleasure before, during, and after sexual intercourse.

—. _____

_____

—. _____

_____

—. _____

_____

SHORT-TERM OBJECTIVES

THERAPEUTIC INTERVENTIONS

1. Describe the signs and symptoms of sexual dysfunction that are experienced and note their impact on daily life. (1, 2)

1. Explore what symptoms of sexual dysfunction are experienced by the patient and how it affects his daily life (e.g., low sexual desire, inability to attain and maintain an erection, inability to have an orgasm, pain with intercourse, premature ejaculation with minimal stimulation, relationship difficulties with a mate).

2. Explore with the patient any history of childhood physical or sexual abuse or sexual trauma as an adult (e.g., rape, sexual coercion).

2. Describe other symptoms or disorders that may also be present. (3, 4)

3. Assess the patient for comorbid psychiatric disorders (e.g., see the Depression or Anxiety chapters in this *Planner*) that may contribute to or result from the sexual dysfunction.

4. Gather detailed personal and family history information

3. Outline a complete and accurate medical and psychiatric history, including treatment received and its effectiveness. (5, 6)

4. Cooperate with a physical examination and laboratory tests. (7, 8)

5. Pursue treatment for concurrent medical or psychiatric problems that may cause sexual dysfunction. (9, 10, 11)

regarding the patient's substance and/or alcohol abuse and its potential contribution to sexual dysfunction; refer him/her for in-depth substance abuse treatment, if indicated (see the Chemical Dependence chapters in this *Planner*).

5. Explore the patient's history of previous treatment for sexual dysfunction and the success and tolerance of that treatment.

6. Assess the patient for the presence of other medical problems and medications used to treat them.

7. Perform or refer the patient for a complete physical, urological, and neurological examination and send his blood and/or urine for analysis to rule out an organic cause for sexual dysfunction (e.g., infection, trauma, hypertension, hypercholesterolemia, smoking, diabetes, neurological disorders, endocrine disease, Peyronie's disease, prostatectomy, history of radiation therapy).

8. Provide feedback to the patient regarding the results and implications of the physical examination and laboratory test results.

9. Treat or refer the patient for treatment for any medical problem that may be causing sexual dysfunction (e.g., infection, hypertension, hypercholesterolemia, smoking, diabetes, neurological disorders, endocrine disease).

6. Complete psychological testing and other questionnaires
   for assessing sexual
   dysfunction. (12)

7. Verbalize an understanding
   of the impact of substance
   abuse on sexual dysfunction.
   (13)

8. Express an understanding of
   treatment options, expected
   results, and potential side
   effects of medication.
   (14, 15)

9. Participate in psychotherapy
   sessions as planned with the
   therapist. (16, 17)

10. Treat the patient for any psychi-
    atric disorder that may be
    causing sexual dysfunction (e.g.,
    see the Depression and Anxiety
    chapters in this *Planner*).

11. Monitor the patient's progress in
    recovery from concomitant
    disorders and the impact on his
    sexual dysfunction.

12. Administer to the patient an
    objective assessment instrument
    for measuring male sexual dys-
    function (e.g., International
    Index of Erectile Dysfunction,
    Brief Index of Sexual Function-
    ing [BISF], Sexual Function
    Questionnaire [SFQ]); evaluate
    the results and give him
    feedback.

13. Emphasize to the patient the
    negative and dangerous interac-
    tion of substance abuse with
    sexual functioning (e.g.,
    decreased desire, reduced
    physical sexual response,
    decreased sensation during
    intercourse).

14. Discuss appropriate treatment
    options with the patient includ-
    ing medications and
    psychotherapy.

15. Educate the patient on medica-
    tion treatment including the
    expected results, potential side
    effects, and dosing strategies.

16. Assess the patient for potential
    benefit from psychotherapy and
    refer him to a psychotherapist, if
    necessary.

17. Monitor the patient's investment
    in and response to psycho-
    therapy; assess his ability to

verbalize a basis for progress in recovery from sexual dysfunction (e.g., increased sexual desire, improved excitement response during sexual encounters, ability to reach orgasm, significantly reduced pain during intercourse).

10. Verbalize an understanding of the use of lubricants during sexual intercourse. (18, 19)

18. Recommend to the patient the use of a water-based lubricant (e.g., KY Jelly®, Astroglide®) if he has pain during sexual intercourse.

19. Educate the patient on the risk of condom failure if a nonwater-based lubricant (e.g., petroleum jelly [Vaseline®]) is used along with condoms.

11. Cooperate with blood draws to measure testosterone level and adhere to any prescribed testosterone replacement therapy. (20, 21)

20. Measure the patient's blood testosterone level.

21. Prescribe testosterone replacement therapy to the patient if he has low testosterone levels (hypogonadism).

12. Verbalize all medications and doses, as well as alcohol and illicit drugs, that are currently being taken. (22)

22. Determine if the patient is taking a substance could cause sexual dysfunction (e.g., antidepressant, antipsychotic, antihypertensive, anticholinergic, antihistamine, benzodiazepine, lithium, psychostimulant, alcohol, cannabis, opioid, barbiturate).

13. Refrain from the use of alcohol and illicit drugs as recommended by the physician. (23)

23. Emphasize to the patient that he refrain from the use of alcohol or other illicit substances if the sexual dysfunction occurs in the context of substance use.

14. Adhere to any changes in medication as prescribed by the physician. (24, 25, 26, 27)

24. Decrease the dose of medication that is thought to contribute to the sexual dysfunction if such a reduction does not adversely affect the patient.

25. Consider changing the patient's antidepressant to an alternative antidepressant without sexual side effects (e.g., mirtazapine [Remeron®], bupropion [Wellbutrin®], nefazodone [Serzone®]), if necessary.

26. Titrate the dose of the alternative medication to the minimum effecttive dose for treating depresssion, as tolerated by the patient.

27. Reduce the dose of the antidepressant medication that appears to be associated with the patient's sexual dysfunction slowly over weeks to months, as tolerated by him, until the medication is stopped.

15. Report as to the effectiveness of the new antidepressant medication and any side effects that develop. (28)

28. Monitor the patient closely for relapse or worsening of symptoms during the cross-titration of medications.

16. Cooperate with the addition of any new medication to help improve sexual functioning. (29, 30, 31, 32)

29. Consider the addition of a second antidepressant (e.g., mirtazapine [Remeron®], bupropion [Wellbutrin®], nefazodone [Serzone®]), or ginkgo biloba if the patient would be adversely affected by changing the current antidepressant medication.

30. Titrate the dose of the added medication every two to three weeks, as tolerated, until the patient has a satisfactory response or the maximum dose is reached.

31. Discuss with the patient the option of taking medication (e.g., sildenafil [Viagra®], alprostadil [Muse®, Caverject®], yohimbine [Yocon®]) to help increase physical sexual response.

32. Prescribe to the patient a sexual response enhancing medication; educate him on the proper use of the medication to enhance sexual response (i.e., taking the medication one to two hours prior to a sexual encounter).

17. Verbalize an understanding of taking a "drug holiday" for temporary improvement in sexual side effects of medication. (33, 34)

33. Discuss with the patient the possibility of taking a "drug holiday" for one to two days if he is currently in remission from depressive symptoms.

34. Educate the patient on the importance of resuming the medication after the "drug holiday."

18. Cooperate with blood draws to measure prolactin levels and adhere to any changes in medication based on the results. (35, 36, 37)

35. Measure the patient's blood prolactin level, especially if he is taking an antipsychotic medication.

36. Consider reducing the dose of the antipsychotic or changing the patient to an antipsychotic with less D_2 dopamine receptor antagonism (e.g., quetiapine [Seroquel®], olanzapine [Zyprexa®], ziprasidone [Geodon®], aripiprazole [Abilify™]).

37. Monitor the patient closely for worsening psychotic symptoms during any change in medication.

19. Verbalize an understanding of treatment options for erectile dysfunction and cooperate with the prescribed treatment. (38, 39, 40, 41)

38. Educate the patient on treatment options (e.g., medication, vacuum pumps, penile implants) for erectile dysfunction that is not caused by a substance or hormone abnormality.

39. Instruct the patient on the use of a vacuum pump for attaining an erection, if necessary.

40. Prescribe to the patient a medication (e.g., sildenafil [Viagra®], alprostadil [Muse®, Caverject®], yohimbine [Yocon®]) to help him attain an erection during sexual intercourse.

41. Refer the patient to an urologist for treatment with a penile implant, if necessary.

20. Adhere to medication for the treatment of premature ejaculation as prescribed by the physician. (42, 43)

42. Prescribe to the patient a selective serotonin reuptake inhibitor (SSRI) (e.g., paroxetine [Paxil®], sertraline [Zoloft®], citalopram [Celexa™], escitalopram [Lexapro™], fluoxetine [Prozac®], fluvoxamine [Luvox®]) if he has premature ejaculation.

43. Titrate the dose as tolerated, until symptoms are improved or the maximum dose is reached.

21. Read books on enhancing sexuality and coping with sexual dysfunction. (44)

44. Recommend that the patient read books on sexuality and coping with sexual dysfunction (e.g., *Sexual Awareness* by McCarthy and McCarthy; *The Gift of Sex* by Penner and Penner; *The New Male Sexuality* by Zilbergeld); process his implementation of coping techniques, reinforcing success and redirecting for failure.

__. _____

    _____

__. _____

    _____

__. _____

    _____

__. _____

    _____

__. _____

    _____

__. _____

    _____

DIAGNOSTIC SUGGESTIONS:

Axis I:

302.71	Hypoactive Sexual Desire Disorder
302.79	Sexual Aversion Disorder
302.72	Male Erectile Disorder
302.74	Male Orgasmic Disorder
302.76	Dyspareunia
302.75	Premature Ejaculation
V61.21	Sexual Abuse of Child (995.5, victim)
V61.1	Sexual Abuse of Adult (995.81, victim)
608.89	Male Hypoactive Sexual Desire Disorder Due to (Axis III Disorder)
607.84	Male Erectile Disorder Due to (Axis III Disorder)
302.70	Sexual Dysfunction NOS
292.89	Substance-Induced Sexual Dysfunction
296.xx	Major Depressive Disorder
_____	_____
_____	_____

Axis II:

_____	_____
_____	_____

MANIA/HYPOMANIA

BEHAVIORAL DEFINITIONS

1. Loquaciousness or pressured speech.
2. Flight of ideas or reports of thoughts racing.
3. An exaggerated, euphoric belief in own capabilities that denies any limitations or realistic obstacles but often sees others as standing in the way.
4. Decreased need for sleep often with little or no appetite.
5. Increased motor activity or agitation.
6. Poor attention span and easy distractibility.
7. Loss of normal inhibition leading to impulsive, pleasure-oriented behavior without regard for painful consequences.
8. Outlandish dress and grooming.
9. Expansive mood that can easily turn to impatience and irritable anger if behavior is blocked or confronted.
10. Rapids shifts in mood state.
11. Lack of follow-through in projects even though energy is very high since behavior lacks discipline and goal-directedness.

__. _____
   _____
__. _____
   _____
__. _____
   _____

LONG-TERM GOALS

1. Achieve controlled behavior, moderated mood, and more deliberative speech and thought process through psychotherapy and medication.

2. Eliminate any accompanying psychotic symptoms.
3. Reduce psychic energy and return to normal activity levels, good judgment, stable mood, and goal-directed behavior.
4. Reduce agitation, impulsivity, and pressured speech, while achieving sensitivity to the consequences of behavior and having more realistic expectations.
5. Talk about underlying feelings of low self-esteem or guilt and fears of rejection, dependency, and abandonment.

—. _____
   _____

—. _____
   _____

—. _____
   _____

SHORT-TERM OBJECTIVES

THERAPEUTIC INTERVENTIONS

1. Describe the nature and history of the hypomanic/manic symptoms and note their impact on daily life. (1, 2, 3)

1. Explore what symptoms are experienced by the patient (e.g., racing thoughts, pressured speech, decreased sleep, expansive mood, irritability, distractibility) and how they affect his/her daily life.

2. Assess stage of the patient's elation (i.e., hypomania, mania without psychosis, or mania with psychosis).

3. Determine the acuity and severity of the patient's symptoms (e.g., threatening or aggressive behavior, lack of judgment resulting in exposure to dangerous situations, impairment in social and occupational functioning).

2. Describe other symptoms or disorders that may also be present. (4, 5)

4. Assess the patient for concurrent symptoms of depression (i.e., a mixed state) or psychosis (see

the Depression and Psychoticism chapters in this *Planner*).

5. Gather detailed personal and family history information regarding substance abuse and its potential interaction with hypomania or mania; refer the patient for in-depth substance abuse treatment, if indicated (see the Chemical Dependence chapters in this *Planner*).

3. Patient or significant other(s) to describe any current or past suicidal thoughts/behavior as well as violent threats or actions. (6, 7, 8)

6. Explore the patient's current and past suicidal thoughts and suicidal behavior; ask about family history of suicide (see the Suicidal Ideation chapter in this *Planner*).

7. Assess the patient's potential for violence and determine the presence of current and past threats or acts of aggression.

8. Arrange for hospitalization, as necessary, when the patient is judged to be harmful to self or others or unable to care for his/her basic needs.

4. Complete psychological testing and other questionnaires for measuring the severity of hypomanic/manic symptoms. (9)

9. Administer an objective mania rating instrument to the patient (e.g., Young Mania Rating Scale [YMRS], Internal State Scale [ISS]); evaluate the results and give him/her feedback.

5. Outline a complete and accurate medical and psychiatric history, including treatment received and its effectiveness. (10, 11)

10. Explore the patient's history of previous treatment for hypomania/mania and the success of, as well as his/her tolerance for and follow through with, that treatment.

11. Assess the patient for the presence of other medical problems and the medications used to treat them.

6. Cooperate with a physical examination and laboratory tests. (12, 13, 14, 15)

12. Perform a complete physical and neurological examination on the patient and send his/her blood and/or urine for analysis to rule out organic contributors to hypomania/mania.

13. Obtain radiologic studies of the patient (i.e., head computed tomography [CT] scan or magnetic resonance imaging [MRI]), if necessary.

14. Provide feedback to the patient regarding the results and implications of the physical examination and laboratory test results.

15. Inquire about any new medications or changes in dose that could contribute to the patient's hypomania/mania (e.g., antidepressants, steroids, amphetamines).

7. Pursue treatment for concurrent medical problems that may contribute to hypomanic/manic symptoms. (16, 17, 18)

16. Treat or refer the patient for treatment for any medical problem that may be contributing to hypomania/mania (e.g., Parkinson's disease, stroke, thyroid disease, viral infections, autoimmune disease, certain cancers).

17. Reduce the dose of or discontinue use of any medications that could be contributing to the patient's hypomania/mania (e.g., antidepressants, steroids, amphetamines).

18. Monitor the patient's progress in recovery from concomitant disorders and the impact of the recovery on his/her hypomania/mania.

8. Verbalize an understanding of the possible causes for hypomania/mania and the

19. Educate the patient on the possible causes (e.g., neurotransmitter abnormalities,

relationship between symptoms and substance abuse. (19, 20)

9. Express an understanding of treatment options, expected results from medication and potential side effects. (21, 22)

10. Take prescribed medications responsibly at times ordered by the physician. (23, 24, 25, 26, 27)

genetic propensity, medical illness, medications) and signs of hypomania/mania.

20. Emphasize to the patient the negative and dangerous impact of substance abuse on hypomania/mania.

21. Discuss appropriate treatment options with the patient including medications and psychotherapy.

22. Educate the patient on mood stabilizer treatment, including expected results, potential side effects, and dosing strategies.

23. Prescribe a mood stabilizing agent (i.e., lithium [Lithonate®, Eskalith®], divalproex sodium [Depakote®], or olanzapine [Zyprexa®]) if the patient is in a euphoric state.

24. Consider using divalproex sodium (Depakote®), carbamazepine (Tegretol®), or olanzapine (Zyprexa®) if the patient is in a rapid cycling or mixed state.

25. Add an atypical antipsychotic agent (i.e., risperidone [Risperdal®], olanzapine [Zyprexa®], aripiprazole [Abilify™], ziprasidone [Geodon®], quetiapine [Seroquel®]) if the patient has psychotic symptoms (e.g., auditory hallucinations, paranoia, delusions).

26. Consider prescribing a long-acting benzodiazepine (e.g., clonazepam [Klonopin®]) if the patient has severe symptoms (e.g., violent or aggressive

11. Participate in psychotherapy sessions as planned with the therapist. (28, 29)

12. Cooperate with blood draws to check medication levels. (30)

13. Report as to the effectiveness of medications and any side effects that develop. (31, 32)

14. Attend follow-up appointments as scheduled by the physician and adhere to any adjustments in medication dose. (33, 34, 35, 36)

behavior, severe anxiety) requiring more rapid treatment.

27. Titrate the patient's medications to the minimum effective dose as tolerated.

28. Assess the patient for potential benefit from psychotherapy; refer him/her to a psychotherapist if necessary.

29. Monitor the patient's response to psychotherapy; assess his/her ability to verbalize a basis for progress in recovery from hypomania/mania (e.g., improvement in social and occupational functioning, increased focus on tasks, sobriety).

30. Measure medication blood levels in four to five days if the patient is taking lithium (Lithonate®, Eskalith®), divalproex sodium (Depakote®), or carbamazepine (Tegretol®); adjust the dose to obtain therapeutic blood levels.

31. Reassess the patient in one to two weeks for response to medication, development of side effects and adherence to treatment.

32. Repeat administration of objective rating instruments for assessment of the patient's hypomania/mania; evaluate the results and give him/her feedback.

33. Add a second mood stabilizer if the patient has little or no response; titrate the second medication to a therapeutic level.

34. Reassess the patient in two to four weeks; add a third mood stabilizer if response is unsatisfactory.

35. Consider adding an atypical antipsychotic agent (i.e., risperidone [Risperdal®], olanzapine [Zyprexa®], aripiprazole [Abilify™], ziprasidone [Geodon®], quetiapine [Seroquel®], clozapine [Clozaril®]) if the patient does not have a satisfactory response to mood stabilizers.

36. Reassess the patient's improvement in hypomanic/manic symptoms in two to four months.

15. Express an understanding of additional treatment options and cooperate with the treatment. (37, 38, 39)

37. Consider alternative treatments if the patient is showing a poor response to all mood stabilizers and atypical antipsychotics; options include electroconvulsive therapy (ECT) and other anticonvulsant medications (e.g., oxcarbazepine [Trileptal®], topiramate [Topamax®], lamotrigine [Lamictal®], gabapentin [Neurontin®]).

38. Maximize adjunctive medications as tolerated.

39. Maintain the patient on current medication indefinitely, especially if he/she has a history of recurrent hypomanic/manic episodes.

16. Retain a remission or significant reduction in hypomanic/manic symptoms. (40)

40. Assess the patient's resistance to continuing on medication (e.g., "I'm better now and in control of myself," "I don't like how I feel on the medication. I'm not normal," "I feel like I've lost my

creative edge and energy."); nor-
malize the resistance while em-
phasizing the need to stay on the
medication or risk returning to
pretreatment complications.

__. _____   __. _____
      _____   _____
__. _____   __. _____
      _____   _____
__. _____   __. _____
      _____   _____

DIAGNOSTIC SUGGESTIONS:

Axis I: 296.xx   Bipolar I Disorder
                 296.89   Bipolar II Disorder
                 301.13   Cyclothymic Disorder
                 296.80   Bipolar Disorder NOS
                 293.83   Mood Disorder due to (Axis III Disorder)
                 292.84   Substance-Induced Mood Disorder
                 295.70   Schizoaffective Disorder
                 292.89   Amphetamine Intoxication
                 292.89   Cocaine Intoxication
                 310.1   Personality Change Due to (Axis III Disorder)

                 _____   _____

                 _____   _____

Axis II: 301.83   Borderline Personality Disorder

                 _____   _____

                 _____   _____

MEDICAL ISSUES—DELIRIUM

BEHAVIORAL DEFINITIONS

1. Disturbance of consciousness manifested by a reduced awareness of the environment.
2. Easy distractibility.
3. Impaired memory.
4. Disorientation as to time, place, and person.
5. Language disturbance.
6. Perceptual disturbances (i.e., hallucinations).
7. Agitation that results from the cognitive impairments.
8. Fluctuation in the level of impairment throughout the day.
9. Impairments have an acute onset and are not better accounted for by a dementia.
10. Evidence that the impairments are a direct result of a general medical condition, substance intoxication, or substance withdrawal.

—. _____

_____

—. _____

_____

—. _____

_____

LONG-TERM GOALS

1. Alleviate perceptual and cognitive disturbances through medication and/ or environmental and behavioral interventions.
2. Medically stabilize the physical condition.
3. Improve the acute medical condition.

4. Control substance withdrawal symptoms and establish chemical dependency recovery.

—. _____

_____

—. _____

_____

—. _____

_____

SHORT-TERM OBJECTIVES

THERAPEUTIC INTERVENTIONS

1. Describe or demonstrate the signs and symptoms of delirium and identify any recent change in medical condition. (1, 2)

1. Explore the symptoms of delirium that the patient is experiencing (e.g., visual, tactile, or auditory hallucinations; agitation; disorientation; distractibility).

2. Determine the time course of the symptoms (i.e., hours to days) and the relation of the symptom onset with a change in medical condition.

2. Describe other symptoms or disorders that may also be present, such as dementia or substance abuse. (3, 4, 5)

3. Assess the patient for comorbid disorders (e.g., see the Dementia, Depression, or Psychosis chapters in this *Planner*).

4. Gather detailed personal and family history information regarding the patient's substance abuse and its potential contribution to delirium; refer the patient for in-depth substance abuse treatment, if indicated (see the Chemical Dependence chapters in this *Planner*).

5. Emphasize to the patient the negative and dangerous impact of substance abuse on confusion/delirium.

3. Complete psychological testing and other questionnaires for measuring delirium. (6)

4. Patient or significant other(s) outline a complete and accurate medical history, including current medication regimen and exposure to toxins. (7, 8)

5. Cooperate with a physical examination and diagnostic tests. (9, 10, 11)

6. Administer objective instruments to assess the patient's delirium (e.g., Mini Mental State Examination [MMSE], Delirium Rating Scale [DRS], Memorial Delirium Assessment Scale [MDAS]); evaluate the results and provide feedback to the patient and/or significant other(s).

7. Assess the patient for the presence of any medical problems and any medications used to treat them.

8. Explore the patient's use of or exposure to any medication or other substance that could produce delirium (i.e., opioids, anticholinergics, anesthesia, antihypertensives, anticonvulsants, muscle relaxants).

9. Perform a complete physical and neurological examination on the patient and send his/her blood and/or urine for analysis to evaluate any organic cause for delirium (e.g., infection, electrolyte abnormality, cardiac disease, neurologic disease, intoxication or poisoning, neuroleptic malignant syndrome [NMS], substance withdrawal).

10. Obtain radiologic studies (e.g., head computed tomography [CT] scan or magnetic resonance imaging [MRI], chest X-ray) of the patient to assess for brain abnormalities or pulmonary disease that might explain the delirium.

11. Provide feedback to the patient and family regarding the results and implications of the physical

6. Pursue treatment for con-current medical problems that may be causing delirium. (12, 13)

7. Express an understanding of the possible causes for and treatment of delirium. (14, 15)

8. Cooperate with the reduction of any medication that might contribute to delirium. (16)

9. Take prescribed antipsychotic medication responsibly at times ordered by the physician. (17, 18, 19, 20)

examination and laboratory test results.

12. Treat or refer the patient for treatment for any medical problem that may be causing delirium; arrange for a hospitali-zation if the patient's medical status is tenuous.

13. Monitor the patient's progress in recovery from concomitant dis-orders and the impact of the recovery on his/her delirium.

14. Educate the patient and family on the possible contributing fac-tors (e.g., advanced age, medical illness, medications) and signs of delirium.

15. Discuss appropriate treatment options with the patient and family including medications and environmental and/or behavioral interventions (e.g., frequently orienting the patient, change lighting to cue night ver-sus day, reducing the amount of stimulation).

16. Minimize the use of or discon-tinue any medication that could be worsening the patient's delir-ium (e.g., opioids, anticholiner-gics, benzodiazepines, steroids, antihistamines).

17. Prescribe to the patient a low dose of an atypical antipsychotic (e.g., risperidone [Risperdal®], olanzapine [Zyprexa®], quetiap-ine [Seroquel®], aripiprazole [Abilify™], ziprasidone [Geodon®]).

18. Avoid the use of ziprasidone (Geodon®) if the patient has suffered a recent myocardial

infarction, has cardiac QTc pro-longation, or has uncompensated cardiac failure.

19. Prescribe to the patient low-dose intravenous haloperidol (Haldol®) or intramuscular ziprasidone (Geodon®) if he/she is unable to take medication by mouth.

20. Titrate the dose of the antipsychotic medication every two to three days, as tolerated, until the patient's behavioral disturbances (i.e., agitation) are controlled.

10. Report on the effectiveness of antipsychotic medication and any side effects that develop. (21, 22, 23)

21. Monitor the patient frequently for development of side effects, response to the antipsychotic medication, and adherence to treatment.

22. Administer objective measures of the patient's delirium on a serial basis to track improvement in his/her cognition; evaluate the results and give feedback to him/her.

23. Continue the antipsychotic medication for one to two weeks after the delirium has resolved; monitor closely for recurrence of symptoms after discontinuation of the medication.

11. Verbalize the type and amount of any anti-cholinergic substance used. (24)

24. Determine if the patient's delirium is caused by anticholinergic intoxication (e.g., anesthesia, overdose of anticholinergic medication, organophosphate insecticide poisoning).

12. Adhere to acetylcholine-sterase inhibitor medication used to treat an anti-cholinergic delirium. (25, 26)

25. Prescribe an acetylcholinesterase inhibitor (e.g., physostigmine [Eserine®], tacrine [Cognex®], donepezil [Aricept®]).

26. Titrate the dose of the acetylcho-linesterase inhibitor every two to three days as tolerated; monitor closely for side effects (e.g., nausea, vomiting, bradycardia, salivation).

13. Verbalize the type and amount of any antipsychotic medication used. (27)

27. Determine if the delirium is a result of NMS (e.g., recent use of an antipsychotic, muscle rigidity, elevated liver enzymes, elevated creatinine phospho-kinase (CPK), rhabdomyolysis, autonomic instability).

14. Adhere to medication and other treatment for neuroleptic malignant syndrome (NMS). (28, 29, 30, 31)

28. Avoid the use of antipsychotic medications.

29. Provide the patient with intrave-nous fluids to assure adequate hydration.

30. Prescribe a benzodiazepine (e.g., lorazepam [Ativan®], clonaze-pam [Klonopin®], diazepam [Valium®]).

31. Titrate the dose of the benzodiazepine every one to two days as tolerated; monitor frequently for signs of improvement in NMS symptoms.

15. Cooperate with electroconvul-sive treatment (ECT) for treat-ing NMS. (32)

32. Refer the patient for electrocon-vulsive therapy (ECT) if the NMS does not improve with other treatments.

16. Verbalize the type, amount, and last use of alcohol and/or other drugs. (4, 33)

4. Gather detailed personal and family history information regarding the patient's substance abuse and its potential contribu-tion to delirium; refer the patient for in-depth substance abuse treatment, if indicated (see the Chemical Dependence chapters in this *Planner*).

33. Determine if the patient's delirium is a result of alcohol or sedative-hypnotic (e.g., benzodiazepines, barbiturates) withdrawal (see the Chemical Dependence—Withdrawal chapter in this *Planner*).

17. Adhere to the prescribed medication regimen for treating a substance withdrawal delirium. (5, 34, 35, 36)

5. Emphasize to the patient the negative and dangerous impact of substance abuse on confusion/delirium.

34. Prescribe to the patient a long-acting benzodiazepine (e.g., diazepam [Valium®], oxazepam [Serax®], chlordiazepoxide [Librium®]).

35. Titrate the dose of the benzodiazepine every one to two days, as tolerated, until withdrawal symptoms (e.g., autonomic instability, hallucinations, confusion, tremor) are controlled; monitor frequently for improvement in withdrawal symptoms.

36. Taper the dose of the benzodiazepine slowly over several days; monitor closely for recurrence of withdrawal symptoms.

__. _____   __. _____

_____   _____

__. _____   __. _____

_____   _____

__. _____   __. _____

_____   _____

__. _____   __. _____

_____   _____

__. _____   __. _____

_____   _____

DIAGNOSTIC SUGGESTIONS:

Axis I:

293.0	Delirium Due to (Axis III Disorder)
290.xx	Dementia
308.3	Acute Stress Disorder
298.8	Brief Psychotic Episode
295.xx	Schizophrenia
296.xx	Major Depression
303.00	Alcohol Intoxication
291.0	Alcohol Withdrawal Delirium
292.89	Sedative, Hypnotic or Anxiolytic Intoxication
292.81	Sedative, Hypnotic or Anxiolytic Withdrawal Delirium
292.81	Hallucinogen Intoxication Delirium
292.81	Phencyclidine Intoxication Delirium

_____   _____

_____   _____

Axis II:

_____   _____

_____   _____

OBSESSIVE-COMPULSIVE DISORDER (OCD)

BEHAVIORAL DEFINITIONS

1. Recurrent and persistent ideas, thoughts, or impulses that are viewed as intrusive, senseless, and time-consuming, or that interfere with daily routine, job performance, or social relationships.
2. Failed attempts to ignore or control these thoughts or impulses or neutralize them with other thoughts and actions.
3. Recognize that obsessive thoughts are a product of the mind.
4. Repetitive and intentional behaviors done in response to obsessive thoughts or according to eccentric rules.
5. Repetitive and excessive behavior done to neutralize or prevent discomfort or some dreaded situation; however, the behavior is not connected in any realistic way with what it is designed to neutralize or prevent.
6. Recognition of repetitive behaviors as excessive and unreasonable.

—. _____
   _____
—. _____
   _____
—. _____
   _____

LONG-TERM GOALS

1. Take the appropriate medication and dose and/or participate in psychotherapy to control obsessive thoughts and compulsive behaviors that interfere with daily living.

2. Reduce time involved with or interference from obsessions and compulsions.

3. Function on a daily basis at a consistent level with minimal interference from obsessions and compulsions.

4. Resolve key life conflicts and the emotional stress that fuels obsessive-compulsive behavior patterns.

5. Let go of key thoughts, beliefs, and past life events in order to maximize time free from obsessions and compulsions.

—. _____

_____

—. _____

_____

—. _____

_____

SHORT-TERM OBJECTIVES

THERAPEUTIC INTERVENTIONS

1. Describe the signs and symptoms of OCD that are experienced and note their impacts on daily life. (1, 2)

1. Explore what obsessions (e.g., thoughts of contamination, somatic concerns, need for order, aggressive or sexual impulses) and compulsions (e.g., checking, washing, ordering, hoarding, counting) are experienced by the patient and how they affect his/her daily life.

2. Determine the acuity and severity of the patient's anxiety symptoms (e.g., incapacitation, inability to work or leave the house).

2. Describe other symptoms or disorders that may also be present, such as depression, generalized anxiety, and substance abuse. (3, 4)

3. Assess the patient for comorbid disorders (e.g., depression, generalized anxiety) (see the Depression and Anxiety chapters in this *Planner*).

4. Gather detailed personal and family history information regarding substance abuse and

3. Verbalize any current suicidal thoughts and any history of suicidal behavior. (5, 6)

4. Complete psychological testing and other questionnaires for measuring the severity of OCD symptoms. (7)

5. Outline a complete and accurate medical and psychiatric history, including treatment received and its effectiveness. (8, 9)

6. Cooperate with a physical examination and laboratory tests. (10, 11)

its potential interaction with anxiety; refer the patient for in-depth substance abuse treatment, if indicated (see the Chemical Dependence chapters in this *Planner*).

5. Explore the patient's current and past suicidal thoughts and suicidal behavior; ask about family history of suicide (see the Suicidal Ideation chapter in this *Planner*).

6. Arrange for hospitalization, as necessary, when the patient is judged to be harmful to self or unable to care for his/her basic needs.

7. Administer an objective OCD assessment instrument to the patient (e.g., Yale-Brown Obsessive Compulsive Scale [Y-BOCS]); evaluate the results and give him/her feedback.

8. Explore the patient's history of previous treatment for OCD and the success of, as well as his/her tolerance for, that treatment.

9. Assess the patient for the presence of other medical problems and what medications are used to treat them.

10. Perform a complete physical and neurological examination on the patient and send his/her blood and/or urine for analysis to rule out organic contributors to anxiety.

11. Provide feedback to the patient regarding the results and implications of the physical examination and laboratory test results.

7. Pursue treatment for concurrent medical problems that may contribute to anxiety/OCD symptoms. (12, 13)

8. Verbalize an understanding of the possible causes for OCD and the relationships between OCD, depression, and substance abuse. (14, 15)

9. Express an understanding of treatment options, expected results from medication, and potential side effects. (16, 17)

10. Take prescribed medications responsibly at times ordered by the physician. (18, 19, 20)

12. Treat or refer the patient for treatment for any medical problem that may be contributing to anxiety/OCD symptoms (e.g., cardiovascular disease, pulmonary disease, endocrine disorders, pheochromocytoma, carcinoid syndrome).

13. Monitor the patient's progress in recovery from concomitant disorders and the impact of the recovery on his/her OCD.

14. Emphasize to the patient the negative and dangerous impact of substance abuse on anxiety.

15. Educate the patient on the possible causes (e.g., neurotransmitter abnormalities, genetic propensity) and signs of OCD.

16. Discuss appropriate treatment options with the patient including medications and psychotherapy.

17. Educate the patient on psychotropic medication treatment including expected results, potential side effects, and dosing strategies.

18. Prescribe to the patient an antidepressant such as a selective serotonin reuptake inhibitor (SSRI) (e.g., paroxetine [Paxil®], sertraline [Zoloft®], citalopram [Celexa™], escitalopram [Lexapro™], fluoxetine [Prozac®], fluvoxamine [Luvox®]), or the tricyclic antidepressant (TCA) clomipramine (Anafranil®).

19. Complete a medical evaluation on the patient, including an electrocardiogram, if necessary,

before starting him/her on a TCA; gradually titrate dose of TCA as necessary to maximum effectiveness.

20. Titrate the antidepressant medication to the minimum effective dose used to treat depression; educate the patient on the likelihood of having to use higher doses to control the OCD symptoms.

11. Participate in psychotherapy sessions as planned with therapist. (21, 22)

21. Assess the patient for potential benefit from psychotherapy and refer him/her to a psychotherapist, if necessary.

22. Monitor the patient's investment in and response to psychotherapy; assess his/her ability to verbalize a basis for progress in OCD recovery (e.g., reduction in obsessions and compulsions, improvement in social and occupational functioning, sobriety).

12. Report as to the effectiveness of medications and any side effects that develop. (23, 24, 25, 26)

23. Monitor the patient frequently for the development of side effects, response to medication, and adherence to treatment.

24. Reassess the patient who is taking an antidepressant at six weeks; determine whether the medication is adequate or needs a dose increase.

25. Educate the patient about the possibility of a delayed response to medication (10 to 12 weeks) when treating OCD.

26. Maximize the antidepressant dose as tolerated; allow for a full 12-week trial at the highest tolerated dose.

13. Attend follow-up appointments as scheduled by the physician. (27)

14. Report evidence of the degree of improvement in OCD symptoms as well as any comorbid disorders. (28)

15. Adhere to medication changes used to augment current medication regimen. (29, 30, 31, 32, 33)

27. Evaluate the patient at twelve weeks for his/her response to medication; determine if he/she has had a full response or partial response to the treatment regimen.

28. Repeat administration of objective rating instruments for assessment of the patient's OCD severity; evaluate the results and give him/her feedback.

29. Discuss other treatment options (e.g., changing medication, augmenting current medication, psychotherapy) with the patient if he/she shows no treatment response or a partial response.

30. Determine if the patient needs additional medication to augment current therapy; partial responders to a single medication should be considered for this strategy.

31. Consider adding buspirone (BuSpar®) or a benzodiazepines (e.g., clonazepam [Klonopin®]), especially if the patient has comorbid anxiety symptoms.

32. Consider prescribing an atypical antipsychotic medication (e.g., risperidone [Risperdal®], olanzapine [Zyprexa®]), ziprasidone [Geodon®], quetiapine [Seroquel®], aripiprazole [Abilify™]; strongly consider this if the patient has comorbid delusions or tics.

33. Prescribe to the patient lithium (Lithonate®, Eskalith®) or trazodone (Desyrel®) if one of the above augmentation medications is not a better

16. Cooperate with changes in type of medication prescribed. (34, 35)

17. Verbalize an understanding of alternative surgical treatments for refractory OCD. (36)

18. Retain a remission of OCD symptoms with a minimum amount of medications. (37, 38, 39)

choice because of comorbid symptoms.

34. Maximize the augmentation medication as tolerated by the patient.

35. Consider changing the patient's medication to another agent if he/she has minimal or no response to the initial medication and the augmentation process; alternatives include a different SSRI and clomipramine [Anafranil™].

36. Discuss neurosurgical options, including benefits and risks, with patients who have extremely severe OCD symptoms that are refractory to all medication options; refer eligible candidates to a neurosurgeon experienced in these procedures for consultation.

37. Maintain the patient on current medication for at least 12 months if he/she has shown a fully successful response; if he/she has had a previous episode of OCD or demonstrates only a partial response, consider continuing treatment indefinitely.

38. Reduce medications gradually (i.e., approximately 25% of the dose every two months); monitor closely for recurrence of symptoms.

39. Taper doses of benzodiazepines slowly to avoid the patient experiencing withdrawal symptoms (e.g., rebound anxiety, tremor, nausea, elevated pulse or blood pressure).

__. _____   __. _____
     _____   _____
__. _____   __. _____
     _____   _____
__. _____   __. _____
     _____   _____

DIAGNOSTIC SUGGESTIONS:

Axis I:	300.3	Obsessive-Compulsive Disorder
	300.7	Hypochondriasis
	300.7	Body Dysmorphic Disorder
	307.23	Tourette's Disorder
	295.xx	Schizophrenia
	297.1	Delusional Disorder
	300.02	Generalized Anxiety Disorder
	300.29	Specific Phobia
	300.23	Social Phobia
	296.2x	Major Depressive Disorder, Single Episode
	296.3x	Major Depressive Disorder, Recurrent
	303.90	Alcohol Dependence
	304.10	Sedative, Hypnotic or Anxiolytic Dependence

_____   _____

_____   _____

Axis II:	301.4	Obsessive-Compulsive Personality Disorder
	301.82	Avoidant Personality Disorder

_____   _____

_____   _____

PHOBIA-PANIC/AGORAPHOBIA

BEHAVIORAL DEFINITIONS

1. A persistent and unreasonable fear of a specific object or situation that promotes avoidance behaviors because an encounter with the phobic stimulus provokes an immediate anxiety response.
2. Unexpected, sudden, debilitating panic symptoms (e.g., shallow breathing, sweating, heart racing or pounding, dizziness, depersonalization or derealization, trembling, chest tightness, fear of dying or losing control, nausea) that have occurred repeatedly, resulting in persistent concern about having additional attacks or behavioral changes to avoid attacks.
3. Fear of being in an environment that may trigger intense anxiety symptoms (panic) and, therefore, avoidance of such situations as leaving home alone, being in a crowd of people, or traveling in an enclosed environment.
4. Avoidance or endurance of the phobic stimulus or feared environment with intense anxiety resulting in interference of normal routines or marked distress.
5. Persistence of fear in spite of recognition that the fear is unreasonable.

—. _____
   _____
—. _____
   _____
—. _____
   _____

LONG-TERM GOALS

1. Take the appropriate medication and dose to not only control symptoms of fear, but to attain a complete remission (i.e., elimination of symptoms).
2. Independently and freely leave home and comfortably function in public environments.
3. Travel away from home by car, train, or bus.
4. Reduce fear of the specific stimulus object or situation that previously provoked immediate anxiety.
5. Eliminate interference in normal routines and remove distress from the feared object or situation.
6. Report the termination of panic symptoms and the fear that they will recur without an ability to cope with and control them.

—. _____

_____

—. _____

_____

—. _____

_____

SHORT-TERM OBJECTIVES

1. Describe the signs and symptoms of panic/fear and identify the specific stimuli for it. (1, 2)

2. Describe other symptoms or disorders that may also be present, such as depression or substance abuse. (3, 4, 5)

THERAPEUTIC INTERVENTIONS

1. Explore what stimuli provoke the patient's fear or panic and the signs and symptoms that arise from the fear (e.g., racing heart, shortness of breath, trembling, sweating, feelings of impending doom).

2. Determine how the fear of specific situations affects the patient's daily life (e.g., avoidance of crowded places, difficulty riding in enclosed vehicles).

3. Assess the patient for comorbid disorders (e.g., depression, social phobia or generalized anxiety) (see the Depression,

Social Discomfort, and/or Anxiety chapters in this *Planner*).

4. Gather detailed personal and family history information regarding substance abuse and its potential interaction with panic; refer the patient for in-depth substance abuse treatment, if indicated (see the Chemical Dependence chapters in this *Planner*).

5. Emphasize to the patient the negative and dangerous impact of substance abuse on panic/fear symptoms.

3. Verbalize any current suicidal thoughts and any history of suicidal behavior. (6, 7)

6. Explore the patient's current and past suicidal thoughts and suicidal behavior; ask about family history of suicide (see the Suicidal Ideation chapter in this *Planner,* if necessary).

7. Arrange for hospitalization, as necessary, when the patient is judged to be harmful to self or unable to care for his/her basic needs.

4. Complete psychological test-ing and other questionnaires for measuring level of fear. (8)

8. Administer objective instru-ments to assess the patient's panic severity and frequency as well as avoidance of situations or stimuli (e.g., Mobility Inven-tory for Agoraphobia, Panic Disorder Severity Scale); evaluate the results and give him/her feedback.

5. Outline a complete and accu-rate medical and psychiatric history, including treatment received and its effectiveness. (9, 10, 11)

9. Explore the patient's history of previous treatment for fear or panic symptoms and the success of, as well as his/her tolerance for, that treatment.

10. Assess the patient for the presence of other medical problems and any medications used to treat them.

11. Explore the patient's use of any medication or other substance that could produce or worsen panic symptoms (i.e., caffeine, ephedrine, pseudoephedrine, amphetamines, bronchodilators, anticholinergics, corticosteroids).

6. Cooperate with a physical examination and laboratory tests. (12, 13)

12. Perform a complete physical and neurological examination on the patient and send his/her blood and/or urine for analysis to rule out an organic cause for panic.

13. Provide feedback to the patient regarding the results and implications of the physical examination and laboratory test results.

7. Pursue treatment for concurrent medical problems that may contribute to panic symptoms. (14, 15)

14. Treat or refer the patient for treatment for any medical problem that may be causing or contributing to panic symptoms (e.g., cardiovascular disease, pulmonary disease, endocrine disorders, pheochromocytoma).

15. Monitor the patient's progress in recovery from concomitant disorders and the impact of the recovery on his/her panic symptoms.

8. Express an understanding of the possible causes for panic and the relationships between panic, depression and substance abuse. (5, 16, 17)

5. Emphasize the negative and dangerous impact of substance abuse on panic/fear.

16. Educate the patient on the possible contributing factors (e.g., stressful life events, specific stimuli, genetic propensity, medical illness, medications) and signs of panic.

17. Ask the patient to identify what he/she believes may be contributing factors and/or specific stimuli for his/her panic or fear.

9. Verbalize an understanding of treatment options, expected results from medication, and potential side effects. (18, 19)

18. Discuss appropriate treatment options with the patient including medications and psychotherapy.

19. Educate the patient on psychotropic medication treatment including expected results, potential side effects, dosing strategies, and dependence liability potential of benzodiazepines.

10. Take prescribed medications responsibly at times ordered by the physician. (20, 21, 22, 23, 24)

20. Prescribe to the patient an antidepressant (e.g., selective serotonin reuptake inhibitor [SSRI]) with documented anti-panic properties (e.g., paroxetine [Paxil®], sertraline [Zoloft®], citalopram [Celexa™], escitalopram [Lexapro™], fluoxetine [Prozac®]); strongly consider this strategy in patients with comorbid depression (see the Depression chapter in this *Planner*).

21. Start the SSRI at a low dose then titrate it to the minimum effective dose for treating the patient's panic; educate the patient about the potential for worsening panic symptoms with initiation of SSRI therapy.

22. Prescribe a long-acting benzodiazepine (e.g., diazepam [Valium®], clonazepam [Klonopin®]) if the patient has frequent panic attacks that impair daily life and he/she has no history of substance abuse.

23. Consider prescribing the patient alprazolam [Xanax®] for short-term use to control acute symptoms of panic.

24. Titrate the dose of benzodiazepines every two to three days until the patient's panic symptoms are controlled or the maximum dose for the medication is reached.

11. Participate in psychotherapy sessions as planned with the therapist. (25, 26)

25. Assess the patient for potential benefit from psychotherapy and refer him/her to a psychotherapist, if necessary.

26. Monitor the patient's investment in and response to psychotherapy; assess his/her ability to verbalize a basis for progress in reducing panic or fear (e.g., fewer and less intense panic attacks, reduced fear of specific stimuli, sobriety).

12. Attend follow-up appointments and report as to the effectiveness of medications and any side effects that develop. (27, 28)

27. Monitor the patient frequently for the development of side effects, response to medication, adherence to treatment or withdrawal symptoms (if he/she takes benzodiazepines).

28. Reassess the patient who is taking an antidepressant in four weeks; determine whether the medication is adequate, needs a dose increase, or another agent needs to be tried.

13. Report evidence of the degree of improvement in panic symptoms as well as any comorbid disorders. (29)

29. Repeat objective measures of the patient's panic and avoidance; evaluate the results and give feedback to him/her.

14. Adhere to changes in medication regimen. (30, 31)

30. Increase medication dose if the patient has had a partial response; titrate his/her dose every two weeks until the maximum

dose is reached or he/she has a full response.

31. Consider changing the patient's medication to another agent if he/she has minimal or no response to the initial medication; alternatives include another SSRI, venlafaxine (Effexor®), tricyclic antidepressant (TCA) (e.g., imipramine [Tofranil®] or clomipramine [Anafranil®]), a monoamine oxidase inhibitor (MAOI) (e.g., phenelzine [Nardil®]), or a long-acting benzodiazepine.

15. Cooperate with additional medical evaluation and dietary restrictions necessary for certain medications. (32, 33, 34)

32. Complete a medical evaluation on the patient including an electrocardiogram, if necessary, before starting him/her on a TCA; gradually titrate dose of TCA as necessary to maximum effectiveness.

33. Educate the patient on dietary restrictions and ask him/her to try the restrictions before starting an MAOI.

34. Prescribe MAOI and titrate dose as necessary, monitoring for effectiveness and side effects as well as the patient's compliance with the dietary restrictions.

16. Attend follow-up appointments and report as to the effectiveness of medications and any side effects that develop. (35, 36)

35. Titrate the patient's dose of the alternative medication until the minimum effective dose is reached for symptom control or until maximum dose for the medication is reached.

36. Reassess the patient in four weeks; determine whether the medication is adequate, needs a dose increase, or another agent needs to be tried.

17. Retain a remission of anxiety symptoms with a minimum amount of medications. (37, 38)

37. Maintain the patient on current medication for nine to twelve months if he/she has shown a fully successful response; if he/she has had previous episodes of panic prior to this treatment regimen, consider continuing treatment indefinitely.

38. Taper benzodiazepines slowly to avoid the patient experiencing withdrawal symptoms (e.g., rebound anxiety, tremor, nausea, elevated pulse or blood pressure).

__. _____

_____

__. _____

_____

__. _____

_____

__. _____

_____

__. _____

_____

__. _____

_____

DIAGNOSTIC SUGGESTIONS:

Axis I:	300.01	Panic Disorder without Agoraphobia
	300.21	Panic Disorder with Agoraphobia
	300.22	Agoraphobia without History of Panic Disorder
	300.29	Specific Phobia
	300.23	Social Phobia
	300.02	Generalized Anxiety Disorder
	293.89	Anxiety Disorder Due to (Axis III Disorder)
	309.81	Posttraumatic Stress Disorder
	300.3	Obsessive-Compulsive Disorder
	308.3	Acute Stress Disorder
	291.8	Alcohol-Induced Anxiety Disorder
	292.89	Substance-Induced Anxiety Disorder
	296.2x	Major Depressive Disorder, Single Episode
	296.3x	Major Depressive Disorder, Recurrent
	309.24	Adjustment Disorder with Anxiety

_____   _____

_____   _____

Axis II: 301.82 Avoidant Personality Disorder
301.5 Histrionic Personality Disorder
301.6 Dependent Personality Disorder

_____ _____

_____ _____

POSTTRAUMATIC STRESS DISORDER (PTSD)

BEHAVIORAL DEFINITIONS

1. Exposure to actual or threatened death or serious injury that resulted in an intense emotional response of fear, helplessness, or horror.
2. Intrusive, distressing thoughts or images that recall the traumatic event.
3. Disturbing dreams associated with the traumatic event.
4. A sense that the event is reoccurring, as in illusions, hallucinations, or flashbacks.
5. Intense distress when exposed to reminders of the traumatic event.
6. Physiological reactivity when exposed to internal or external cues that symbolize the traumatic event.
7. Avoidance of thoughts, feelings, or conversations about the traumatic event.
8. Avoidance of activity, places, or people associated with the traumatic event.
9. Inability to recall some important aspect of the traumatic event.
10. Lack of interest and participation in significant activities.
11. A sense of detachment from self and/or others.
12. Inability to experience the full range of emotions, including love.
13. A pessimistic, fatalistic attitude regarding the future.
14. Sleep disturbance.
15. Irritability and/or angry outbursts.
16. Increased impulsive and/or aggressive behaviors.
17. Lack of concentration.
18. Hypervigilance.
19. Exaggerated startle response.
20. Symptoms have been present for more than one month.
21. Sad or guilty affect and other signs of depression.
22. Alcohol and/or drug abuse.

23. Suicidal thoughts.
24. A pattern of interpersonal conflict, especially in intimate relationships.
25. Verbally and/or physically violent threats or behavior.
26. Inability to maintain employment due to authority/coworker conflict or anxiety symptoms.

__· _____
   _____
__· _____
   _____
__· _____
   _____

LONG-TERM GOALS

1. Take the appropriate medication and dose to control unpleasant symptoms that occur when thinking about the traumatic event.
2. Reduce the negative impact that the traumatic event has had on many aspects of life and return to pretrauma level of functioning.
3. Develop and implement effective coping skills to carry out normal responsibilities and participate constructively in relationships.
4. Recall the traumatic event without becoming overwhelmed with emotion.
5. Terminate the destructive behaviors that maintain escape and denial while implementing behaviors that promote healing, acceptance of the past events, and responsible living.

__· _____
   _____
__· _____
   _____
__· _____
   _____

SHORT-TERM OBJECTIVES

THERAPEUTIC INTERVENTIONS

1. Describe the signs and symptoms that are experienced

1. Assess the patient for exposure to traumatic event(s) (e.g.,

when recalling the traumatic event(s) and note their impact on daily life. (1, 2, 3)

    physical or sexual assault, motor vehicle accident, combat exposure, childhood physical or sexual abuse) that could have precipitated symptoms.

2. Explore what PTSD symptoms are experienced by the patient and how they affect his/her daily life (e.g., intrusive thoughts, avoiding particular situations and/or thoughts, insomnia, irritability).

3. Determine the acuity and severity of the patient's PTSD symptoms (e.g., aggressiveness, suicidal thoughts) and the urgency with which they need to be controlled.

2. Describe other symptoms or disorders that may also be present, such as depression or substance abuse. (4, 5)

4. Assess the patient for comorbid disorders (e.g., depression, generalized anxiety or panic) (see the Depression, Anxiety and/or Phobia-Panic/Agoraphobia chapters in this *Planner*).

5. Gather detailed personal and family history information regarding substance abuse and its potential interaction with PTSD; refer the patient for in-depth substance abuse treatment, if indicated (see the Chemical Dependence chapters in this *Planner*).

3. Verbalize any current suicidal thoughts and any history of suicidal behavior. (6, 7)

6. Explore the patient's current and past suicidal thoughts and suicidal behavior; ask about family history of suicide (see the Suicidal Ideation chapter in this *Planner,* if necessary).

7. Arrange for hospitalization, as necessary, when the patient is judged to be harmful to himself/

4. Complete psychological testing and other questionnaires for measuring PTSD symptoms and severity. (8)

5. Outline a complete and accurate medical and psychiatric history, including treatment received and its effectiveness. (9, 10)

6. Cooperate with a physical examination and laboratory tests. (11, 12)

7. Pursue treatment for concurrent medical problems that may contribute to PTSD symptoms. (13, 14)

herself or others or is unable to care for his/her basic needs.

8. Administer an objective PTSD assessment instrument to the patient (e.g., Treatment Outcome PTSD Scale [TOP-8], Clinician Administered PTSD Scale [CAPS]); evaluate the results and give him/her feedback.

9. Explore the patient's history of previous treatment for PTSD and the success of, as well as his/her tolerance for, that treatment.

10. Assess the patient for the presence of other medical problems and what medications are used to treat them.

11. Perform a complete physical and neurological examination on the patient and send his/her blood and/or urine for analysis to rule out an organic cause for PTSD symptoms.

12. Provide feedback to the patient regarding the results and implications of the physical examination and laboratory test results.

13. Treat or refer the patient for treatment of any medical problem that may be causing or contributing to PTSD symptoms (e.g., cardiovascular disease, pulmonary disease, endocrine disorders, pheochromocytoma, carcinoid syndrome).

14. Monitor the patient's progress in recovery from concomitant disorders and the impact of the recovery on his/her PTSD.

8. Express an understanding of the possible causes for PTSD and the relationships between PTSD, depression, and substance abuse. (15, 16)

15. Educate the patient on the possible causes (e.g., experiencing or witnessing a life threatening event, childhood abuse, burn injury, war) and signs of PTSD.

16. Emphasize to the patient the negative and dangerous impact of substance abuse on depression, anxiety, or other PTSD symptoms.

9. Express an understanding of treatment options, expected results from medication and potential side effects. (17, 18)

17. Discuss appropriate treatment options with the patient including medications and psychotherapy.

18. Educate the patient on psychotropic medication treatment (e.g., expected results, potential side effects, dosing strategies).

10. Take prescribed medications responsibly at times ordered by the physician. (19, 20)

19. Prescribe to the patient a selective serotonin reuptake inhibitor (SSRI) (e.g. fluoxetine [Prozac®], sertraline [Zoloft®], paroxetine [Paxil®], citalopram [Celexa™], escitalopram [Lexapro™], or fluvoxamine [Luvox®]); strongly consider this strategy if the patient presents with comorbid depression (see the Depression chapter in this *Planner*).

20. Titrate the patient's antidepressant medication to the minimum effective dose for treating the patient's symptoms.

11. Report as to the effectiveness of medications and any side effects that develop. (21)

21. Monitor the patient frequently for the development of side effects, response to medication, and adherence to treatment.

12. Participate in psychotherapy sessions as planned with therapist. (22, 23)

22. Assess the patient for potential benefit from psychotherapy and refer him/her to a psychotherapist, if necessary.

23. Monitor the patient's investment in and response to psychotherapy; assess his/her ability to verbalize a basis for progress in PTSD recovery (e.g., reduction in intrusive thoughts, less avoidance and/or withdrawal, improved relationships).

13. Attend follow-up appointments as scheduled by the physician. (24, 25)

24. Reassess the patient who is taking an antidepressant in four weeks; if the patient has had no response, consider switching to another SSRI antidepressant agent.

25. Evaluate the patient at six weeks for his/her response to the SSRI medication; determine if he/she has had a full response or partial response to the treatment regimen.

14. Report evidence of the degree of improvement in PTSD symptoms as well as any comorbid disorders. (26)

26. Repeat administration of objective rating instruments to the patient for assessment of his/her PTSD severity; evaluate the results and give him/her feedback.

15. Cooperate with any changes in medication dose. (27)

27. Increase medication dose if the patient has had a partial response; titrate his/her dose every two weeks until the maximum dose is reached.

16. Adhere to augmentation medication regimen. (28, 29, 30, 31)

28. Determine if the patient displays impulsive and/or aggressive behavior that is not controlled with an SSRI; if so, consider adding a mood stabilizer (e.g., carbamazepine [Tegretol®], lithium [Eskalith®, Lithonate®], divalproex sodium [Depakote®], or lamotrigine [Lamictal®]).

29. Consider the use of β-blockers (i.e., atenolol [Tenormin®] or nadolol [Corgard®]) or

long-acting benzodiazepines (i.e., clonazepam [Klonopin®]) in conjunction with an antidepressant if the patient's sympathomimetic hyperactivity (e.g., elevated heart rate, exaggerated startle) is not controlled.

30. Maximize augmentation medication as tolerated by the patient; measure blood levels for carbamazepine (Tegretol®), lithium (Lithonate®, Eskalith®), or divalproex sodium (Depakote®) to determine if dose is in the therapeutic range.

31. Consider prescribing an atypical antipsychotic (e.g., risperidone [Risperdal®], olanzapine [Zyprexa®], ziprasidone [Geodon®], aripiprazole [Abilify™], or quetiapine [Seroquel®]) if the patient's aggression/anger is not controlled or if he/she has hallucinations or self-mutilative behavior.

17. Cooperate with changes in type of medication prescribed as well as additional medical tests and dietary restrictions. (32, 33, 34, 35, 36)

32. Consider changing the patient's medication to another agent if he/she has minimal or no response to the initial medication and the augmentation process; alternatives include an SSRI, tricyclic antidepressants (TCAs) (e.g., imipramine [Tofranil®], amitriptyline [Elavil®]), venlafaxine (Effexor®), nefazodone (Serzone®), or monoamine oxidase inhibitors (MAOIs) (i.e., phenelzine [Nardil®]).

33. Complete a medical evaluation on the patient including an

electrocardiogram, if necessary, before starting him/her on a TCA.

34. Educate the patient on dietary restrictions and ask him/her to try the restrictions before starting an MAOI; closely monitor compliance with dietary restrictions during treatment.

35. Titrate the dose of the alternative medication until the patient's symptoms are controlled or maximum dose for the medication is reached.

36. Monitoring the patient frequently for effectiveness and side effects of any new medication.

18. Retain a remission of anxiety symptoms with a minimum amount of medications. (37, 38)

37. Maintain the patient on effective medication for six to twelve months if he/she has shown a fully successful response; if he/she has had previous episodes of PTSD symptoms, consider continuing treatment indefinitely.

38. Taper off the patient's medications slowly and monitor closely for return of PTSD symptoms.

19. Read books on coping with anxiety and implement newly learned techniques. (39)

39. Recommend that the patient read books on coping with anxiety (e.g., *The Relaxation and Stress Reduction Workbook* by Davis, Eschelman, and McKay; *Feel the Fear and Do It Anyway* by Jeffers; *I Can't Get Over It: A Handbook for Trauma Survivors* by Matsakis; *Exercising Your Way to Better Mental Health* by Leith; or *The Anxiety Disease* by Sheehan); process his/her implementation

of coping techniques, reinforcing success and redirecting for failure.

—. _____   —. _____
_____   _____
—. _____   —. _____
_____   _____
—. _____   —. _____
_____   _____

DIAGNOSTIC SUGGESTIONS:

Axis I:	309.81	Posttraumatic Stress Disorder
	308.3	Acute Stress Disorder
	300.02	Generalized Anxiety Disorder
	309.xx	Adjustment Disorder
	300.15	Dissociative Disorder NOS
	300.6	Depersonalization Disorder
	300.01	Panic Disorder without Agoraphobia
	300.21	Panic Disorder with Agoraphobia
	296.xx	Major Depression
	995.54	Physical Abuse of Child (Victim)
	995.81	Physical Abuse of Adult (Victim)
	995.5	Sexual Abuse of Child (Victim)
	995.81	Sexual Abuse of Adult (Victim)
	304.80	Polysubstance Dependence
	305.0	Alcohol Abuse
	303.90	Alcohol Dependence
	304.30	Cannabis Dependence
	304.20	Cocaine Dependence
	304.0	Opioid Dependence

_____ _____
_____ _____

Axis II:	301.83	Borderline Personality Disorder
	301.9	Personality Disorder NOS

_____ _____
_____ _____

PSYCHOTICISM

BEHAVIORAL DEFINITIONS

1. Bizarre content of thoughts (delusions of grandeur, persecution, reference, influence, control, somatic sensations, or infidelity).
2. Illogical form of thought/speech (loose association of ideas in speech; incoherence; illogical thinking; vague, abstract, or repetitive speech; neologisms; perseverations; clanging).
3. Perceptual disturbances (hallucinations, primarily auditory but occasionally visual, tactile, or olfactory).
4. Disturbed affect (blunted, none, flattened, or inappropriate).
5. Lost sense of self (loss of ego boundaries, lack of identity, blatant confusion).
6. Diminished volition (inadequate interest, drive, or ability to follow a course of action to its logical conclusion; pronounced ambivalence or cessation of goal-directed activity).
7. Relationship withdrawal (withdrawal from involvement with the external world, preoccupation with egocentric ideas and fantasies, feelings of alienation).
8. Psychomotor abnormalities (marked decrease in reactivity to environment; various catatonic patterns such as stupor, rigidity, excitement, posturing, or negativism; unusual mannerisms or grimacing).
9. Cognitive abnormalities (impaired memory or attention, difficulty with abstraction).

—. _____

_____

—. _____

_____

—. _____

_____

LONG-TERM GOALS

1. Take the appropriate medication to best control positive and negative psychotic symptoms with minimal side effects.
2. Control or eliminate active psychotic symptoms such that supervised functioning is positive and medication is taken consistently.
3. Significantly reduce or eliminate hallucinations and/or delusions.
4. Eliminate acute, reactive psychotic symptoms and return to normal functioning in affect, thinking, and relating.

—. _____

_____

_____

—. _____

_____

_____

—. _____

_____

SHORT-TERM OBJECTIVES

1. Describe the nature and history of the psychotic symptoms and note their impact on daily life. (1, 2, 3)

THERAPEUTIC INTERVENTIONS

1. Explore what symptoms are experienced by the patient (e.g., hallucinations, delusions, ideas of reference, lack of interest or motivation, loose associations, catatonia) and how they affect his/her daily life.

2. Determine the acuity and severity of the patient's psychotic symptoms (e.g., threatening or aggressive behavior, lack of judgment resulting in exposure to dangerous situations, bizarre behavior, inability to leave the house).

3. Probe for causes if the patient's psychotic symptoms are thought to be reactive.

2. Describe other symptoms or disorders that may also be present. (4, 5)

3. Patient or significant other to describe any current or past suicidal thoughts/behavior as well as violent threats or actions. (6, 7, 8)

4. Complete psychological testing and other questionnaires for measuring the severity of psychotic symptoms. (9)

5. Outline a complete and accurate medical and psychiatric history, including treatment received and its effectiveness. (10, 11)

4. Assess the patient for comorbid disorders (e.g., depression, mania) (see the Depression and Mania chapters in this *Planner*).

5. Gather detailed personal and family history information regarding substance abuse and its potential interaction with psychosis; refer the patient for in-depth substance abuse treatment, if indicated (see the Chemical Dependence chapters in this *Planner*).

6. Explore the patient's current and past suicidal thoughts and suicidal behavior; ask about family history of suicide (see the Suicidal Ideation chapter in this *Planner*).

7. Assess the patient's potential for violence and determine the presence of current and past threats or acts of aggression.

8. Arrange for hospitalization, as necessary, when the patient is judged to be harmful to self or others or unable to care for his/her basic needs.

9. Administer an objective psychosis rating instrument to the patient (e.g., Brief Psychotic Rating Scale [BPRS], Positive and Negative Symptom Scale [PANSS]); evaluate the results and give him/her feedback.

10. Explore the patient's history of previous treatment for psychosis and the success of, as well as his/her tolerance for, that treatment.

11. Assess the patient for the presence of other medical problems

and what medications are used to treat them.

6. Cooperate with a physical examination and laboratory tests. (12, 13, 14)

12. Perform a complete physical and neurological examination on the patient and send his/her blood and/or urine for analysis to rule out organic contributors to psychosis.

13. Obtain radiologic studies (i.e., head computed tomography [CT] scan or magnetic resonance imaging [MRI]) of the patient if necessary.

14. Provide feedback to the patient regarding the results and implications of the physical examination and laboratory test results.

7. Pursue treatment for concurrent medical problems that may contribute to psychotic symptoms. (15, 16)

15. Treat or refer the patient for treatment of any medical problem that may be contributing to the psychotic symptoms (e.g., brain lesions or tumors, seizures, dementia, endocrine disorders, intoxication, delirium).

16. Monitor the patient's progress in recovery from concomitant disorders and the impact of the recovery on his/her psychosis.

8. Express an understanding of the possible causes for psychosis and the relationship between psychosis and substance abuse. (17, 18)

17. Emphasize the negative and dangerous impact of substance abuse on psychosis.

18. Educate the patient on the possible causes (e.g., neurotransmitter abnormalities, genetic propensity, medical illness) and signs of psychosis.

9. Verbalize an understanding of treatment options, expected results from medication, and potential side effects. (19, 20)

19. Discuss appropriate treatment options with the patient including medications and psychotherapy.

20. Educate the patient on antipsychotic medication treatment including expected results, potential side effects, and dosing strategies.

10. Take prescribed medications responsibly at times ordered by the physician. (21, 22)

21. Prescribe an atypical antipsychotic (i.e., risperidone [Risperdal®], olanzapine [Zyprexa®], aripiprazole [Abilify™], ziprasidone [Geodon®], quetiapine [Seroquel®]); initial dose should be appropriate for the patient's age and medical status.

22. Titrate the patient's medication to the minimum effective dose as tolerated.

11. Report on the effectiveness of medications and any side effects that develop. (23, 24, 25)

23. Monitor the patient frequently for the development of side effects, response to medication, and adherence to treatment.

24. Reassess the patient who is taking an antipsychotic at four to six weeks; determine whether the medication is adequate or needs a dose increase.

25. Repeat administration of objective rating instruments for assessment of the patient's psychosis; evaluate the results and give him/her feedback.

12. Participate in psychotherapy sessions as planned with the therapist. (26, 27)

26. Assess the patient for potential benefit from psychotherapy and/or vocational and social therapy (e.g., day treatment, vocational training); refer him/her to a psychotherapist or rehabilitation program, if necessary.

27. Monitor the patient's response to psychotherapy; assess his/ her ability to verbalize a basis for progress in recovery from

psychosis (e.g., improvement in social and occupational functioning, improvement in coping skills, increased ability to deal with symptoms, sobriety).

13. Attend follow-up appointments as scheduled by the physician and adhere to any adjustments in medication dose. (28, 29)

28. Increase the antipsychotic dose every three to four weeks, as tolerated, if the patient has only a partial response.

29. Evaluate the patient at ten to twelve weeks for his/her response to medication; determine if he/she has had a full response or partial response to the treatment regimen.

14. Cooperate with a change to a prescription of an alternate atypical antipsychotic. (30, 31)

30. Discuss other treatment options with the patient if he/she shows no treatment response or a partial response.

31. Switch the patient's medication to another atypical antipsychotic agent if patient has no response or a partial response; give each individual atypical antipsychotic a full trial, if necessary.

15. Verbalize an understanding of treatment with clozapine (Clozaril®) for refractory psychotic symptoms and cooperate with treatment guidelines. (32, 33, 34)

32. Consider prescribing clozapine (Clozaril®) if the patient has had a poor response to all atypical antipsychotics.

33. Educate patient on the potential risks and side effects of clozapine (Clozaril®) (e.g., agranulocytosis, weight gain, elevated blood glucose, sedation).

34. Perform a full medical evaluation and check baseline laboratory values, including a complete blood count, prior to starting clozapine (Clozaril®) therapy; follow published guidelines for prescribing clozapine.

16. Cooperate with a change to a prescription of a typical antipsychotic medication. (35, 36)

35. Prescribe a typical antipsychotic (e.g., haloperidol [Haldol®], fluphenazine [Prolixin®], trifluoperazine [Stelazine®], perphenazine [Trilafon®], chlorpromazine [Thorazine®]) if the patient has failed to respond to all atypical antipsychotics; allow for a full trial at a therapeutic dose.

36. Monitor for side effects of typical antipsychotics (e.g., stiffness, tremor, dystonic reactions); prescribe an anticholinergic medication (e.g., benztropine [Cogentin®], diphenhydramine [Benadryl®], trihexyphenidyl [Artane®]) as necessary.

17. Patient and family members report on the patient's compliance with medication. (37)

37. Determine if the patient is compliant with oral medication; if not, prescribe a long-acting intramuscular agent (i.e., haloperidol decanoate or fluphenazine decanoate).

18. Adhere to augmentation strategies used to reduce psychotic symptoms. (38, 39, 40, 41)

38. Determine if the patient needs additional medication to augment current therapy.

39. Consider adding an atypical or typical antipsychotic agent to the current medication to augment the symptom response.

40. Consider other augmentation strategies such as antidepressants, mood stabilizers (lithium [Lithonate®, Eskalith®], divalproex sodium [Depakote®]) or, electroconvulsive therapy (ECT); strongly consider these strategies if the patient has congruent mood symptoms.

19. Retain a remission or significant reduction in psychotic
symptoms with a minimum
amount of medications.
(42, 43)

41. Maximize the augmentation
medication as tolerated by the
patient.

42. Maintain the patient on current
medication indefinitely if the
patient has a chronic, primary
psychotic disorder (e.g., schizophrenia, schizoaffective disorder).

43. Taper medications slowly one to
two months after resolution of
symptoms if the psychosis is
secondary to another disorder
(e.g., depression, delirium) or if
it is related to a brief psychotic
disorder; monitor closely for
recurrence of symptoms.

__. _____   __. _____
    _____   _____
__. _____   __. _____
    _____   _____
__. _____   __. _____
    _____   _____
__. _____   __. _____
    _____   _____

DIAGNOSTIC SUGGESTIONS:

Axis I:
295.xx	Schizophrenia
295.4	Schizophreniform Disorder
298.8	Brief Psychotic Disorder
297.1	Delusional Disorder
295.70	Schizoaffective Disorder
296.xx	Bipolar I Disorder
296.xx	Major Depressive Disorder
292.1x	Substance-Induced Psychotic Disorder
310.1	Personality Change Due to (Axis III Disorder)

_____   _____

_____   _____

Axis II: 301.22   Schizotypal Personality Disorder
301.20   Schizoid Personality Disorder
301.0   Paranoid Personality Disorder
301.83   Borderline Personality Disorder

_____   _____

_____   _____

SLEEP DISTURBANCE

BEHAVIORAL DEFINITIONS

1. Difficulty getting to or maintaining sleep.
2. Sleeping adequately but not feeling refreshed or rested after waking.
3. Predominant daytime sleepiness or falling asleep too easily during the daytime.
4. Insomnia or hypersomnia complaints due to a reversal of the sleep-wake schedule normal for the patient's environment.
5. Distress resulting from repeated awakening with detailed recall of extremely frightening dreams involving threats to self.
6. Abrupt awakening with a panicky scream followed by intense anxiety and autonomic arousal, no detailed scream recall, and confusion or disorientation.
7. Repeated incidents of sleep walking accompanied by amnesia for the episode.
8. Episodes of cataplexy (sudden bilateral loss of muscle tone), usually in association with intense emotion.
9. Recurrent episodes of hypnopompic/hypnagogic hallucinations or sleep paralysis that occur during the transition between sleep and wakefulness.

—. _____
   _____
—. _____
   _____
—. _____
   _____

LONG-TERM GOALS

1. Restore restful sleep pattern.
2. Feel refreshed and energetic during wakeful hours.
3. Terminate anxiety-producing dreams that cause awakening.
4. End abrupt awakening in terror and return to peaceful, restful sleep pattern.
5. Restore restful sleep with reduction of sleep-walking incidents.
6. Control episodes of cataplexy and/or hypnopompic/hypnagogic hallucinations and sleep paralysis.

—. _____
_____

—. _____
_____

—. _____
_____

SHORT-TERM OBJECTIVES

1. Describe the signs and symptoms of sleep disorder that are experienced and note their impact on daily life. (1, 2)

2. Describe other symptoms or disorders that may also be present. (3, 4)

THERAPEUTIC INTERVENTIONS

1. Explore the symptoms of sleep disturbance that are experienced by the patient (e.g. insomnia, excessive daytime sleepiness, unrefreshing sleep, sudden loss of muscle tone).

2. Assess what impact the sleep disturbance has on the patient's daily life (e.g., impaired job performance, inability to accomplish routine chores).

3. Assess the patient for comorbid psychiatric disorders (e.g., see the Depression, Anxiety, Mania/ Hypomania, or Panic Disorder chapters in this *Planner*).

4. Gather detailed personal and family history information regarding the patient's substance abuse and its potential

3. Outline a complete and accurate medical and psychiatric history, including treatment received and its effectiveness. (5, 6, 7)

4. Cooperate with a physical examination and diagnostic tests. (8, 9, 10)

contribution to sleep disturbance; refer the patient for in-depth substance abuse treatment, if indicated (see the Chemical Dependence chapters in this *Planner*).

5. Explore the patient's history of previous treatment for any sleep disturbance and the success of, as well as tolerance for, that treatment.

6. Assess the patient for the presence of other medical problems and any medications used to treat them.

7. Explore the patient's use of any medication or other substance that could produce or worsen sleep disturbance (e.g., alcohol, caffeine, nicotine, central nervous system stimulants, antihypertensives, bronchodilators, anticholinergics, corticosteroids).

8. Perform a complete physical and neurological examination on the patient and send his/her blood and/or urine for analysis to rule out an organic cause for sleep disturbance (e.g., obesity, Parkinson's disease, congestive heart failure, pain).

9. Refer the patient for an overnight sleep study, if necessary, to evaluate him/her for physical or neurological disorders (e.g., obstructive sleep apnea, restless legs syndrome) that manifest during sleep.

10. Provide feedback to the patient regarding the results and implications of the physical examination and diagnostic test results.

5. Pursue treatment for concurrent medical problems that may contribute to the sleep disturbance. (11, 12)

6. Complete psychological testing and other questionnaires for measuring sleep disturbance. (13)

7. Express an understanding of possible causes for sleep disturbance and the relationship between substance abuse and sleep disturbance. (14, 15)

8. Keep a written daily record of hours and times of sleep. (16)

9. Verbalize an understanding of treatment options, including medication, psychotherapy, and sleep hygiene techniques. (17, 18)

11. Treat or refer the patient for treatment of any medical problem that may be causing or contributing to the sleep disturbance (e.g., obstructive sleep apnea, restless legs syndrome, congestive heart failure).

12. Monitor the patient's progress in recovery from concomitant disorders and the impact of the recovery on his/her sleep disturbance.

13. Administer objective instruments to assess the patient's sleep disturbance (e.g., Sleep Disorders Questionnaire [SDQ], Pittsburgh Sleep Quality Scale [PSQI], Epworth Sleepiness Scale [ESS]); evaluate the results and give him/her feedback.

14. Educate the patient on the possible contributing factors (e.g., stressful life events, daytime naps, medical illness, psychiatric illness, medications, travel across time zones) to sleep disturbance.

15. Emphasize the negative and dangerous impact of substance abuse on sleep.

16. Recommend the patient keep a sleep log for two weeks to help define the exact symptoms and sleep pattern.

17. Discuss appropriate treatment options with the patient including medication, psychotherapy, and sleep hygiene techniques.

18. Educate the patient on techniques for good sleep hygiene (e.g., daily exercise, set routine times for going to bed and

getting up, avoid stimulating activity prior to sleep, relaxation techniques).

10. Participate in psychotherapy sessions as planned with therapist. (19, 20)

19. Assess the patient for potential benefit from psychotherapy and refer to a psychotherapist, if necessary.

20. Monitor the patient's response to psychotherapy and/or sleep hygiene techniques; assess his/her ability to verbalize a basis for progress in recovery from sleep disturbance (e.g., less daytime sleepiness, more refreshing sleep, improved productivity).

11. Verbalize an understanding of medication treatment options, expected results from medication, and potential side effects. (21)

21. Educate the patient on pharmacologic treatment including expected results, potential side effects, expected time course of treatment (e.g., days to weeks for acute primary insomnia, months to years for chronic insomnia or narcolepsy), and potential dependence liability with long-term use.

12. Take prescribed anxiolytic or hypnotic medications responsibly at times ordered by the physician. (22, 23, 24)

22. Prescribe to the patient an anxiolytic or hypnotic agent (e.g., zolpidem [Ambien®], zaleplon [Sonata®], lorazepam [Ativan®], flurazepam [Dalmane®], triazolam [Halcion®], diazepam [Valium®], chloral hydrate [Noctec®], estazolam [ProSom®], temazepam [Restoril®]).

23. Avoid the use of anxiolytic or hypnotics in patients with a history of substance abuse.

24. Titrate the anxiolytic or hypnotic medication dose every two to three days until the patient shows a good response or the maximum dose is reached.

13. Report as to the effectiveness of the anxiolytic or hypnotic medications and any side effects that develop. (25, 26)

14. Adhere to changes in medication regimen as prescribed by the physician. (27, 28)

15. Cooperate with any additional medical evaluation necessary for taking tricyclic antidepressants (TCAs). (29)

16. Report as to the effectiveness of the alternative medication and adhere to any changes in dose as prescribed. (30, 31)

25. Recommend to the patient that he/she limit the use of the anxiolytic or hypnotic medication to two to four times per week if possible.

26. Monitor the patient frequently for daytime sedation or grogginess as well as excessive use of the medication.

27. Consider the use of an alternative medication for patients who do not respond to anxiolytic or hypnotics, who have a history of substance abuse or who do not want to be exposed to a potentially addictive medication.

28. Prescribe to the patient an alternative medication (e.g., trazodone [Desyrel®], amitriptyline [Elavil®], doxepin [Sinequan®, Zonalon®], diphenhydramine [Benadryl®], mirtazapine [Remeron®], quetiapine [Seroquel®]).

29. Complete a medical evaluation on the patient including an electrocardiogram (EKG), if necessary, before starting him/her on a tricyclic antidepressant (e.g., amitriptyline [Elavil®], doxepin [Sinequan®, Zonalon®]).

30. Titrate the dose of the alternative medication every two to three days, as tolerated.

31. Monitor the patient for side effects (e.g., dizziness, dry mouth, blurred vision, constipation) and effectiveness of the alternative medication.

17. Cooperate with the medication taper as recommended by the physician. (32, 33)

32. Reduce the medication after one to four weeks by gradually decreasing the frequency and/or dose of the medication over several days to weeks.

33. Monitor the patient for rebound insomnia during the medication taper.

18. Adhere to medications for treating restless legs syndrome. (34, 35, 36)

34. Assess the patient for restless legs syndrome (e.g., restless feelings in the legs, muscle twitching, sensation of "pins and needles," muscle cramps, or aches).

35. Prescribe to the patient a low dose of carbidopa/levodopa (Sinemet®) or pramipexole (Mirapex®) at bedtime.

36. Titrate the dose of carbidopa/levodopa (Sinemet®) or pramipexole (Mirapex®), as tolerated, until symptoms are controlled or the maximum dose is reached.

19. Adhere to medications for treating narcolepsy as prescribed by the physician. (37, 38, 39)

37. Assess the patient for symptoms of narcolepsy (e.g., excessive daytime sleepiness, sudden loss of muscle tone, hypnagogic hallucinations, or sleep paralysis).

38. Prescribe to the patient a stimulant medication (e.g., modafinil [Provigil®], methylphenidate [Ritalin®], amphetamine [Adderall®], dextroamphetamine [Dexedrine®]) to treat daytime sleepiness and cataplexy.

39. Titrate the dose of stimulant medication every three to four days, as tolerated, until the patient's symptoms are controlled or the maximum dose is reached.

20. Take antidepressant augmentation medication that is added to the current regimen. (40, 41)

40. Consider the addition of an antidepressant agent (e.g., a selective serotonin reuptake inhibitor [SSRI] or TCA) if the patient's cataplexy is not fully controlled with stimulant medication.

41. Titrate the antidepressant dose, as tolerated, until the patient's cataplexy is controlled or the maximum dose is reached.

21. Retain a remission of narcolepsy symptoms. (42)

42. Continue effective treatment for narcolepsy indefinitely.

__. _____

__. _____

__. _____

__. _____

DIAGNOSTIC SUGGESTIONS:

Axis I:		
	307.42	Primary Insomnia
	307.44	Primary Hypersomnia
	347	Narcolepsy
	780.59	Breathing-Related Sleep Disorder
	307.45	Circadian Rhythm Sleep Disorder
	307.47	Nightmare Disorder
	307.46	Sleep Terror Disorder
	307.46	Sleepwalking Disorder
	780.xx	Sleep Disorder Due to (Axis III Disorder)
	309.81	Posttraumatic Stress Disorder
	296.xx	Major Depressive Disorder
	300.4	Dysthymic Disorder
	296.xx	Bipolar I Disorder
	296.89	Bipolar II Disorder
	300.01	Panic Disorder without Agoraphobia

_____ _____

_____ _____

Axis II: _____ _____

_____ _____

SOCIAL DISCOMFORT

BEHAVIORAL DEFINITIONS

1. Overall pattern of anxiety, shyness, or timidity that presents itself in most social situations.
2. Hypersensitivity to criticism or disapproval of others.
3. No close friends or confidants outside of first-degree relatives.
4. Avoidance of situations that require a degree of interpersonal contact.
5. Reluctant involvement in social situations out of fear of saying or doing something foolish or of becoming emotional in front of others.
6. Abuse of alcohol or chemicals to help ease the anxiety associated with social situations.
7. Isolation or involvement in solitary activities during most waking hours.
8. Increased heart rate, sweating, dry mouth, muscle tension, and shakiness in most social situations.
9. Recognizes that the fear is excessive or unreasonable.

__. _____

_____

__. _____

_____

__. _____

_____

LONG-TERM GOALS

1. Interact socially without excessive fear or anxiety.
2. Take the appropriate medication and dose to control or reduce symptoms of social anxiety.

3. Develop the essential social skills that will enhance the quality of re-relationship life.
4. Form relationships that will enhance a support system for recovery.
5. Reach a personal balance between solitary time and interpersonal interaction with others.
6. Terminate use of alcohol or nonprescribed chemicals to relieve social anxiety and learn constructive coping behaviors.

—. _____

_____

—. _____

_____

—. _____

_____

SHORT-TERM OBJECTIVES

THERAPEUTIC INTERVENTIONS

1. Identify and clarify the signs and symptoms of anxiety connected to social situations. (1, 2, 3, 4)

1. Assist the patient in expressing fears that stem from being in social situations.

2. Explore for physical signs and symptoms that the patient experiences when he/she is around others (e.g., blushing, sweating, dry mouth, muscle tension, elevated heart rate, tremor).

3. Explore the unpleasant emotions he/she experiences when relating to others (e.g., anxiety, fear, embarrassment, shame).

4. Ask the patient about a personal history of separation anxiety or school phobia.

2. Describe other symptoms or disorders that may also be present. (5, 6, 7, 8)

5. Assess the patient for comorbid disorders (e.g., depression, generalized anxiety or panic) (see the Depression, Anxiety, and/or Phobia-Panic/Agoraphobia chapters in this *Planner*).

6. Gather detailed information regarding the patient's use of alcohol or other nonprescribed chemicals to help him/her cope with social situations.

7. Determine if the patient is abusing substances; refer him/her for in-depth substance abuse treatment, if indicated (see the Chemical Dependence chapters in this *Planner*).

8. Assess whether the patient's fears are irrational or related to psychotic symptoms (e.g., paranoia or delusions) (see the Psychoticism chapter in this *Planner*).

3. Identify the types of social situations that produce anxiety. (9)

9. Establish whether the patient's signs and symptoms occur in all or most social settings (generalized) or in specific situations such as performing or public speaking (nongeneralized).

4. Complete psychological testing and other questionnaires for measuring the level of social anxiety. (10)

10. Administer to the patient the Liebowitz Social Anxiety Scale, Brief Social Phobia Scale, or other objective assessment instrument; evaluate results and give feedback to him/her.

5. Outline a complete and accurate medical and psychiatric history, including treatment received and its effectiveness. (11, 12, 13)

11. Explore the patient's history of previous treatment for social phobia and the success of, as well as his/her tolerance for, that treatment.

12. Assess the patient for the presence of other medical problems and what medications are used to treat them.

13. Explore the patient's use of any medication or other substance that could produce or worsen anxiety (i.e., caffeine, ephedrine,

6. Verbalize an understanding of social anxiety, treatment options, and the potential for substance abuse. (14, 15, 16, 17)

pseudoephedrine, amphetamines, bronchodilators, anticholinergics, corticosteroids).

14. Educate the patient on the signs and symptoms of social phobia and the high prevalence of the disorder; reassure him/her that the symptoms can be reduced or eliminated.

15. Emphasize the potential for the development of a substance abuse disorder if the patient uses substances to control the anxiety symptoms.

16. Discuss appropriate treatment options with the patient including medications and psychotherapy (e.g., cognitive behavioral therapy [CBT]).

17. Educate the patient on psychotropic medication treatment including expected results, potential side effects, and dosing strategies.

7. Participate in psychotherapy sessions as planned with the therapist. (18, 19)

18. Assess the patient's interest in pursuing CBT or other psychotherapy; refer him/her to a psychotherapist, if necessary.

19. Monitor the patient's investment in and response to CBT or other psychotherapy; assess his/her ability to verbalize a basis for progress in reducing social anxiety (e.g., decrease in fear, more realistic self-talk, engagement in more social activities, improved relationships, sobriety).

8. Describe the purpose and correct usage of medications for treating nongeneralized social phobia. (20, 21, 22)

20. Prescribe a β-blocker (i.e., atenolol [Tenormin®] or nadolol [Corgard®]) or a long-acting benzodiazepine (i.e. clonazepam [Klonopin®]) for patients who

have nongeneralized social anxiety.

21. Avoid β-blockers in patients with medical problems that are sensitive to this class of medication (e.g., asthma, congestive heart failure); do not use benzodiazepines in patients with a history of substance abuse.

22. Educate the patient on taking the medication shortly before entering a situation known to cause anxiety.

9. Take prescribed medications for generalized social phobia responsibly at times ordered by physician. (23, 24, 25)

23. Initiate treatment with a selective serotonin reuptake inhibitor (SSRI) (e.g., paroxetine [Paxil®], fluvoxamine [Luvox®], or sertraline [Zoloft®]) if the patient has generalized social phobia.

24. Start treatment with an SSRI at a lower dose in patients who have concurrent panic disorder.

25. Titrate the SSRI to the minimum effective dose for treatment of the patient's symptoms.

10. Report as to the effectiveness of medications and any side effects that develop. (26, 27)

26. Monitor the patient for development of side effects, response to medication, and adherence to treatment.

27. Evaluate the patient at six weeks for his/her response to medication; determine if he/she has had a full response or partial response to the treatment regimen.

11. Report evidence of improvement in social anxiety symptoms. (28)

28. Repeat administration of objective rating instruments for social anxiety to assess the patient's improvement; evaluate the results and give him/her feedback.

12. Adhere to changes in medication dosing or augmentation. (29, 30, 31)

29. Increase the SSRI dose if the patient has had a partial response; titrate his/her dose every two weeks until the maximum dose is reached.

30. Consider the addition of long-acting benzodiazepines (i.e., clonazepam [Klonopin®]) for patients showing only a partial response to an SSRI; use buspirone (BuSpar®) in patients who have a history of substance abuse.

31. Maximize augmentation medication as tolerated by the patient.

13. Cooperate with changes in type of medication prescribed. (32, 33)

32. Discuss other treatment options with the patient if he/she shows only a partial treatment response.

33. Consider the use of a monoamine oxidase inhibitor (MAOI) (e.g., phenelzine [Nardil®]) for patients who do not respond to an SSRI; other alternatives to consider are venlafaxine (Effexor®) or nefazodone (Serzone®).

14. Follow dietary restrictions for treatment with monoamine oxidase inhibitors (MAOIs). (34)

34. Educate the patient on dietary restrictions and ask him/her to try the restrictions before starting an MAOI.

15. Maintain a remission of social anxiety symptoms with a minimum amount of medication. (35, 36)

35. Maintain the patient on current medication for six to twelve months if he/she has shown a fully successful response.

36. Taper medications slowly; if symptoms recur, restart therapy and continue indefinitely.

16. Read books on improving self-image and implement any new techniques that are learned. (37)

37. Assign the patient to read books on improving self-image (e.g., *Ten Days to Self Esteem! by* Burns; *Born to Win* by James

and Jongeward; *I'm OK, You're OK* by Harris and Harris); process his/her implementation of coping techniques, reinforcing success and redirecting for failure.

__. _____   __. _____

_____   _____

__. _____   __. _____

_____   _____

__. _____   __. _____

_____   _____

DIAGNOSTIC SUGGESTIONS:

Axis I:	300.23	Social Phobia
	300.02	Generalized Anxiety Disorder
	293.89	Anxiety Disorder Due to (Axis III Disorder)
	300.01	Panic Disorder without Agoraphobia
	300.21	Panic Disorder with Agoraphobia
	300.29	Specific Phobia
	309.81	Posttraumatic Stress Disorder
	292.89	Substance-Induced Anxiety Disorder
	296.2x	Major Depressive Disorder, Single Episode
	296.3x	Major Depressive Disorder, Recurrent
	297.1	Delusional Disorder
	295.xx	Schizophrenia
	_____	_____
	_____	_____
Axis II:	301.82	Avoidant Personality Disorder
	301.20	Schizoid Personality Disorder
	301.0	Paranoid Personality Disorder
	301.22	Schizotypal Personality Disorder
	_____	_____
	_____	_____

SOMATIZATION

BEHAVIORAL DEFINITIONS

1. One or more physical complaints (usually vague) that have no known organic basis, or the complaining and impairment in life function in excess of what is expected.
2. A physical malady caused by a psychosocial stressor triggering a psychological conflict.
3. Preoccupation with the fear of having a serious physical disease without any medical basis for concern.
4. A multitude of physical complaints that have no organic foundation and have caused the patient to change his/her life (e.g., seeing doctors often, taking prescriptions, withdrawing from responsibilities).
5. Preoccupation with chronic pain grossly beyond what is expected for a physical malady or in spite of no known organic cause.
6. Preoccupation with pain in one or more anatomical sites with both psychological factors and a medical condition as a basis for the pain.
7. Preoccupation with some imagined defect in appearance or excessive concern regarding a small physical disability.

—. _____
   _____
—. _____
   _____
—. _____
   _____

LONG-TERM GOALS

1. Reduce the frequency of physical complaints and improve the level of independent functioning through medication and psychotherapy.

2. Reduce verbalizations focusing on pain while increasing productive activities.
3. Accept body appearance as normal even with insignificant flaws.
4. Accept self as relatively healthy with no known medical illness.
5. Improve physical functioning due to development of adequate coping mechanisms for stress management.

—. _____

_____

—. _____

_____

—. _____

_____

SHORT-TERM OBJECTIVES

THERAPEUTIC INTERVENTIONS

1. Describe the signs and symptoms of somatization that are experienced and note their impact on daily life. (1)

1. Explore the symptoms that are experienced by the patient and how they affect his/her daily life (e.g. complaints of multiple physical symptoms, persistent worries of having a serious disease, preoccupation with a perceived physical abnormality, impaired social and/or occupational functioning).

2. Describe other symptoms or disorders that may also be present. (2, 3)

2. Assess the patient for comorbid disorders (e.g., see the Depression, Anxiety, Panic Disorder chapters in this *Planner*).

3. Gather detailed personal and family history information regarding substance abuse and its potential contribution to somatization; refer the patient for in-depth substance abuse treatment, if indicated (see the Chemical Dependence chapters in this *Planner*).

3. Outline a complete and accurate medical and psychiatric history, including treatment received and its effectiveness. (4, 5, 6)

4. Explore the patient's history of previous treatment for somatization or body dysmorphic disorder and the success of, as well as tolerance for, that treatment.

5. Assess the patient for the presence of specific medical problems and gather a thorough medical and surgical history.

6. Take a careful and thorough medication history that includes all prescription medications as well as over the counter medications; consider that the patient may get medications from several different physicians.

4. Cooperate with a physical examination and laboratory tests. (7, 8)

7. Perform an initial complete physical and neurological examination and send his/her blood and/or urine for analysis to rule out the presence of any medical illness (e.g., infection, hypertension, hypercholesterolemia, diabetes, neurological disorders, endocrine disease, gastrointestinal disease).

8. Provide feedback to the patient regarding the results and implications of the physical examination and laboratory test results.

5. Identify one physician who will provide routine medical care and determine if additional procedures are necessary. (9, 10, 11, 12)

9. Encourage the patient to identify one primary care physician who can see the patient every four to six weeks for a regularly scheduled visit and brief physical examination.

10. Discourage the patient from visiting the physician on an "as needed" basis.

11. Avoid scheduling the patient for unnecessary diagnostic procedures, medications, and surgeries.

12. Avoid making referrals for the patient to multiple medical specialists.

6. Complete psychological testing and other questionnaires for assessing somatization. (13)

13. Administer objective instruments to assess the patient's somatic preoccupation (e.g., Somatoform Disorders Symptom Checklist, Whiteley Index of Hypochondriasis, Body Dysmorphic Disorder Examination [BDDE]); evaluate the results and give him/her feedback.

7. Express an understanding of possible contributors to somatization. (14)

14. Educate the patient on the possible contributing factors (e.g., stressful life events, depression, anxiety) to somatization.

8. Verbalize an understanding of treatment options, expected results from medication, and potential side effects. (15, 16)

15. Discuss appropriate treatment options with the patient including medication and psychotherapy.

16. Educate the patient on psychotropic medication treatment including the expected results, potential side effects, and dosing strategies.

9. Participate in psychotherapy sessions as planned with therapist. (17, 18)

17. Assess the patient for potential benefit from psychotherapy and refer to a psychotherapist, if necessary.

18. Monitor the patient's response to psychotherapy; assess his/her ability to verbalize a basis for progress in recovery from somatization (e.g., development of a realistic image of his/her body, reduction in preoccupation with physical symptoms,

10. Take prescribed medications responsibly at times ordered by the physician. (19, 20)

11. Attend follow-up appointments and report as to the effectiveness of the SSRI medications and any side effects that develop. (21, 22, 23, 24)

12. Report evidence of the degree of improvement in somatization symptoms. (25, 26)

improved social and occupational functioning).

19. Prescribe to the patient a selective serotonin reuptake inhibitor (SSRI) (e.g., paroxetine [Paxil®], sertraline [Zoloft®], citalopram [Celexa™], escitalopram [Lexapro™], fluoxetine [Prozac®], fluvoxamine [Luvox®]).

20. Titrate the SSRI antidepressant medication to the minimum effective dose used to treat depression.

21. Monitor the patient regularly for the development of side effects, response to SSRI medication and adherence to treatment.

22. Reassess the patient who is taking an SSRI antidepressant at six weeks; determine whether the medication is adequate or needs a dose increase.

23. Educate the patient about the possibility of a delayed response to medication (10 to 12 weeks), especially when treating body dysmorphic disorder.

24. Maximize the SSRI antidepressant dose as tolerated; allow for a full 12-week trial at the highest tolerated dose.

25. Evaluate the patient at 12 weeks for his/her response to the SSRI medication; determine if he/she has had a full response or partial response to the treatment regimen.

26. Repeat administration of objective rating instruments for assessment of the patient's

somatization; evaluate the results and give him/her feedback.

13. Adhere to any additional medication used to augment current SSRI medication regimen. (27, 28, 29, 30, 31)

27. Determine if the patient needs additional medication to augment current SSRI therapy; partial responders to a single medication should be considered for this strategy.

28. Consider adding an augmentation medication (e.g., buspirone [BuSpar®], clomipramine [Anafranil®], nefazodone [Serzone®], trazodone [Desyrel®], mirtazapine [Remeron®]) to the current SSRI therapy.

29. Prescribe a benzodiazepine (e.g., clonazepam [Klonopin®]), if the patient has comorbid anxiety symptoms (e.g., excessive worry and/or nervousness, muscle tension, panic attacks).

30. Consider prescribing an atypical antipsychotic medication (e.g., risperidone [Risperdal®], olanzapine [Zyprexa®], ziprasidone [Geodon®], quetiapine [Seroquel®], aripiprazole [Abilify™]) if the patient has comorbid delusions about his/her body.

31. Titrate the dose of the augmentation medication, as tolerated, until the patient has a satisfactory response or the maximum dose is reached.

14. Adhere to changes in medication regimen. (32)

32. Consider changing the patient's medication to another agent (e.g., a different SSRI, clomipramine [Anafranil®], venlafaxine [Effexor®], a monoamine oxidase inhibitor [MAOI]) if he/she has minimal or no

15. Cooperate with any additional medical tests or dietary restrictions. (33, 34)

response to the initial medication and augmentation process.

33. Complete a medical evaluation on the patient, including an electrocardiogram, if necessary, before starting him/her on clomipramine (Anafranil®).

34. Educate the patient on dietary restrictions and ask him/her to try the restrictions before starting an MAOI; closely monitor compliance with dietary restrictions during treatment.

16. Adhere to any changes in the alternative medication dose. (35)

35. Titrate the dose of the alternative medication, as tolerated, until the patient's symptoms are controlled or maximum dose is reached.

17. Retain a remission or significant reduction in dissociative symptoms. (36, 37, 38)

36. Maintain the patient on current medication for at least 12 months if he/she has shown a fully successful response.

37. Continue treatment indefinitely if he/she has had a previous episode of somatization or body dysmorphic disorder or he/she has demonstrated only a partial response to medication.

38. Reduce medications gradually (i.e., approximately 25% of the dose every two months); monitor closely for recurrence of symptoms.

__. _____

_____

__. _____

_____

__. _____

_____

__. _____

_____

__. _____

_____

__. _____

_____

DIAGNOSTIC SUGGESTIONS:

Axis I:

300.7	Body Dysmorphic Disorder
300.11	Conversion Disorder
300.7	Hypochondriasis
300.81	Somatization Disorder
307.80	Pain Disorder Associated with Psychological Factors
307.89	Pain Disorder Associated with Both Psychological Factors and an Axis III Disorder
300.81	Undifferentiated Somatoform Disorder
300.81	Somatoform Disorder NOS
296.xx	Major Depression
300.4	Dysthymic Disorder
300.01	Panic Disorder without Agoraphobia
300.02	Generalized Anxiety Disorder

———   ————————————————————

———   ————————————————————

Axis II:

301.6	Dependent Personality Disorder
301.9	Personality Disorder NOS

———   ————————————————————

———   ————————————————————

SUICIDAL IDEATION

BEHAVIORAL DEFINITIONS

1. Recurrent thoughts of or preoccupation with death.
2. Recurrent or ongoing suicidal ideation without any plans.
3. Ongoing suicidal ideation with a specific plan.
4. Recent suicide attempt.
5. History of suicide attempts that required professional or family/friend intervention on some level (i.e., inpatient, safe house, outpatient, or supervision).
6. Positive family history of depression and/or a preoccupation with suicidal thoughts or suicide attempts.
7. A bleak, hopeless attitude regarding life coupled with recent life events that support this (e.g., divorce, death of a friend or family member, loss of a job).
8. Social withdrawal, lethargy, and apathy coupled with expressions of wanting to die.
9. Sudden change from being depressed to upbeat and at peace while actions indicate the patient is "putting his/her house in order" and there has been no genuine resolution of conflict.

—. _____
   _____
—. _____
   _____
—. _____
   _____

LONG-TERM GOALS

1. Alleviate the suicidal impulses/ideation and return to the highest level of previous daily functioning through the use of medication and/or participation in psychotherapy.
2. Stabilize the suicidal crisis.
3. Placement in an appropriate level of care to safely address the suicidal crisis.
4. Reestablish a sense of hope for self and the future.
5. Cease the perilous lifestyle and resolve the emotional conflicts that underlie the suicidal pattern.

—. _____

_____

—. _____

_____

—. _____

_____

SHORT-TERM OBJECTIVES	THERAPEUTIC INTERVENTIONS
1. Patient and/or significant others to describe any current suicidal thoughts and/or behavior. (1, 2, 3)	1. Explore any current suicidal ideation the patient expresses (e.g., acuity of the suicidality, intent to harm himself/herself, plan for suicide, means to carry out the plan, moral views of suicide).
	2. Assess thoroughly any recent suicidal behavior on the part of the patient (e.g., method, intent, recent stressors, possibility of "rescue" by others, emotional reaction to the behavior).
	3. Gather information from the patient's significant others regarding recent suicidal threats or behaviors that the patient has made.

2. Describe current social support structure and history of suicidal behavior. (4, 5)

4. Gather detailed personal and family history information regarding previous suicidal behavior and the intention of the behavior at the time.

5. Assess the patient's social support structure (e.g., involved family, close friends, involvement with social and/or religious groups).

3. Cooperate with inpatient care as arranged by the clinician. (6)

6. Arrange for hospitalization, as necessary, when the patient is judged to be harmful to self or unable to care for his/her basic needs.

4. Describe other symptoms or disorders that may also be present, such as depression or substance abuse. (7, 8)

7. Gather detailed personal and family history information regarding substance abuse and its potential contribution to suicidal ideation; refer the patient for in-depth substance abuse treatment, if indicated (see the Chemical Dependence chapters in this *Planner*).

8. Assess the patient for comorbid psychiatric disorders (e.g., see the Depression, Anxiety, Panic Disorder, Mania/Hypomania, Psychoticism chapters in this *Planner*).

5. Outline a complete and accurate medical and psychiatric history, including treatment received and its effectiveness. (9, 10, 11)

9. Explore the patient's history of previous treatment for suicidal ideation and/or psychiatric illness, including the success of, as well as tolerance for, that treatment.

10. Assess the patient for the presence of other medical problems and medications used to treat them.

11. Explore the patient's use of any medication or other substance

6. Complete psychological testing and other questionnaires
   for assessing suicidal ideation.
   (12)

7. Express an understanding of
   possible contributing factors to
   suicidality and the relationship
   between substance abuse and
   suicidal ideation. (13, 14)

8. Cooperate with a physical examination and laboratory tests.
   (15, 16)

9. Pursue treatment for concurrent medical problems that
   may contribute to suicidal
   ideation. (17, 18)

that could contribute to suicidal
ideation because of side effects
(e.g., depression, psychosis,
akathisia, panic attacks,
confusion).

12. Administer objective instru-
    ments to assess the patient's
    suicidal ideation and intent (e.g.,
    Beck Scale for Suicide Ideation
    [BSS], Suicide Intent Scale
    [SIS], Beck Hopelessness Scale
    [BHS]); evaluate the results and
    give him/her feedback.

13. Educate the patient on the possi-
    ble contributing factors (e.g.,
    stressful life events, history of
    abuse or other traumatic experi-
    ence) to suicidal ideation.

14. Emphasize to the patient the
    negative and dangerous impact
    of substance abuse on suicidal
    ideation.

15. Perform a complete physical and
    neurological examination on the
    patient and send his/her blood
    and/or urine for analysis to
    assess any current medical
    problems.

16. Provide feedback to the patient
    regarding the results and impli-
    cations of the physical examina-
    tion and laboratory test results.

17. Treat or refer the patient for
    treatment for any medical prob-
    lem that may be contributing to
    suicidal ideation (e.g., cardio-
    vascular disease, pulmonary dis-
    ease, diabetes, cancer, endocrine
    disorders, dementia).

18. Monitor the patient's progress in
    recovery from concomitant dis-
    orders and the impact of the

recovery on his/her suicidal ideation.

10. Verbalize an understanding of treatment options for suicidal ideation. (19)

19. Discuss appropriate treatment options with the patient including medication, psychotherapy, and electroconvulsive therapy (ECT).

11. Participate in psychotherapy sessions as planned with therapist. (20, 21)

20. Assess the patient for potential benefit from psychotherapy and refer to a psychotherapist, if necessary.

21. Monitor the patient's response to psychotherapy; assess his/her ability to verbalize a basis for progress in recovery from suicidal ideations (e.g., decreased frequency and duration of suicidality, improved skills for coping with adversity, increased ability to cope with chronic suicidality).

12. Describe any recent substance use in relation to the suicidal ideation. (14, 22, 23)

14. Emphasize to the patient the negative and dangerous impact of substance abuse on suicidal ideation.

22. Determine if the patient's suicidal ideation is a consequence of substance intoxication or withdrawal.

23. Monitor the patient in a secure environment until the substance intoxication and/or withdrawal has resolved.

13. Take prescribed SSRI medications responsibly at times ordered by the physician. (24, 25, 26)

24. Prescribe to the patient a selective serotonin reuptake inhibitor (SSRI) (e.g., paroxetine [Paxil®], sertraline [Zoloft®], citalopram [Celexa™], escitalopram [Lexapro™], fluoxetine [Prozac®], fluvoxamine [Luvox®]) if he/she has

symptoms of depression (see the Depression chapter in this *Planner*).

25. Avoid the use of medications with a narrow therapeutic index (i.e., tricyclic antidepressants [TCAs]) that are potentially fatal in overdose.

26. Titrate the SSRI antidepressant medication, as tolerated, to gain maximal therapeutic effect.

14. Report on the effectiveness of medications and any side effects that develop. (27)

27. Monitor the patient frequently for the development of side effects, response to medication, and adherence to treatment.

15. Adhere to the addition of lithium to the treatment regimen and cooperate with blood draws. (28, 29)

28. Consider adding a medication (e.g., bupropion [Wellbutrin®], mirtazapine [Remeron®], nefazodone [Serzone®], trazodone [Desyrel®], lithium [Eskalith®, Lithobid®, Lithonate®], an atypical antipsychotic) to augment the patient's current regimen if he/she has only a partial response or displays significant mood instability.

29. Measure the patient's blood level of lithium in four to five days; titrate the dose, as tolerated, to obtain therapeutic blood levels.

16. Verbalize symptoms of anxiety and take medication for anxiety as prescribed. (30, 31)

30. Consider the addition of a benzodiazepine (e.g., clonazepam [Klonopin®], diazepam [Valium®], lorazepam [Ativan®]) if the patient expresses and/or displays high levels of anxiety (e.g., restlessness, emotional discomfort, panic attacks).

31. Titrate the dose of the benzodiazepine every two to

three days, as tolerated, until the patient has a satisfactory response.

17. Describe any symptoms of psychosis and adhere to the prescribed antipsychotic medication regimen. (32, 33, 34, 35)

32. Explore the patient's symptoms and signs of psychosis; prescribe to the patient an atypical antipsychotic (e.g., risperidone [Risperdal®], olanzapine [Zyprexa®], aripiprazole [Abilify™], ziprasidone [Geodon®], quetiapine [Seroquel®]) (see the Psychoticism chapter in this *Planner*).

33. Titrate the antipsychotic medication dose every two to four weeks, as tolerated, until psychotic symptoms have resolved.

34. Consider changing the patient's antipsychotic medication to clozapine (Clozaril®) if he/she continues to have suicidal ideation despite adequate trials of other atypical antipsychotics.

35. Prescribe clozapine (Clozaril®) and follow the patient's blood counts according to published guidelines and prescribing regulations.

18. Cooperate with recommended electroconvulsive therapy (ECT). (36, 37)

36. Refer the patient for ECT if his/her suicidality is severe, requiring rapid treatment.

37. Monitor the patient frequently for improvement in suicidal ideation and any comorbid psychiatric conditions.

19. Retain a remission in suicidal ideation. (38, 39)

38. Maintain the patient on current medication for at least 12 months if he/she has shown a fully successful response.

39. Continue treatment indefinitely if he/she has had a previous episode of psychiatric illness or attains only a partial response in symptoms.

__. _____   __. _____

_____   _____

__. _____   __. _____

_____   _____

__. _____   __. _____

_____   _____

DIAGNOSTIC SUGGESTIONS:

Axis I: 296.xx   Major Depressive Disorder
           300.4   Dysthymic Disorder
           296.xx   Bipolar I Disorder
           296.89   Bipolar II Disorder
           295.xx   Schizophrenia
           300.01   Panic Disorder without Agoraphobia
           309.81   Posttraumatic Stress Disorder
           290.xx   Dementia
           303.90   Alcohol Dependence
           304.20   Cocaine Dependence

           _____   _____

           _____   _____

Axis II: 301.83   Borderline Personality Disorder
           301.7   Antisocial Personality Disorder

           _____   _____

           _____   _____

Appendix A

COMMONLY USED PSYCHIATRIC MEDICATIONS

TABLE 1. SORTED BY CLASS

Generic	Trade	Class	Common Uses	Indication*	Usual Dose (mg/day)
Antidepressants					
amitriptyline	Elavil	TCA	Depression, Anxiety	11	50–150
bupropion	Wellbutrin, Zyban	Atypical	Depression	11, 22	100–450
citalopram	Celexa	SSRI	Depression, Anxiety	11	20–60
clomipramine	Anafranil	TCA	OCD	14	100–250
desipramine	Norpramin	TCA	Depression, Anxiety	11	100–200
doxepin	Sinequan	TCA	Depression, Anxiety	4, 11	75–150
escitalopram	Lexapro	SSRI	Depression, Anxiety	11	10–30
fluoxetine	Prozac, Sarafem	SSRI	Depression, Anxiety	6, 11, 14, 16, 18	20–80
fluvoxamine	Luvox	SSRI	OCD	14	100–300
imipramine	Tofranil	TCA	Depression, Anxiety	11	50–150
maprotiline	Ludiomil	TCA	Depression, Anxiety	11	50–150
mirtazapine	Remeron	Atypical	Depression, Anxiety	11	15–45
nefazodone	Serzone	SARI	Depression, Anxiety	11	300–600
nortriptyline	Aventyl, Pamelor	TCA	Depression, Anxiety	11	50–150
paroxetine	Paxil	SSRI	Depression, Anxiety	7, 11, 14, 16, 17, 24	20–60
phenelzine	Nardil	MAOI	Depression, Anxiety	11	60–90
protriptyline	Vivactil	TCA	Depression, Anxiety	11	15–40
sertraline	Zoloft	SSRI	Depression, Anxiety	11, 14, 16, 17, 18, 23	50–200
tranylcypromine	Parnate	MAOI	Depression, Anxiety	11	30–60
trazodone	Desyrel	SARI	Depression, Insomnia	11	150–400
trimipramine	Surmontil	TCA	Depression, Anxiety	11	100–200
venlafaxine	Effexor	SNRI	Depression, Anxiety	7, 11, 23	75–375

Antipsychotics

aripiprazole	Abilify	Atypical	Psychosis	20	10–20
chlorpromazine	Thorazine	Typical	Psychosis	12, 20	500–1000
clozapine	Clozaril	Atypical	Psychosis	20	100–900
fluphenazine	Prolixin	Typical	Psychosis	19	5–20
haloperidol	Haldol	Typical	Psychosis	19, 25	5–20
loxapine	Loxitane	Typical	Psychosis	20	60–100
mesoridazine	Serentil	Typical	Psychosis	20	100–400
molindone	Moban	Typical	Psychosis	19	100–200
olanzapine	Zyprexa	Atypical	Psychosis, Mania	12, 20	5–20
perphenazine	Trilafon	Typical	Psychosis	20	16–64
pimozide	Orap	Typical	Psychosis	25	5–10
quetiapine	Seroquel	Atypical	Psychosis	20	300–600
risperidone	Risperdal	Atypical	Psychosis	20	2–8
thioridazine	Mellaril	Typical	Psychosis	20	200–800
thiothixene	Navane	Typical	Psychosis	20	20–30
trifluoperazine	Stelazine	Typical	Psychosis	4, 20	15–20
ziprasidone	Geodon	Atypical	Psychosis, Agitation	1, 20	40–160

Anxiolytics

alprazolam	Xanax	Benzodiazepine	Anxiety	4, 16	1–10
buspirone	BuSpar	Atypical	Anxiety	4	20–30
chlordiazepoxide	Librium	Benzodiazepine	Anxiety, Alcohol Withdrawal	3, 4	100–400
clonazepam	Klonopin	Benzodiazepine	Anxiety	16, 21	1–4
clorazepate	Tranxene	Benzodiazepine	Anxiety	3, 16, 21	30–60
diazepam	Valium	Benzodiazepine	Anxiety, Alcohol Withdrawal	3, 16, 21	5–20
hydroxyzine	Vistaril	Antihistamine	Anxiety	4	200–400
lorazepam	Ativan	Benzodiazepine	Anxiety, Alcohol Withdrawal	4	2–6
oxazepam	Serax	Benzodiazepine	Anxiety, Alcohol Withdrawal	3, 4	30–120

Sleep Agents

chloral hydrate	Noctec	Hypnotic	Insomnia	9	500–1000
estazolam	ProSom	Benzodiazepine	Insomnia	9	1–2
flurazepam	Dalmane	Benzodiazepine	Insomnia	9	15–30
temazepam	Restoril	Benzodiazepine	Insomnia	9	7.5–30
triazolam	Halcion	Benzodiazepine	Insomnia	9	0.25–0.5
zaleplon	Sonata	Hypnotic	Insomnia	9	5–10
zolpidem	Ambien	Hypnotic	Insomnia	9	5–10

Mood Stabilizers

carbamazepine	Tegretol	Anticonvulsant	Mood Stabilization, Impulsivity	21	400–800
divalproex sodium	Depakote	Anticonvulsant	Mood Stabilization, Impulsivity	12, 21	1000–2000
gabapentin	Neurontin	Anticonvulsant	Mood Stabilization, Impulsivity	21	900–2400
lamotrigine	Lamictal	Anticonvulsant	Mood Stabilization	21	100–400
lithium	Eskalith, Lithane, Lithobid	Mood Stabilizer	Mood Stabilization, Impulsivity	12	900–1200
topiramate	Topamax	Anticonvulsant	Mood Stabilization	21	400–1200

Stimulants and Other ADHD Agents

amphetamine	Adderall	Stimulant	ADHD, Narcolepsy	5, 13	5–60
atomoxetine	Strattera	NRI	ADHD	5	40–100
d–amphetamine	Dexedrine	Stimulant	ADHD, Narcolepsy	5, 13	5–60
methylphenidate	Ritalin	Stimulant	ADHD, Narcolepsy	5, 13	10–60
pemoline	Cylert	Stimulant	ADHD	5	56.25–75

Substance Abuse Agents

clonidine	Catapres	α–adrenergic Agonist	Opioid Withdrawal	8	0.1–0.6
disulfiram	Antabuse	Alcohol Oxidation Inhibitor	Alcohol Relapse Prevention	2	125–500
methadone	Dolophine, Methadose	Opioid Agonist	Opioid Withdrawal, Opioid Relapse Prevention	10, 15	20–120
naltrexone	ReVia	Opioid Antagonist	Alcohol Relapse Prevention, Opioid Relapse Prevention	2	25–50

*Indications

1	Acute Agitation	14	Obsessive-Compulsive Disorder
2	Alcohol Dependence	15	Opioid Detoxification
3	Alcohol Withdrawal	16	Panic Disorder
4	Anxiety	17	Posttraumatic Stress disorder
5	Attention Deficit/Hyperactivity Disorder	18	Premenstrual Dysphoric Disorder
6	Bulimia	19	Psychosis
7	Generalized Anxiety Disorder	20	Schizophrenia
8	Hypertension	21	Seizure Disorder
9	Insomnia	22	Smoking Cessation
10	Maintenance Treatment of Opioid Dependence	23	Social Anxiety Disorder
11	Major Depressive Disorder	24	Social Phobia
12	Mania	25	Tourette's Syndrome
13	Narcolepsy		

Abbreviations

ADHD	Attention Deficit/Hyperactivity Disorder	SARI	Serotonin Antagonist and Reputake Inhibitor
MAOI	Monoamine Oxidate Inhibitor	SNRI	Serotonin/Norepinephrine Reuptake Inhibitor
NRI	Norepinephrine Reuptake Inhibitor	SSRI	Selective Serotonin Reuptake Inhibitor
OCD	Obsessive-Compulsive Disorder	TCA	Tricyclic Antidepressant

TABLE 2. SORTED BY INDICATION

Generic	Trade	Class	Common Uses	Indication*	Usual Dose (mg/day)
Anxiety					
alprazolam	Xanax	Benzodiazepine	Anxiety	4, 16	1–10
buspirone	BuSpar	Atypical Anxiolytic	Anxiety	4	20–30
chlordiazepoxide	Librium	Benzodiazepine	Anxiety, Alcohol Withdrawal	3, 4	100–400
citalopram	Celexa	SSRI	Depression, Anxiety	11	20–60
clonazepam	Klonopin	Benzodiazepine	Anxiety	16, 21	1–4
clorazepate	Tranxene	Benzodiazepine	Anxiety	3, 16, 21	30–60
diazepam	Valium	Benzodiazepine	Anxiety, Alcohol Withdrawal	3, 16, 21	5–20
doxepin	Sinequan	TCA	Depression, Anxiety	4, 11	75–150
escitalopram	Lexapro	SSRI	Depression, Anxiety	11	10–30
fluoxetine	Prozac, Sarafem	SSRI	Depression, Anxiety	6, 11, 14, 16, 18	20–80
hydroxyzine	Vistaril	Antihistamine	Anxiety	4	200–400
lorazepam	Ativan	Benzodiazepine	Anxiety, Alcohol Withdrawal	4	2–6
oxazepam	Serax	Benzodiazepine	Anxiety, Alcohol Withdrawal	3, 4	30–120
paroxetine	Paxil	SSRI	Depression, Anxiety	7, 11, 14, 16, 17, 24	20–60
sertraline	Zoloft	SSRI	Depression, Anxiety	11, 14, 16, 17, 18, 23	50–200
venlafaxine	Effexor	SNRI	Depression, Anxiety	7, 11, 23	75–375
Attention Deficit/Hyperactivity					
amphetamine	Adderall	Stimulant	ADHD, Narcolepsy	5, 13	5–60
atomoxetine	Strattera	NRI	ADHD	5	40–100
d–amphetamine	Dexedrine	Stimulant	ADHD, Narcolepsy	5, 13	5–60
methylphenidate	Ritalin	Stimulant	ADHD, Narcolepsy	5, 13	10–60
pemoline	Cylert	Stimulant	ADHD	5	56.25–75
Chemical Dependence					
chlordiazepoxide	Librium	Benzodiazepine	Anxiety, Alcohol Withdrawal	3, 4	100–400
clonidine	Catapres	α–adrenergic Agonist	Opioid Withdrawal	8	0.1–0.6
diazepam	Valium	Benzodiazepine	Anxiety, Alcohol Withdrawal	3, 16, 21	5–20

disulfiram	Antabuse	Alcohol Oxidation Inhibitor	Alcohol Relapse Prevention	2	125–500
lorazepam	Ativan	Benzodiazepine	Anxiety, Alcohol Withdrawal	4	2–6
methadone	Dolophine, Methadose	Opioid Agonist	Opioid Withdrawal, Opioid Relapse Prevention	10, 15	20–120
naltrexone	ReVia	Opioid Antagonist	Alcohol Relapse Prevention, Opioid Relapse Prevention	2	25–50
oxazepam	Serax	Benzodiazepine	Anxiety, Alcohol Withdrawal	3, 4	30–120

Depression

amitriptyline	Elavil	TCA	Depression, Anxiety	11	50–150
bupropion	Wellbutrin, Zyban	Atypical Antidepressant	Depression	11, 22	100–450
citalopram	Celexa	SSRI	Depression, Anxiety	11	20–60
desipramine	Norpramin	TCA	Depression, Anxiety	11	100–200
doxepin	Sinequan	TCA	Depression, Anxiety	4, 11	75–150
escitalopram	Lexapro	SSRI	Depression, Anxiety	11	10–30
fluoxetine	Prozac, Sarafem	SSRI	Depression, Anxiety	6, 11, 14, 16, 18	20–80
imipramine	Tofranil	TCA	Depression, Anxiety	11	50–150
maprotiline	Ludiomil	TCA	Depression, Anxiety	11	50–150
mirtazapine	Remeron	Atypical Antidepressant	Depression, Anxiety	11	15–45
nefazodone	Serzone	SARI	Depression, Anxiety	11	300–600
nortriptyline	Aventyl, Pamelor	TCA	Depression, Anxiety	11	50–150
paroxetine	Paxil	SSRI	Depression, Anxiety	7, 11, 14, 16, 17, 24	20–60
phenelzine	Nardil	MAOI	Depression, Anxiety	11	60–90
protriptyline	Vivactil	TCA	Depression, Anxiety	11	15–40
sertraline	Zoloft	SSRI	Depression, Anxiety	11, 14, 16, 17, 18, 23	50–200
tranylcypromine	Parnate	MAOI	Depression, Anxiety	11	30–60
trazodone	Desyrel	SARI	Depression, Insomnia	11	150–400
trimipramine	Surmontil	TCA	Depression, Anxiety	11	100–200
venlafaxine	Effexor	SNRI	Depression, Anxiety	7, 11, 23	75–375

Impulsivity

carbamazepine	Tegretol	Anticonvulsant	Mood Stabilization, Impulsivity	21	400–800
citalopram	Celexa	SSRI	Depression, Anxiety	11	20–60
clonazepam	Klonopin	Benzodiazepine	Anxiety	16, 21	1–4
divalproex sodium	Depakote	Anticonvulsant	Mood Stabilization, Impulsivity	12, 21	1000–2000
escitalopram	Lexapro	SSRI	Depression, Anxiety	11	10–30
fluoxetine	Prozac, Sarafem	SSRI	Depression, Anxiety	6, 11, 14, 16, 18	20–80
gabapentin	Neurontin	Anticonvulsant	Mood Stabilization, Impulsivity	21	900–2400
lithium	Eskalith, Lithane, Lithobid	Mood Stabilizer	Mood Stabilization, Impulsivity	12	900–1200
paroxetine	Paxil	SSRI	Depression, Anxiety	7, 11, 14, 16, 17, 24	20–60
sertraline	Zoloft	SSRI	Depression, Anxiety	11, 14, 16, 17, 18, 23	50–200

Mania/Hypomania

carbamazepine	Tegretol	Anticonvulsant	Mood Stabilization, Impulsivity	21	400–800
clonazepam	Klonopin	Benzodiazepine	Anxiety	16, 21	1–4
divalproex sodium	Depakote	Anticonvulsant	Mood Stabilization, Impulsivity	12, 21	1000–2000
gabapentin	Neurontin	Anticonvulsant	Mood Stabilization, Impulsivity	21	900–2400
lamotrigine	Lamictal	Anticonvulsant	Mood Stabilization	21	100–400
lithium	Eskalith, Lithane, Lithobid	Mood Stabilizer	Mood Stabilization, Impulsivity	12	900–1200
olanzapine	Zyprexa	Atypical Antipsychotic	Psychosis, Mania	12, 20	5–20
topiramate	Topamax	Anticonvulsant	Mood Stabilization	21	400–1200

Obsessive-Compulsive Disorder

citalopram	Celexa	SSRI	Depression, Anxiety, OCD	11	20–60
clomipramine	Anafranil	TCA	OCD	14	100–250
escitalopram	Lexapro	SSRI	Depression, Anxiety, OCD	11	10–30
fluoxetine	Prozac, Sarafem	SSRI	Depression, Anxiety, OCD	6, 11, 14, 16, 18	20–80
fluvoxamine	Luvox	SSRI	OCD	14	100–300
paroxetine	Paxil	SSRI	Depression, Anxiety, OCD	7, 11, 14, 16, 17, 24	20–60
sertraline	Zoloft	SSRI	Depression, Anxiety, OCD	11, 14, 16, 17, 18, 23	50–200

Psychoticism

aripiprazole	Abilify	Atypical Antipsychotic	Psychosis	20	10–20
chlorpromazine	Thorazine	Typical Antipsychotic	Psychosis	12, 20	500–1000
clozapine	Clozaril	Atypical Antipsychotic	Psychosis	20	100–900
fluphenazine	Prolixin	Typical Antipsychotic	Psychosis	19	5–20
haloperidol	Haldol	Typical Antipsychotic	Psychosis	19, 25	5–20
loxapine	Loxitane	Typical Antipsychotic	Psychosis	20	60–100
mesoridazine	Serentil	Typical Antipsychotic	Psychosis	20	100–400
molindone	Moban	Typical Antipsychotic	Psychosis	19	100–200
olanzapine	Zyprexa	Atypical Antipsychotic	Psychosis, Mania	12, 20	5–20
perphenazine	Trilafon	Typical Antipsychotic	Psychosis	20	16–64
pimozide	Orap	Typical Antipsychotic	Psychosis	25	5–10
quetiapine	Seroquel	Atypical Antipsychotic	Psychosis	20	300–600
risperidone	Risperdal	Atypical Antipsychotic	Psychosis	20	2–8
thioridazine	Mellaril	Typical Antipsychotic	Psychosis	20	200–800
thiothixene	Navane	Typical Antipsychotic	Psychosis	20	20–30
trifluoperazine	Stelazine	Typical Antipsychotic	Psychosis	4, 20	15–20
ziprasidone	Geodon	Atypical Antipsychotic	Psychosis, Agitation	1, 20	40–160

Sleep Disturbance

amphetamine	Adderall	Stimulant	ADHD, Narcolepsy	5, 13	5–60
chloral hydrate	Noctec	Hypnotic	Insomnia	9	500–1000
d–amphetamine	Dexedrine	Stimulant	ADHD, Narcolepsy	5, 13	5–60
estazolam	ProSom	Benzodiazepine	Insomnia	9	1–2
flurazepam	Dalmane	Benzodiazepine	Insomnia	9	15–30
methylphenidate	Ritalin	Stimulant	ADHD, Narcolepsy	5, 13	10–60
temazepam	Restoril	Benzodiazepine	Insomnia	9	7.5–30
trazodone	Desyrel	SARI	Depression, Insomnia	11	150–400
triazolam	Halcion	Benzodiazepine	Insomnia	9	0.25–0.5
zaleplon	Sonata	Hypnotic	Insomnia	9	5–10
zolpidem	Ambien	Hypnotic	Insomnia	9	5–10

*Indications

1	Acute Agitation	14	Obsessive-Compulsive Disorder
2	Alcohol Dependence	15	Opioid Detoxification
3	Alcohol Withdrawal	16	Panic Disorder
4	Anxiety	17	Posttraumatic Stress Disorder
5	Attention Deficit/Hyperactivity Disorder	18	Premenstrual Dysphoric Disorder
6	Bulimia	19	Psychosis
7	Generalized Anxiety Disorder	20	Schizophrenia
8	Hypertension	21	Seizure Disorder
9	Insomnia	22	Smoking Cessation
10	Maintenance Treatment of Opioid Dependence	23	Social Anxiety Disorder
11	Major Depressive Disorder	24	Social Phobia
12	Mania	25	Tourette's Syndrome
13	Narcolepsy		

Abbreviations

ADHD	Attention Deficit/Hyperactivity Disorder	SARI	Serotonin Antagonist and Reputake Inhibitor
MAOI	Monoamine Oxidate Inhibitor	SNRI	Serotonin/Norepinephrine Reuptake Inhibitor
NRI	Norepinephrine Reuptake Inhibitor	SSRI	Selective Serotonin Reuptake Inhibitor
OCD	Obsessive-Compulsive Disorder	TCA	Tricyclic Antidepressant

Appendix B

BIBLIOTHERAPY

Adjustment Disorder with Depression or Anxiety

Grateful Members of Emotional Health Anonymous. (1977). *The Twelve Steps for Everyone Who Really Wants Them*. Minneapolis: CompCare Publications.

Anger Management

Ellis, A. and Harper, R. A. (1998). *A Guide to Rational Living*. North Hollywood, CA: Wilshire Book Co.

Lerner, H. G. (1986). *The Dance of Anger: A Woman's Guide to Changing the Patterns of Intimate Relationships*. New York: Perennial Library.

McKay, M. (2003). *The Anger Control Workbook*. New York: MJF Books.

McKay, M., Rogers, P. D., McKay, J. and Johnson, K. (1989). *When Anger Hurts: Quieting the Storm Within*. Oakland, CA: New Harbinger Publications.

Rosellini, G. and Worden, M. (1997). *Of Course You're Angry: A Guide to Dealing with the Emotions of Substance Abuse*. Center City, MN: Hazelden.

Rubin, T. I. (1993). *The Angry Book*. New York: Collier Books.

Smedes, L. B. (1984). *Forgive and Forget: Healing the Hurts We Don't Deserve*. San Francisco: Harper & Row.

Smedes, L. B. (1997). *The Art of Forgiving: When You Need to Forgive and Don't Know How*. New York: Ballantine Books.

Tavris, C. (1989). *Anger: The Misunderstood Emotion*. New York: Simon & Schuster.

Weisinger, H. (1985). *Dr. Weisinger's Anger Work-out Book*. New York: Quill.

Antisocial Behavior

Carnes, P. (2001). *Out of the Shadows: Understanding Sexual Addiction*. Center City, MN: Hazelden

Katherine, A. (1993). *Boundaries: Where You End and I Begin*. New York: Simon & Schuster.

Pittman, F. S. (1998). *Grow Up!: How Taking Responsibility Can Make You a Happy Adult*. New York: Golden Books.

Williams, R. B. and Williams, V. P. (1994). *Anger Kills: Seventeen Strategies for Controlling the Hostility That Can Harm Your Health*. New York: Harper Collins Publishers.

Anxiety

Benson, H. and Klipper, M. Z. (1992). *The Relaxation Response*. New York: Wings Books.

Burns, D. D. (1993). *Ten Days to Self-Esteem!* New York: Quill.

Davis, M., McKay, M. and Eschelman, E. R. (2002). *The Relaxation & Stress Reduction Workbook*. New York: MJF Books.

Hauck, P. A. (1977). *Overcoming Worry and Fear*. Philadelphia: Westminster Press.

Jeffers, S. J. (1987). *Feel the Fear and Do It Anyway*. San Diego: Harcourt Brace Jovanovich.

Marks, I. M. (2002). *Living with Fear: Understanding and Coping with Anxiety*. New York: McGraw-Hill.

Sheehan, D. V. (1983). *The Anxiety Disease*. New York: Scribner.

Attention Deficit/Hyperactivity Disorder (ADHD)—Adult

Hallowell, E. M. and Ratey, J. J. (1995). *Driven to Distraction: Recognizing and Coping with Attention Deficit Disorder from Childhood through Adulthood*. New York: Simon & Schuster.

Kelly, K. and Ramundo, P. (1995). *You Mean I'm Not Lazy, Stupid, or Crazy?!: A Self-Help Book for Adults with Attention Deficit Disorder*. New York: Scribner.

Nadeau, K. G. (1996). *Adventures in Fast Forward: Life, Love, and Work for the ADD Adult*. New York: Brunner/Mazel.

Quinn, P. O. and Stern, J. M. (2001). *Putting on the Brakes: Young People's Guide to Understanding Attention Deficit Hyperactivity Disorder*. Washington, DC: Magination Press.

Weiss, L. (1994). *The Attention Deficit Disorder in Adults Workbook*. Dallas, TX: Taylor Publishing.

Weiss, L. (1997). *Attention Deficit Disorder in Adults*. Dallas, TX: Taylor Publishing.

Wender, P. H. (1998). *Attention-Deficit Hyperactivity Disorder in Adults*. New York: Oxford University Press.

Borderline Personality

Cudney, M. R. and Hardy, R. E. (1991). *Self-Defeating Behaviors: Free Yourself from the Habits, Compulsions, Feelings, and Attitudes That Hold You Back*. San Francisco, CA: Harper San Francisco.

Katherine, A. (1993). *Boundaries: Where You End and I Begin*. New York: Simon & Schuster.

Puerito, R. (1997). *Overcoming Anxiety*. New York: Henry Holt.

Chemical Dependence—Relapse Prevention

Alcoholics Anonymous. (1975). *Living Sober*. New York: A.A. World Services.

Alcoholics Anonymous. (1976). *Alcoholics Anonymous: The Big Book*. New York: A.A. World Service.

Carnes, P. (1993). *A Gentle Path through the Twelve Steps: The Classic Guide for All People in the Process of Recovery*. Minneapolis, MN: CompCare Publishers.

Drews, T. R. (1998). *Getting Them Sober: You Can Help!* Baltimore, MD: Recovery Communications.

Gorski, T. T. (1989-92). *The Staying Sober Workbook*. Independence, MO: Herald House Press.

Gorski, T. T., Miller, M. and Cenaps Corporation. (1986). *Staying Sober: A Guide for Relapse Prevention*. Independence, MO: Independence Press.

Johnson, V. E. (1990). *I'll Quit Tomorrow*. San Francisco: Harper & Row.

Kasl, C. D. (1992). *Many Roads, One Journey: Moving Beyond the Twelve Steps*. New York: Harper Perennial.

Nuckals, C. (1989). *Cocaine: From Dependence to Recovery*. Blue Ridge Summit, PA: TAB Books.

Wilson, B. (1967). *As Bill Sees It*. New York: A. A. World Service.

Chemical Dependence—Withdrawal

Alcoholics Anonymous. (1975). *Living Sober*. New York: A.A. World Services.

Alcoholics Anonymous. (1976). *Alcoholics Anonymous: The Big Book*. New York: A.A. World Service.

Carnes, P. (1993). *A Gentle Path through the Twelve Steps: The Classic Guide for All People in the Process of Recovery*. Minneapolis, MN: CompCare Publishers.

Drews, T. R. (1998). *Getting Them Sober: You Can Help!* Baltimore, MD: Recovery Communications.

Gorski, T. T. (1989–1992). *The Staying Sober Workbook*. Independence, MO: Herald House Press.

Gorski, T. T., Miller, M. and Cenaps Corporation. (1986). *Staying Sober: A Guide for Relapse Prevention*. Independence, MO: Independence Press.

Johnson, V. E. (1990). *I'll Quit Tomorrow*. San Francisco: Harper & Row.

Kasl, C. D. (1992). *Many Roads, One Journey: Moving Beyond the Twelve Steps*. New York: Harper Perennial.

Nuckals, C. (1989). *Cocaine: From Dependence to Recovery*. Blue Ridge Summit, PA: TAB Books.

Wilson, B. (1967). *As Bill Sees It*. New York: A. A. World Service.

Chronic Fatigue Syndrome

Benson, H. (1979). *The Mind-Body Effect: How Behavioral Medicine Can Show You the Way to Better Health*. New York: Simon and Schuster.

Berne, K. H. (1995). *Running on Empty: The Complete Guide to Chronic Fatigue Syndrome*. Alameda, CA: Hunter House.

Berne, K. H. (2002). *Chronic Fatigue Syndrome, Fibromyalgia and Other Invisible Illnesses: The Comprehensive Guide*. Alameda, CA: Hunter House.

Teitelbaum, J. (2001). *From Fatigued to Fantastic!: A Proven Program to Regain Vibrant Health, Based on a New Scientific Study Showing Effective Treatment for Chronic Fatigue and Fibromyalgia*. New York: Avery.

Chronic Pain

Benson, H. (1979). *The Mind-Body Effect: How Behavioral Medicine Can Show You the Way to Better Health*. New York: Simon and Schuster.

Benson, H. and Klipper, M. Z. (1992). *The Relaxation Response*. New York: Wings Books.

Burns, D. D. (1993). *Ten Days to Self-Esteem!* New York: Quill.

Burns, D. D. (1999). *The Feeling Good Handbook*. New York: Plume.

Caudill, M. (2001). *Managing Pain before It Manages You*. New York: Guilford Press.

Duckro, P. N., Richardson, W. D. and Marshall, J. E. (1995). *Taking Control of Your Headaches: How to Get the Treatment You Need*. New York: Guilford Press.

Fields, H. L. (2002). *Pain: Mechanisms and Management*. New York: McGraw-Hill.

Hunter, M. E. (1996). *Making Peace with Chronic Pain: A Whole-Life Strategy*. New York: Brunner/Mazel Publishers.

Leshan, L. L. (1999). *How to Meditate: A Guide to Self-Discovery*. Boston: Little, Brown.

Morris, D. B. (1991). *The Culture of Pain*. Berkeley: University of California Press.

Siegel, B. S. (1989). *Peace, Love & Healing: Body-Mind Communication and the Path to Self-Healing*. New York: Harper & Row.

Cognitive Deficits—Dementia

Davis, R. and Davis, B. (1989). *My Journey into Alzheimer's Disease*. Wheaton, IL: Tyndale House Publishers.

Heckman-Owen, C. (1992). *Life with Charlie: Coping with an Alzheimer Spouse or Other Dementia Patient and Keeping Your Sanity*. Ventura, CA: Pathfinder Publications of California.

Knittweis, J. and Harch, J. (2002). *Alzheimer Solutions: A Personal Guide for Caregivers*. Sausalito, CA: Lucid Press.

Cognitive Deficits—Developmental Disorder

Keller, M. J. (1991). *Activities with Developmentally Disabled Elderly and Older Adults*. New York: Haworth Press.

Luchterhand, C. and Murphy, N. (1998). *Helping Adults with Mental Retardation Grieve a Death Loss*. Philadelphia, PA: Accelerated Development.

Stumpf, S. H. (1990). *Pathways to Success: Training for Independent Living*. Washington, DC: American Association on Mental Retardation.

Depression

Burns, D. D. (1980). *Feeling Good: The New Mood Therapy*. New York: Morrow.

Burns, D. D. (1999). *The Feeling Good Handbook*. New York: Plume.

Butler, P. (1991). *Talking to Yourself: Learning the Language of Self-Affirmation*. San Francisco, CA: Harper San Francisco.

Dyer, W. W. (1991). *Your Erroneous Zones*. New York: Harper Perennial.

Frankl, V. E. (1992). *Man's Search for Meaning: An Introduction to Logotherapy*. Boston: Beacon Press.

Geisel, T. S. (1990). *Oh, the Places You'll Go!* New York: Random House.

Hallinan, P. K. (1989). *One Day at a Time*. Center City, MN: Hazelden.

Hazelden Staff. (1991). *Each Day a New Beginning: Daily Meditations for Women*. Center City, MN: Hazelden.

Helmstetter, S. (1992). *What to Say When You Talk to Yourself*. New York: MJF Books.

Knauth, P. (1975). *A Season in Hell*. New York: Harper & Row.

Leith, L. M. (1998). *Exercising Your Way to Better Mental Health: Combat Stress, Fight Depression, and Improve Your Overall Mood and Self-Concept with These Simple Exercises*. Morgantown, WV: Fitness Information Technology.

Styron, W. (1992). *Darkness Visible: A Memoir of Madness*. New York: Vintage Books.

Zonnebelt-Smeenge, S. J. and De Vries, R. C. (1998). *Getting to the Other Side of Grief: Overcoming the Loss of a Spouse*. Grand Rapids, MI: Baker Books.

Dissociation

Grateful Members of Emotional Health Anonymous. (1977). *The Twelve Steps for Everyone Who Really Wants Them*. Minneapolis: CompCare Publications.

Eating Disorder

Fairburn, C. G. (1995). *Overcoming Binge Eating*. New York: Guilford Press.

Hirschmann, J. R. and Munter, C. H. (1988). *Overcoming Overeating: Living Free in a World of Food*. Reading, MA: Addison-Wesley Publishing.

Hollis, J. (2003). *Fat Is a Family Affair: How Food Obsessions Affect Relationships*. Center City, MN: Hazelden.

Rodin, J. (1991). *Body Traps: Breaking the Binds That Keep You from Feeling Good About Your Body*. New York: Morrow.

Sacker, I. M. and Zimmer, M. A. (2001). *Dying to Be Thin*. New York: Warner Books.

Siegel, M., Brisman, J. and Weinshel, M. (1997). *Surviving an Eating Disorder: Strategies for Family and Friends*. New York: Harper Perennial.

Female Sexual Dysfunction

Barbach, L. G. (2001). *For Each Other: Sharing Sexual Intimacy*. New York: Signet.

Comfort, A. (1992). *The New Joy of Sex*. New York: Pocket Books.

Heiman, J. and Lopiccolo, J. (1988). *Becoming Orgasmic: A Sexual and Personal Growth Program for Women*. New York: Prentice Hall.

Kaplan, H. S. (1987). *The Illustrated Manual of Sex Therapy*. New York: Brunner/Mazel.

McCarthy, B. W. and McCarthy, E. J. (1993). *Sexual Awareness: Enhancing Sexual Pleasure*. New York: Carroll & Graf Publishers.

Penner, C. and Penner, J. (1981). *The Gift of Sex: A Guide to Sexual Fulfillment*. Waco, TX: Word Books.

Valins, L. (1992). *When a Woman's Body Says No to Sex: Understanding and Overcoming Vaginismus*. New York: Penguin Books.

Zilbergeld, B. (1999). *The New Male Sexuality*. New York: Bantam Books.

Impulse Control Disorder

Helmstetter, S. (1992). *What to Say When You Talk to Yourself*. New York: MJF Books.

Kelly, K. and Ramundo, P. (1995). *You Mean I'm Not Lazy, Stupid, or Crazy?!: A Self-Help Book for Adults with Attention Deficit Disorder*. New York: Scribner.

Wender, P. H. (1998). *Attention-Deficit Hyperactivity Disorder in Adults*. New York: Oxford University Press.

Male Sexual Dysfunction

Comfort, A. (1992). *The New Joy of Sex*. New York: Pocket Books.

Kaplan, H. S. (1987). *The Illustrated Manual of Sex Therapy*. New York: Brunner/Mazel.

McCarthy, B. W. and McCarthy, E. J. (1993). *Sexual Awareness: Enhancing Sexual Pleasure*. New York: Carroll & Graf Publishers.

Penner, C. and Penner, J. (1981). *The Gift of Sex: A Guide to Sexual Fulfillment*. Waco, TX: Word Books.

Zilbergeld, B. (1999). *The New Male Sexuality*. New York: Bantam Books.

Mania/Hypomania

Grateful Members of Emotional Health Anonymous. (1977). *The Twelve Steps for Everyone Who Really Wants Them*. Minneapolis: CompCare Publications.

Torrey, E. F. and Knable, M. B. (2001). *Surviving Manic Depression: A Manual on Bipolar Disorder for Patients, Families, and Providers*. New York: Basic Books.

Medical Issues—Delirium

Lynn, J., Harrold, J. K. and Center to Improve Care of the Dying. (1999). *Handbook for Mortals: Guidance for People Facing Serious Illness*. New York: Oxford University Press.

Obsessive-Compulsive Disorder (OCD)

Burns, D. D. (1999). *The Feeling Good Handbook*. New York: Plume.

Foa, E. B. and Wilson, R. R. (2001). *Stop Obsessing!: How to Overcome Your Obsessions and Compulsions*. New York: Bantam Books.

Levenkron, S. (1991). *Obsessive-Compulsive Disorders: Treating & Understanding Crippling Habits*. New York: Warner Books.

Phobia-Panic/Agoraphobia

Gold, M. S. (1990). *The Good News About Panic, Anxiety & Phobias*. New York: Bantam Books.

Marks, I. M. (2002). *Living with Fear: Understanding and Coping with Anxiety*. New York: McGraw-Hill.

Swede, S. and Jaffe, S. (2000). *The Panic Attack Recovery Book*. New York: New American Library.

Wilson, R. R. (1996). *Don't Panic: Taking Control of Anxiety Attacks*. New York: Harper Perennial.

Posttraumatic Stress Disorder (PTSD)

Frankl, V. E. (1992). *Man's Search for Meaning: An Introduction to Logotherapy*. Boston: Beacon Press.

Jeffers, S. J. (1987). *Feel the Fear and Do It Anyway*. San Diego: Harcourt Brace Jovanovich.

Leith, L. M. (1998). *Exercising Your Way to Better Mental Health: Combat Stress, Fight Depression, and Improve Your Overall Mood and Self-Concept with These Simple Exercises*. Morgantown, WV: Fitness Information Technology.

Matsakis, A. (1996). *I Can't Get over It: A Handbook for Trauma Survivors*. Oakland, CA: New Harbinger Publications.

Sheehan, D. V. (1986). *The Anxiety Disease*. New York: Bantam Books.

Simon, S. B. and Simon, S. (1990). *Forgiveness: How to Make Peace with Your Past and Get on with Your Life*. New York: Warner Books.

Psychoticism

Torrey, E. F. (2001). *Surviving Schizophrenia: A Manual for Families, Consumers, and Providers*. New York: Quill.

Sleep Disturbance

Dotto, L. (1990). *Losing Sleep: How Your Sleeping Habits Affect Your Life*. New York: Morrow.

Hewish, J. (1985). *Relaxation*. Chicago: NTC Publishing Group.

Leith, L. M. (1998). *Exercising Your Way to Better Mental Health: Combat Stress, Fight Depression, and Improve Your Overall Mood and Self-Concept with These Simple Exercises*. Morgantown, WV: Fitness Information Technology.

Social Discomfort

Bradshaw, J. (2001). *Healing the Shame That Binds You*. New York: MJF Books.

Burns, D. D. (1993). *Ten Days to Self-Esteem!* New York: Quill.

Burns, D. D. and Presbyterian-University of Pennsylvania Medical Center. (1985). *Intimate Connections: The New Clinically Tested Program for Overcoming Loneliness*. New York: W. Morrow.

Dyer, W. W. (1991). *Your Erroneous Zones*. New York: Harper Perennial.

Fossum, M. A. and Mason, M. J. (1989). *Facing Shame: Families in Recovery*. New York: W.W. Norton & Co.

Harris, T. A. (1999). *I'm OK You're OK: A Practical Guide to Transactional Analysis*. New York: BBS Publishing.

James, M. and Jongeward, D. (1996). *Born to Win: Transactional Analysis with Gestalt Experiments*. Reading, MA: Addison-Wesley Publishing.

Nouwen, H. J. M. (1986). *Reaching Out: The Three Movements of the Spiritual Life*. Garden City, NY: Image Books.

Zimbardo, P. G. (1989). *Shyness: What It Is, What to Do About It*. Cambridge, MA: Perseus Books.

Somatization

Benson, H. (1979). *The Mind-Body Effect: How Behavioral Medicine Can Show You the Way to Better Health*. New York: Simon and Schuster.

Grateful Members of Emotional Health Anonymous (1977). *The Twelve Steps for Everyone Who Really Wants Them*. Minneapolis: CompCare Publications.

Suicidal Ideation

Butler, P. (1991). *Talking to Yourself: Learning the Language of Self-Affirmation*. San Francisco, CA: Harper San Francisco.

Hutschnecker, A. A. (1986). *The Will to Live*. New York: Simon & Schuster.

Seligman, M. E. P. (1991). *Learned Optimism*. New York: A.A. Knopf.

Appendix C

INDEX OF *DSM-IV-TR* CODES ASSOCIATED WITH PRESENTING PROBLEMS

Acute Stress Disorder   308.3
Adjustment Disorder with
   Depression or Anxiety
Anxiety
Medical Issues—Delirium
Phobia-Panic/Agoraphobia
Posttraumatic Stress Disorder
   (PTSD)

Adjustment Disorder   309.xx
Adjustment Disorder with
   Depression or Anxiety
Posttraumatic Stress Disorder
   (PTSD)

**Adjustment Disorder
Unspecified**   309.9
Adjustment Disorder with
   Depression or Anxiety

**Adjustment Disorder with
Anxiety**   309.24
Adjustment Disorder with
   Depression or Anxiety
Anxiety
Phobia-Panic/Agoraphobia

**Adjustment Disorder with
Depressed Mood**   309
Adjustment Disorder with
   Depression or Anxiety
Depression

**Adjustment Disorder with
Disturbance of Conduct**   309.3
Adjustment Disorder with
   Depression or Anxiety
Anger Management
Antisocial Behavior
Suicidal Ideation

**Adjustment Disorder with
Mixed Anxiety and
Depressed Mood**   309.28
Adjustment Disorder with
   Depression or Anxiety

**Adjustment Disorder with
Mixed Disturbance of
Conduct and Emotions**   309.4
Adjustment Disorder with
   Depression or Anxiety
Suicidal Ideation

**Agoraphobia without History
of Panic Disorder**   300.22
Phobia-Panic/Agoraphobia

Alcohol Aubse   305
Adjustment Disorder with
   Depression or Anxiety
Attention Deficit/Hyperactivity
   Disorder (ADHD)—Adult
Chemical Dependence—Relapse
   Prevention
Chronic Fatigue
Depression
Posttraumatic Stress Disorder
   (PTSD)

Sexual Abuse of Adult (Victim)   995.81
Female Sexual Dysfunction
Male Sexual Dysfunction
Posttraumatic Stress Disorder (PTSD)

Sexual Abuse of Child (Victim)   995.5
Female Sexual Dysfunction
Male Sexual Dysfunction
Posttraumatic Stress Disorder (PTSD)

Sexual Aversion Disorder   302.79
Female Sexual Dysfunction
Male Sexual Dysfunction

Sexual Dysfunction NOS   302.7
Chronic Pain
Female Sexual Dysfunction
Male Sexual Dysfunction

Sleep Disorder Due to (Axis III Disorder)   780.xx
Sleep Disturbance

Sleep Terror Disorder   307.46
Sleep Disturbance

Sleepwalking Disorder   307.46
Sleep Disturbance

Social Phobia   300.23
Anxiety
Obsessive-Compulsive Disorder (OCD)
Phobia-Panic/Agoraphobia
Social Discomfort

Somatization Disorder   300.81
Chronic Pain
Somatization

Somatoform Disorder NOS   300.81
Somatization

Specific Phobia   300.29
Anxiety
Obsessive-Compulsive Disorder (OCD)
Phobia-Panic/Agoraphobia
Social Discomfort

Substance-Induced Anxiety Disorder   292.89
Anxiety
Phobia-Panic/Agoraphobia
Social Discomfort

Substance-Induced Mood Disorder   292.84
Chemical Dependence—Relapse Prevention
Chemical Dependence—Withdrawal
Depression
Mania or Hypomania

Substance-Induced Psychotic Disorder   292.1x
Psychoticism

Substance-Induced Sexual Dysfunction   292.89
Female Sexual Dysfunction
Male Sexual Dysfunction

Tourette's Disorder   307.23
Obsessive-Compulsive Disorder (OCD)

Trichotillomania   312.39
Impulse Control Disorder

Undifferentiated Somatoform Disorder   300.81
Somatization

Vaginismus   306.51
Female Sexual Dysfunction

Vascular Dementia   290.4x
Cognitive Deficits—Dementia